central hall leads past a powder room to the breakfast room. Placing chimneys at the ends of the house, rather than in the middle, was a development in the Southern colonies, making possible the corner fireplaces in both the living room and the dining room. A media room with a full-wall multi-media center opens off the living room, adding to entertainment possibilities. Casual dining areas, to the rear of the home, include a large eat-in country kitchen with a snack bar and a breakfast room with a planning desk. A good-sized pantry is nearby, as are also a broom closet and a laundry room with counter space.

Upstairs, the master suite is highlighted by an expansive walk-in closet, a dressing room and a bath with twin vanities. A second suite has a fireplace, a dressing room and private access to another fine bath. A third bedroom could be left open to create a study or nursery connected to the master suite.

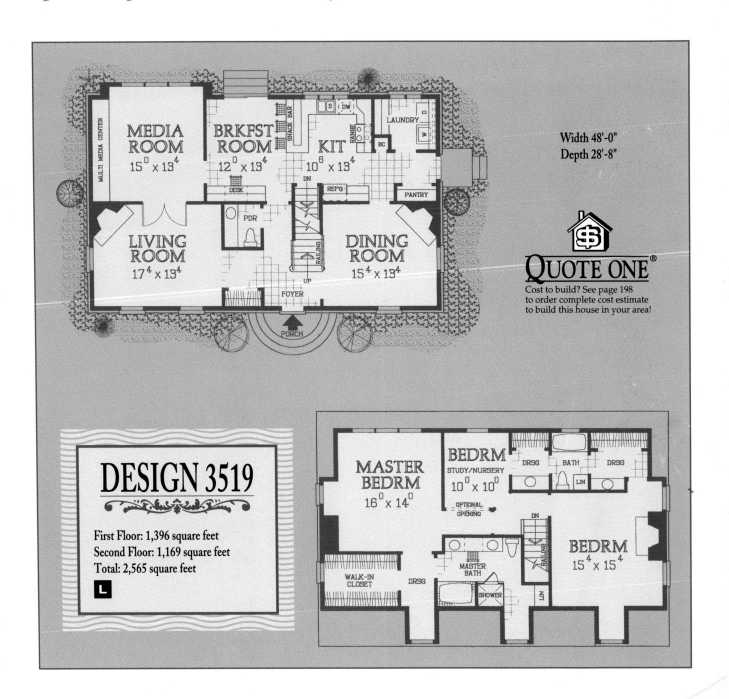

Width 48'-0"
Depth 28'-8"

QUOTE ONE®

Cost to build? See page 198 to order complete cost estimate to build this house in your area!

DESIGN 3519

First Floor: 1,396 square feet
Second Floor: 1,169 square feet
Total: 2,565 square feet

L

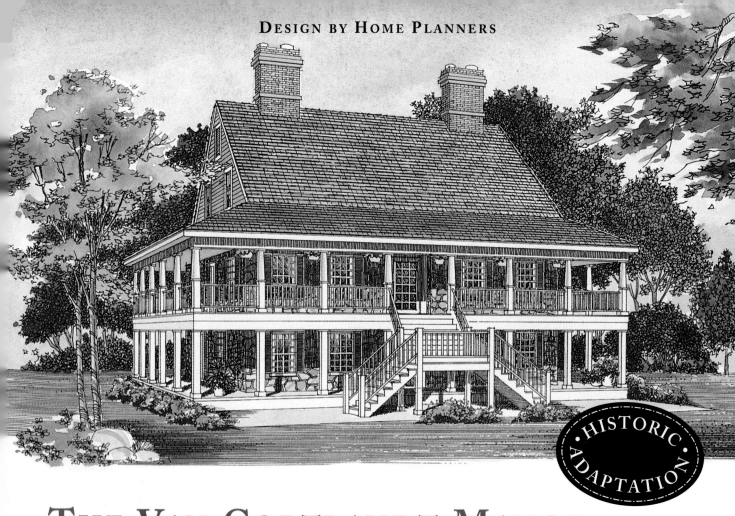

THE VAN CORTLANDT MANOR

THIS DESIGN RECALLS the Van Cortlandt Manor, a good example of the fieldstone farmhouses built in New York's Hudson Valley during the 18th Century. Original portions of the manor date to the 1600s, when the house was used as hunting lodge. In 1749, the third Lord of the Manor moved his family from New York City for year-round living in this estate. The upper stories were added at that time. The house soon became a center for social life and political history, with visits from Benjamin Franklin, the Marquis de Lafayette and George Washington.

The wonderful wraparound porches on both levels give this home the look of a Louisiana plantation house, but Dutch Colonial style is there in the stone exterior, the double-sloped roof and the massive chimneys. A dramatic split staircase creates a grand entrance leading to the second floor,

> **Van Cortlandt Manor is located on South River Avenue in Croton-on-Hudson, NY, and is open from 10 a.m. to 5 p.m. daily, except Tuesdays, April through October, and on weekends in November and December.**
>
> •
>
> **For information, contact: Historic Hudson Valley at 914-631-8200; or the Manor at 914-271-8981.**
>
> •

the main living area of the house. To the left of the foyer, the formal living room shares a through-fireplace with the family room. Both rooms have built-in cabinetry, as does the den, which also has a fireplace. The U-shaped kitchen features a breakfast counter that separates the work area from the living space. The laundry area provides a

COLONIAL
HOUSES

HOME PLANNERS, LLC
Wholly owned by Hanley-Wood, Inc.
TUCSON, ARIZONA

COLONIAL HOUSES

Published by Home Planners, LLC
Wholly owned by Hanley-Wood, Inc.
Editorial and Corporate Offices:
3275 West Ina Road, Suite 110
Tucson, Arizona 85741

Distribution Center:
29333 Lorie Lane
Wixom, Michigan 48393

Rickard D. Bailey, *CEO and Publisher*
Cindy Coatsworth Lewis, *Director of Publishing*
Jan Prideaux, *Senior Editor*
Sarah P. Smith, *Editor*
Matthew S. Kauffman, *Graphic Designer*

Design/Photography Credits
Front and Back Covers:
    Plan 2683 by Home Planners
    Photos by Laszlo Regos

First Printing, September 1998

10 9 8 7 6 5 4 3 2 1

Printed in the United States of America

Library of Congress
Catalog Card Number: 98-072351

ISBN softcover: 1-881955-47-8

TABLE OF CONTENTS

HISTORIC ADAPTATION

This symbol indicates designs that are historic adaptations. The exteriors of more than 90 plans in this book are based on actual Colonial houses. In many cases, the history of the house or its occupants is included. The floor plans are not historically accurate, but are designed for today's homeowners.

An Introduction To Colonial Architecture

Ranging from the prim New England saltbox to the grandiose Greek Revival mansion, Colonial homes reflect not only diverse cultural customs brought from Europe, but also varying climates, geography and economic conditions encountered in the New World. The earliest dwellings were crude huts, dug into the ground and covered over with mud, turf and branches—at first, shelter from the elements was the most important consideration. But it wasn't long before the settlers started building better dwellings—essentially re-creations of the medieval houses they'd left behind in their native lands.

Most of the first settlers in New England were English immigrants who had come to America in quest of religious freedom. Their houses were simple and free of ostentation. Distinguishing characteristics included a single file of rooms, tiny casement windows, steep (sometimes thatched) roofs, sharply angled gables and lean-to additions. Wood, which was plentiful, was the favored building material. The houses were built of sturdy timbers, hewn from the trees felled as farmland was cleared.

The Cape Cod house originated with the Pilgrims around 1670 and was built throughout coastal regions of the Northeast. Small and snug, Cape Cods generally had only one or two rooms, often with a lean-to addition in the rear. Typically one-and-one-half stories high, they sat low in the landscape, providing minimal resistance to harsh coastal winds. A particularly recognizable feature is the gable roof,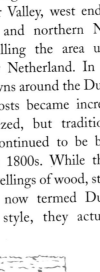

CAPE COD

which slopes down from the peak at a 45-degree angle, stopping just above the front door and multi-pane windows. Cape Cods generally faced south in order to take advantage of the winter sun.

Dutch immigrants settled the Hudson River Valley, west end of Long Island and northern New Jersey, controlling the area until 1664 as New Netherland. In the 1700s, the towns around the Dutch fur-trading posts became increasingly Anglicized, but traditional farmhouses continued to be built well into the 1800s. While these low, broad dwellings of wood, stone or brick are now termed Dutch Colonial in style, they actually reflect an amalgam of building traditions brought together by many groups. The distinguishing feature of many so-called Dutch Colonial houses—a sloping roofline with flared eaves—has no known precedent in Holland, but may be Flemish in origin. Numerous Dutch Colonial houses were also built with gambrel roofs, which have a double slope on each side. The gambrel, an economical roofing system also used by the English, developed during the 1700s to increase the roof span and provide more space on the upper story of the house. Still other Dutch houses have a simple peaked roof, often steeply pitched in the medieval tradition.

The interior plans of Dutch houses could vary, but, like those of the New England Colonial houses, they featured a best room, or *dotenkammer* (parlor-bedroom) furnished with a master bed.

Pennsylvania, founded by the English Quaker William Penn, became a haven for numerous groups that were fleeing persecution in Europe. Their farmhouses, built up into the 1800s and associated in particular with parts of Pennsylvania and Maryland, display a mixture of Germanic design traditions. Because these colonies were English, the houses invariably incorporated English elements as

EARLY COLONIAL

well—a door made in an English carpentry shop or a Georgian floor plan featuring a central hall and end chimneys.

FARMHOUSE

Generally, houses built in the Germanic tradition can be recognized by their solid and rectangular forms, often with thick masonry walls made from fieldstone. Dormers frequently protruded from the roof to light the second story. Other distinguishing features included a projecting hood over the door and a long, narrow pent roof jutting out over the first story.

At the same time that colonists were establishing towns in the north, communities were also prospering in well-populated southern regions like the Virginia Tidewater. Among the Tidewater homesteaders were many skilled craftsmen, including bricklayers from regions in England where masonry was an established building tradition. Thus, while wood was still the dominant building material for Virginia houses, brick was also frequently used—particularly as the area offered a ready supply of clay for making bricks and oyster shells for lime to make mortar.

Like their New England counterparts, early Colonial Virginia farmhouses were simple and practical dwellings, often having a two-story center section flanked by low

wings and usually containing one or two rooms on the ground floor. While there were various floor plans, it was not uncommon for the chimney (or chimneys) to be placed on the end of the structure rather than in the center (as was typical of New England houses). The end chimneys may have been designed to draw heat away from the rooms, an important consideration during the hot southern summers. A central passageway running from front to back was also frequently incorporated, to help channel cooling breezes throughout the house.

French immigrants, mostly Huguenots facing religious persecution, began settling in Southern colonies in the 17th Century. For the most part, they built simple homes distinguished by a steep gabled roof that broke near the peak and sloped easily over the front and rear "galleries" or porches. The French farmhouse in America became a cozy cottage and soon could be found all of the way from the Carolinas north to Maryland.

In Louisiana, the French built one-story homes surrounded by a gallery or porch and topped with a hip roof. In regions that were prone to flooding, builders used stone piers to raise the houses off the ground. Eventually, such raised cottages became a popular style

GEORGIAN

throughout the South, regardless of flood conditions.

As the nation entered the 18th Century, a prosperous merchant class developed. The presence of Royal Governors in the colonies ignited interest in whatever fashions were currently the rage across the Atlantic. From approximately 1700 until 1780, Georgian was the dominant style for the landed gentry who could afford its grandeur. Commerce was thriving, with plantations in the South and seaports in the North, and the prosperous welcomed the pretentious Georgian design as a statement of their wealth and elegant lifestyle.

With vastly improved communications, news—and trends—traveled rapidly. Consequently, the Georgian house developed a somewhat similar look in all the colonies. That look—ordered symmetry—was rooted in the formal principles of classical design set forth in the treatises of Andrea Palladio, a 16th-Century Italian Renaissance architect. Many Georgian homes were built from patterns and carpentry books shipped from Europe.

The basic Georgian house was a one- or two-story box with symmetrical windows and doors and two rooms deep. It usually included a massive chimney, dentils and pedimented dormers. The front door was a major feature, often flanked with pilasters (esssentially flattened columns) and topped with a pediment or cornice. Generally, Georgians in the South were of brick or stone construction, while New England Georgians were mainly of wood.

American architecture in the late 1700s was influenced by two related trends—a surge of nationalism following independence and a deepened interest in classical design, heightened by recent archaeological discoveries in Rome and Greece. With the new Federal government came what is now known as the Federal style, favored until about 1820. Exterior designs became simpler, yet more elegant, with elongated proportions as the heavier massing of the Georgian period gave way to a graceful lightness. The box shape of Georgian homes was often expanded to include wings. While classical detail still prevailed, the facades were generally plain—perhaps gently broken into a rhythmic sequence of slightly projecting arches. The smoothness of flush-boarded walls or painted brick or stucco demonstrates this understatement, as does the bare simplicity of painted plaster walls. A more elongated Palladian window was in favor, as were circular and elliptical window shapes. The Federal house often featured a curved or polygon-shaped bay added to an exterior wall and a balustrade or parapet over the eaves (rather than high on the roof).

The so-called Federal doorway typically featured an arched fanlight and sidelights. There might also be an elegant portico, centrally positioned to emphasize the classical symmetry of the overall design. Doorways kept their pilasters and

columns, and were often topped with flat entablature. Corners were usually unmarked by quoins or ornamental pilasters.

The 1820s marked yet another new beginning for America. With the War of 1812 over, it was a time of peace and prosperity; the country regarded the future with a renewed sense of optimism. Mindful of their own recently gained freedom, Americans also looked on with interest and sympathy as the Greeks engaged in a war of independence from Turkey during the early years of the century.

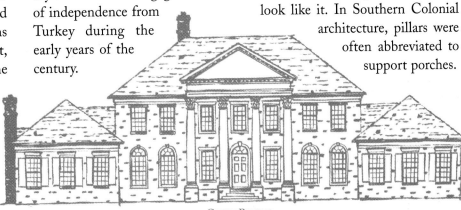

GREEK REVIVAL.

A passion for all things Greek soon swept the United States. Embodying beauty, breadth and permanence, no other architecture seemed better suited to the national ideal than the splendid temples of Classical Greece—the earliest democracy in recorded history.

In its purest form, the Greek Revival differed from the Federal style in its far stricter adherence to the Greek—as distinct from Roman—vocabulary of architecture. Columns were sturdier, profiles were squarer, lines were straighter. As was true in other periods, the style was modified to suit particular needs, local materials and personal preferences; every architect, builder and carpenter in the nation, it seemed, tried his hand at a Greek temple!

In all cases, however, there was some reference to classical design, no matter how remote. Invariably the facade was crowned by a pediment, which might be a full-blown design or merely suggested by a molding at the gable end of the roof. The front door was typically framed with pilasters and an entablature, or with sidelights and a transom of simple, square glass panes. Columns were featured on major houses, and if a house was not built of marble, it was painted white to look like it. In Southern Colonial architecture, pillars were often abbreviated to support porches.

The Greek Revival period, which prevailed until the time of the Civil War, represented the culmination of classical expression in America. Lying ahead was the age of Romanticism, which would popularize an eclectic range of architectural styles. The Colonial period, by contrast, stands on its own, an enduring testament to fine design. ▪

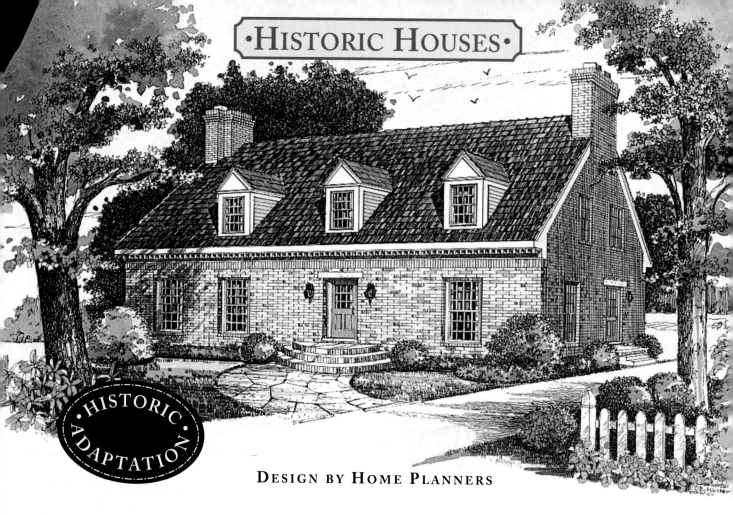

·HISTORIC· ADAPTATION

DESIGN BY HOME PLANNERS

THE ADAM THOROUGHGOOD HOUSE

ADAM THOROUGHGOOD was born in Norfolk County, England, in the town of Lynn. Like many of his country-men, he came to the Colonies as an indentured servant, arriving in Virginia in 1621. After gaining his liberty, he became active in politics and by 1629 had been elected to the House of Burgesses. In 1635, he was granted ten square miles of land near Norfolk, Virginia, for bringing more than a hundred settlers to the colony. On this land he built what is believed to be the first brick house in America and the oldest house in Virginia.

This stately cottage was built of sunbaked, straw-bound bricks and demonstrates many of the features of the simple home-building style that early settlers brought with them from England, including a steeply pitched gabled roof, case-ment windows and a two-room "hall-and-parlor" floor plan. The massive chim-neys were pyramidal in shape, a Tudor feature, and origi-nally extended out from the ends of the house. The dormers were a later addi-tion, as was the den-tiled cornice along the roofline. The fan-shaped stoop makes an attractive approach to the original home—and to this adaption.

Inside, the floor plan is totally up-to-date. The

The Adam Thoroughgood House is located at 1636 Parish Road, Virginia Beach, VA 23455.

•

It is open to the public from Tuesday through Saturday, 10 a.m. to 5 p.m.; Sunday 1 p.m. to 5 p.m.

•

For information, call 757-460-0007.

•

handy closet and a powder room that will be appreciated by both family members and guests. Note that there are also closets in the foyer, the den and the hall. The upper-level wrap-around porch can be reached through doors in the living room, the family room and the laundry.

Sleeping quarters are on the lower level. The spacious master suite features a fourth fireplace and a private bath with a windowed garden tub, a separate shower and twin lavatories. Two closets, including a walk-in, provide plenty of storage. Two additional bedrooms share a full bath.

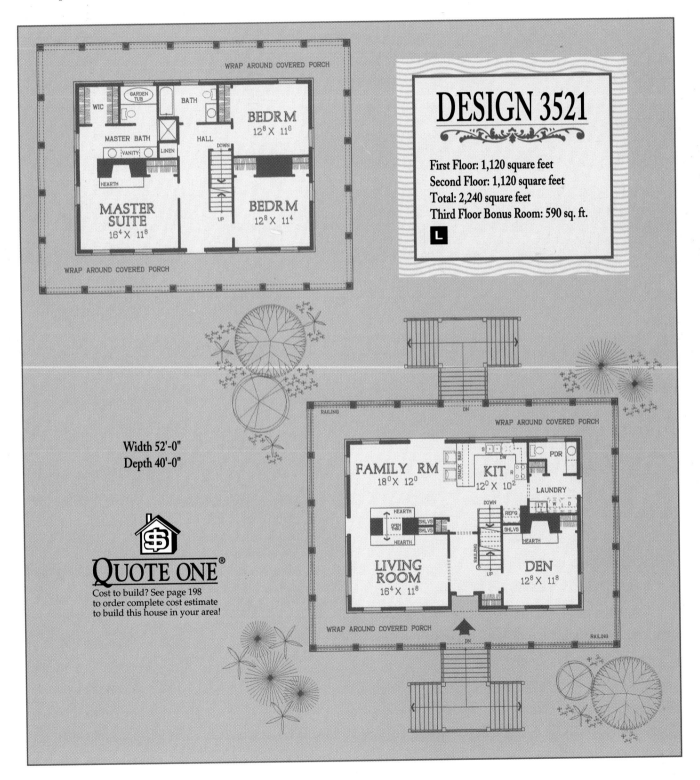

DESIGN 3521

First Floor: 1,120 square feet
Second Floor: 1,120 square feet
Total: 2,240 square feet
Third Floor Bonus Room: 590 sq. ft.

L

Width 52'-0"
Depth 40'-0"

QUOTE ONE®

Cost to build? See page 198 to order complete cost estimate to build this house in your area!

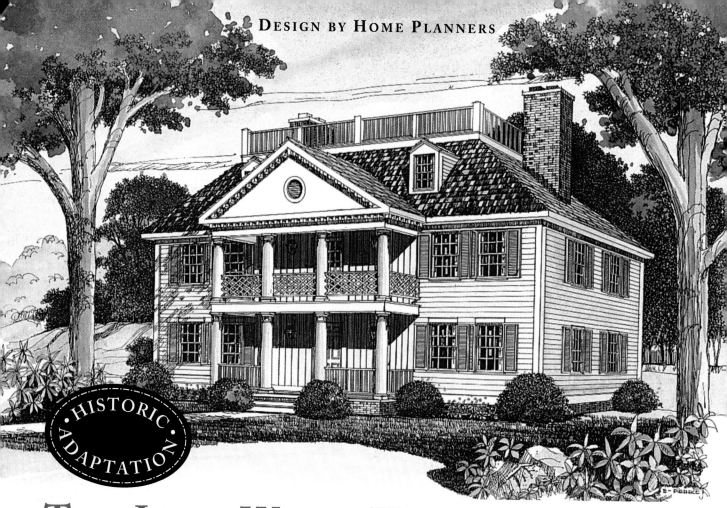

HISTORIC · ADAPTATION

THE JULIA WOOD HOUSE

THIS CAPE COD GEOR-gian recalls the Julia Wood House, built in 1790 in Falmouth, Massachusetts, by Dr. Francis Wicks as his home and office. Dr. Wicks is remembered as a pioneer of smallpox vaccination and for serving in the medical corps of the Revolutionary Army. He was a respected citizen of Falmouth, who charged his patients according to what they could afford and whose office was always open to those who needed him.

Like the original, this elegant adaptation combines elements of Georgian, Federal and Greek Revival architecture. The exterior is sheathed in clap-boards and topped by a hip roof. The two-story portico supported by col-umns creates a par-ticularly attractive entrance. Like many homes along the seacoast, the Julia Wood House was topped with a bal-ustraded roof deck, where wives of sea captains looked for signs of returning ships. The fact

The Julia Wood House, located at 15 Palmer Avenue in Falmouth, Massachusetts, is open Wednesday through Sunday, 2 to 5 p.m., from mid-June through mid-September.

•

For information, call 508-548-4857.

•

that they often searched in vain gave rise to the name "widow's walk" for this structure.

The elegance con-tinues inside, where formal rooms flank the foyer. The din-ing room features an impressive fireplace and a niche for dis-playing family trea-sures. A two-way fireplace warms both the formal living room and the family room, which also provides a built-in wood box and a media niche. Cooks will enjoy the U-shaped kitchen and family members will appreciate quick meals at the snack bar in the breakfast nook. The utility area includes a pantry, space for laundry facilities and plenty of storage. A small porch here leads to the backyard, as do sliding glass doors in the breakfast nook.

Upstairs, the master suite features a walk-in closet, a garden tub, a shower with a seat, and twin vanities. Two family bedrooms with built-in shelves share a full bath and linen closet. A third-floor studio lit by dormers is perfect for the artist or craftsperson in the family. With its own full bathroom, it could also become a fourth bedroom. A ladder leads up to the widow's walk, a pleasant place for sunning or even, perhaps, for entertaining.

DESIGN 3520

First Floor: 1,232 square feet
Second Floor: 1,232 square feet
Third Floor: 421 square feet
Total: 2,885 square feet

D

QUOTE ONE®

Cost to build? See page 198 to order complete cost estimate to build this house in your area!

Width 44'-0"
Depth 34'-0"

HISTORIC · ADAPTATION

MAGNOLIA MOUND

THIS SOUTHERN DESIGN is based on one of Louisiana's oldest wood structures, a typical Creole house called Magnolia Mound. Originally just four rooms, it was built in 1791 by an Irish merchant, John Joyce, for the overseer of his 900-acre indigo plantation. Following Joyce's death by drowning in 1798, his widow married Armand Duplantier, a French cavalry officer who had served with Lafayette in the American Revolution. The Duplantiers made Magnolia Mound their home, adding to it as their family grew.

The house was built of cypress and included a hip roof to dispel rainwater and pilings to raise the structure off the ground, protecting it from floods while also helping to dispel the heat and humidity. The "umbrella" roof extended out in a smooth line to cover porches, or galleries, which were an essential part of family living space, especially during the summer, when furniture was moved outside. Wide doorways allowed breezes to sweep through the house. A feature not included in our adaptation was the use of *bousillage*, a mixture of mud and Spanish moss packed between the broad wooden studs of the walls.

The floor plan of Magnolia Mound was a typical French design in that each room opened to another, rather than being served by a central hallway. In the one-story original, as in this version, all first-floor rooms opened to a porch. In all other ways, our floor plan is totally up-to-date. Formal living and dining rooms are located to

Now a museum, Magnolia Mound is open Tuesday through Saturday, from 10 a.m. to 4 p.m., and Sunday from 1 p.m. to 4 p.m.

•

For more information, contact Magnolia Mound, 2161 Nicholson Drive, Baton Rouge, LA 70802; 504-343-4955.

•

the front of the home. Each boasts a fireplace and two French doors to the front porch. A powder room and storage/coat closets are nearby. Informal living areas function with the rear covered porch for excellent indoor/outdoor relationships. The spacious family room has a ten-foot beam ceiling, its own fireplace and a handy snack bar for casual meals. The efficient U-shaped kitchen features a work island and an indoor barbecue grill. The nearby laundry room has a large closet and access to the back porch.

The master suite is on the second floor and includes two walk-in closets plus a luxury bath with two lava-tories, a linen closet, an ultra tub and a separate shower. Dormers provide natural light for the two front bedrooms, one of which has a private bath. The other shares a bath with the fourth bedroom.

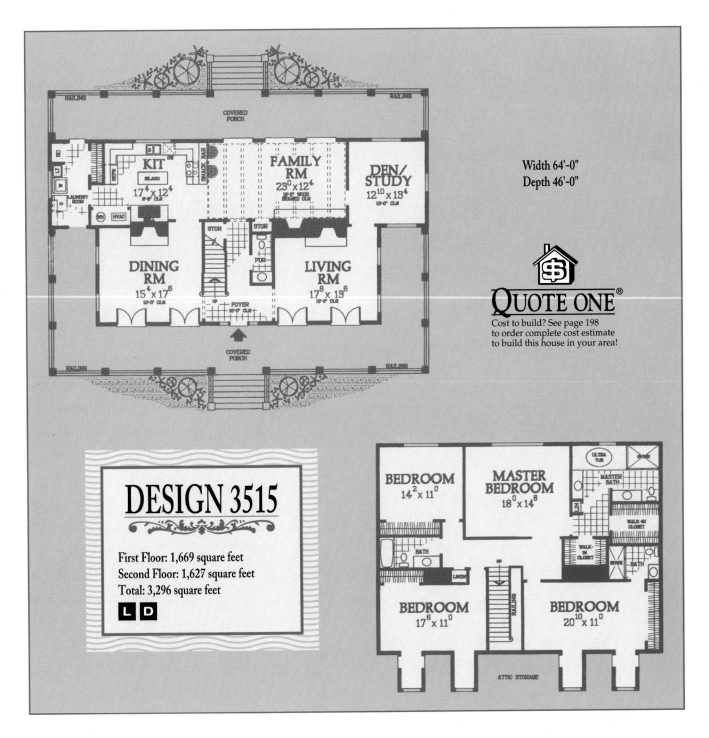

Width 64'-0"
Depth 46'-0"

Quote One®

Cost to build? See page 198
to order complete cost estimate
to build this house in your area!

DESIGN 3515

First Floor: 1,669 square feet
Second Floor: 1,627 square feet
Total: 3,296 square feet

L D

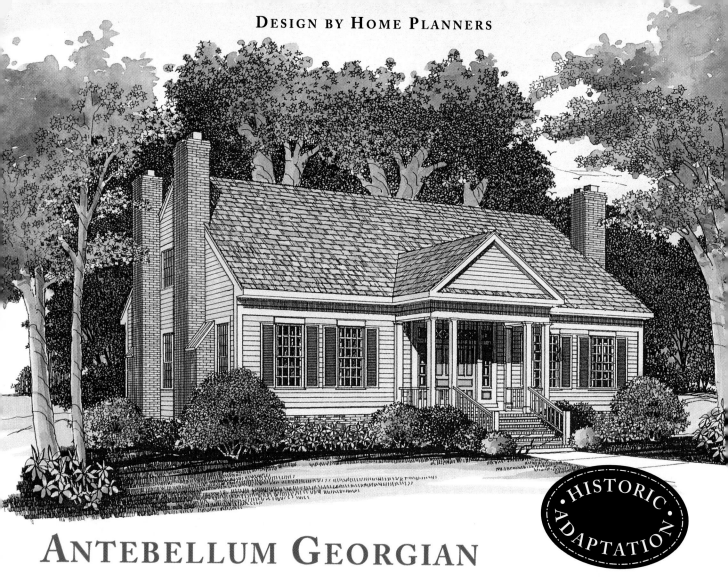

ANTEBELLUM GEORGIAN

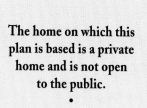

HISTORIC ADAPTATION

THIS DESIGN RECALLS the style of an antebellum house built in Georgia in 1828 and believed to have been built by Henry Houton, who won the land in a lottery. Both the original and the reproduction exhibit elements of Greek Revival style—raised-panel doors with sidelights and a transom, a pedimented front portico with square columns and a symmetrical arrangement of windows. The outside chimneys are a distinctively Southern feature, designed to draw heat away from the interior of the house before the advent of air-conditioning.

This adaptation is a timber-frame structure with a masonry foundation covered by a brick veneer, wood siding (or vinyl) and a shingle roof. Inside, the floor plan provides plenty of living space for a family of four, with the possibility of expansion in the full basement. With the master suite on the first floor, the upstairs can be kept for guests, making this ideal as a starter or retirement home.

The heart of this home will be the country kitchen, which features an efficient work space with an island snack bar, a pantry, a planning desk

The home on which this plan is based is a private home and is not open to the public.

•

and glass doors to the brick back porch. There's plenty of room here for a kitchen table or for a grouping of casual furniture in front of the fireplace. The living room is separate, providing a quiet space for entertaining or relaxing. It also has a fireplace. A coat closet and a powder room are nearby for the convenience of guests and family members.

The master bedroom has its own fireplace, a romantic touch that transforms the room into a welcome retreat. The large master bath has a whirlpool tub, a separate shower, twin vanities and a walk-in closet.

The laundry room is nearby, with access to the back porch. Upstairs, two bedrooms share a full hall bath and a linen closet. A good-sized open lounge area with a built-in desk would make a perfect study, sleeping loft or playroom.

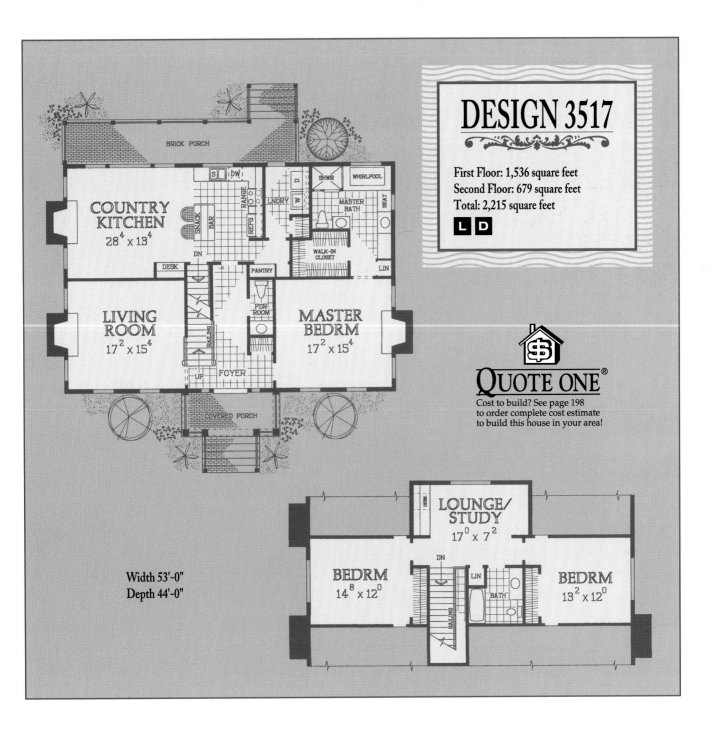

DESIGN 3517

First Floor: 1,536 square feet
Second Floor: 679 square feet
Total: 2,215 square feet

L D

QUOTE ONE®

Cost to build? See page 198 to order complete cost estimate to build this house in your area!

Width 53'-0"
Depth 44'-0"

OLIVER LOUD'S TAVERN

O LIVER LOUD'S TAVERN, built in 1812, was originally a stagecoach stop in the hamlet of Egypt, New York. The owner had grown up in Massachusetts, which may explain the New England farmhouse-style construction. Loud was also a sawmill operator, a pamphleteer, an amateur astronomer and a public official—a true Renaissance man. His tavern reflected this, boasting refined Federal and Greek Revival moldings, French wallpapers, and doors that were painted to resemble mahogany. Unfortunately, after many years of catering to weary travelers, the tavern's business began to decline. In 1825, the Erie Canal opened just a few miles away, and people and goods traveled by water rather than by road. Fortunately, before the tavern could be demolished, it was moved to nearby Pittsford, where it was restored and reopened as Oliver Loud's Country Inn.

This adaptation of the tavern retains the charming wraparound porch, as well as decorative touches such as the paneled front door with sidelights and the cornice returns. Expansive roof planes, symmetrically placed windows, effectively stationed columns and a massive brick chimney add to the appeal. The central foyer is flanked by the formal dining room and the living room, which features one of the home's three stone fireplaces.

Oliver Loud's Country Inn is open for business at 1474 Marsh Road, Pittsford, NY 14534, four miles from its original location.

•

For more information, call 716-248-5200.

•

Conveniently located near the dining room is the step-saving kitchen, which boasts an island cooktop, a pantry and a built-in planning desk. The kitchen is open to the nook, with access to the back porch, and the family room. Casual gatherings in the family room are enhanced by a blazing fire in the fireplace, and a built-in cabinet designed to hold favorite movies or family games. A spacious laundry room and a powder room complete the first floor.

Upstairs, two family bedrooms share a full bath with a double-sink vanity. The master suite will be a homeowners' retreat with its own warming fireplace and built-in shelves. A wealth of closet space—including a walk-in closet with a built-in seat and cabinet—serves the large dressing area. A luxurious master bath pampers with a whirlpool tub, a separate shower, a compartmented toilet and twin vanities.

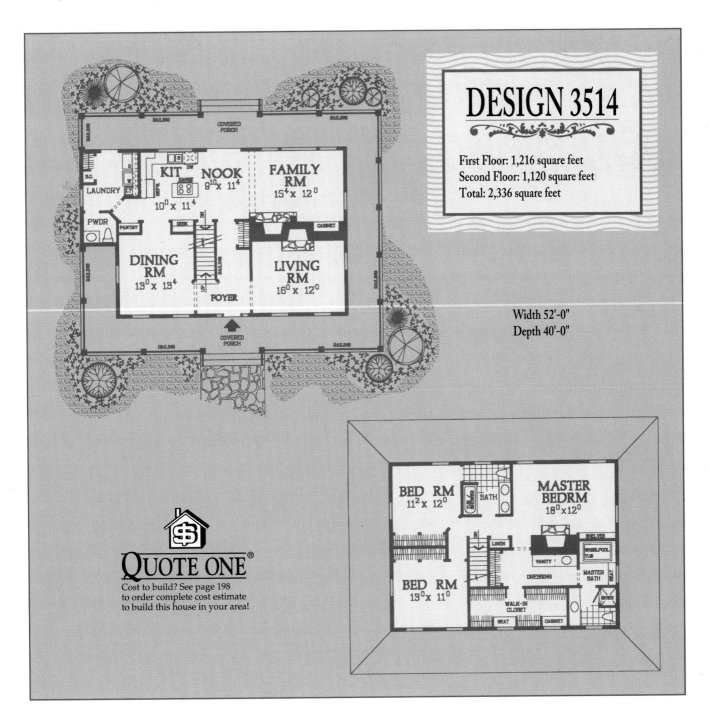

DESIGN 3514

First Floor: 1,216 square feet
Second Floor: 1,120 square feet
Total: 2,336 square feet

Width 52'-0"
Depth 40'-0"

QUOTE ONE®
Cost to build? See page 198
to order complete cost estimate
to build this house in your area!

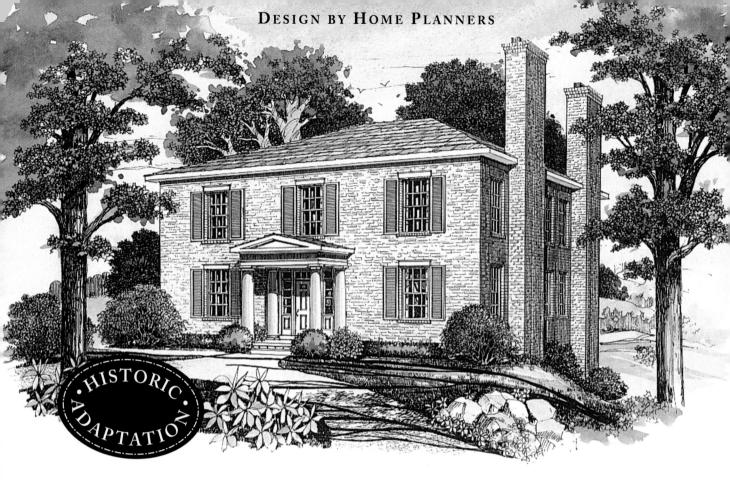

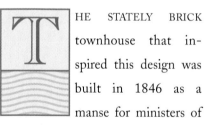

WOODROW WILSON BIRTHPLACE

THE STATELY BRICK townhouse that inspired this design was built in 1846 as a manse for ministers of the Presbyterian Church in Staunton, Virginia. The Rev. Joseph Wilson was called to serve as the church's minister in 1855. His son, future President Woodrow Wilson was born there on December 12, 1856. The family moved to a larger church in Augusta, Georgia, less than two years later, but the house is now a National Historic Landmark, telling the story of Wilson's presidency and providing an authentic picture of family life of that time.

Like many structures built in the mid-1830s, especially in the South, this one featured such trademark Greek Revival elements as an overall block-like shape, a hip roof and a pedimented porch supported by columns. A two-story columned portico in the rear also recalls the style.

Three levels of living potential are found inside. The foyer is flanked by the formal dining room and the parlor, which has a commanding fireplace. A coat closet and a powder room are nearby for the convenience of guests. The L-shaped kitchen will be a delight for the family cook. It has an island cooktop with cabinets below, a pantry, a planning desk, a broom closet and built-in ovens. It is open to the spacious great room with a fireplace and rear-portico access. The second floor offers exceptional livability. The media room, with its

> **The Woodrow Wilson Birthplace is now a museum and displays memorabilia of our 28th President.**
>
> •
>
> **It is located at 24 North Coalter Street, Staunton, VA 24401, and is open daily from 9 a.m. to 5 p.m.**
>
> •
>
> **For more information, call 703-885-0897.**
>
> •

entertainment center and access to the upper railed portico, may also serve as a fourth bedroom. The master bedroom has a fireplace and a fine bath. The lower level offers a guest bedroom and an incredible activities room with a mini-kitchen.

REAR VIEW

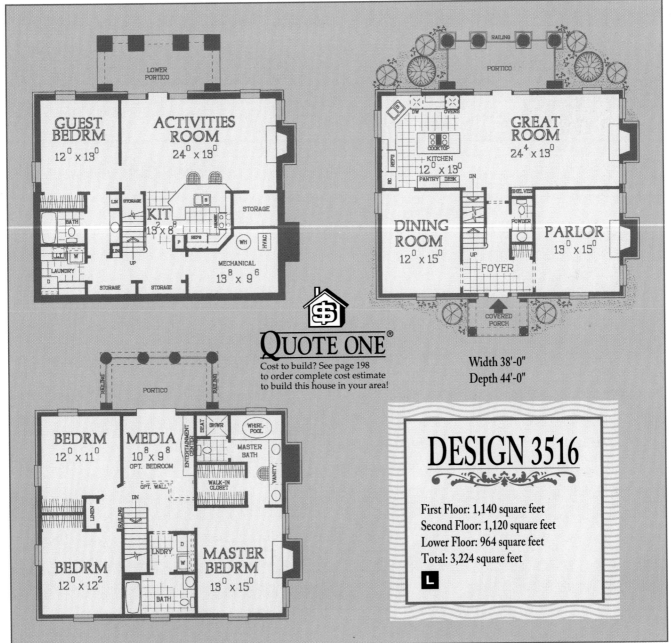

LOWER PORTICO

GUEST BEDRM
12⁰ x 13⁰

ACTIVITIES ROOM
24⁰ x 13⁰

BATH

LIN STORAGE

KIT
13⁸ x 8⁰

STORAGE

LAUNDRY

W

D

UP

STORAGE

STORAGE

WH

HVAC

MECHANICAL
13⁸ x 9⁶

PORTICO

RAILING

GREAT ROOM
24⁴ x 13⁰

DW

OVENS

COOK TOP

KITCHEN
12⁰ x 13⁰

PANTRY

DESK

SHELVES

DINING ROOM
12⁰ x 15⁰

DN

UP

POWDER

PARLOR
13⁰ x 15⁰

FOYER

COVERED PORCH

Width 38'-0"
Depth 44'-0"

QUOTE ONE®
Cost to build? See page 198 to order complete cost estimate to build this house in your area!

PORTICO

RAILING

BEDRM
12⁰ x 11⁰

MEDIA
10⁸ x 9⁸
OPT. BEDROOM

ENTERTAINMENT CENTER

SEAT

SHWR

WHIRLPOOL

MASTER BATH

VANITY

OPT. WALL

WALK-IN CLOSET

DN

BEDRM
12⁰ x 12²

RAILING

LINEN

LNDRY

D

W

MASTER BEDRM
13⁰ x 15⁰

BATH

DESIGN 3516

First Floor: 1,140 square feet
Second Floor: 1,120 square feet
Lower Floor: 964 square feet
Total: 3,224 square feet

L

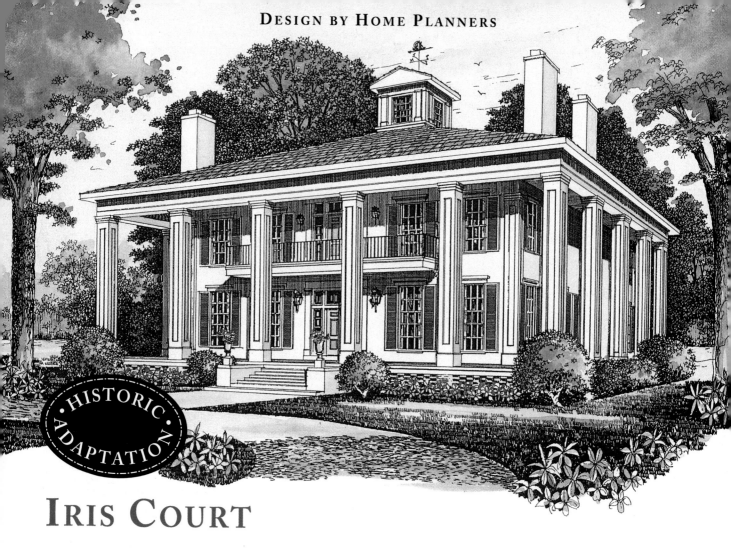

HISTORIC · ADAPTATION

IRIS COURT

I

N 1853, WHEN ALBANY, Georgia, was still in the middle of nowhere, itinerant house builders were the best sources of information about house fashions then popular in Atlanta and Savannah. After consulting such a traveler, Judge John Jackson chose the most elaborate design available, in a popular Greek Revival format called "Creole-Hellenic." Following the Civil War, the house served for a while as the headquarters for the Federal general in charge of occupation troops. A descendant of Judge

Jackson loved flowers and chose the name Iris Court after filling her front yard with irises. After her death in 1962, the house was saved from destruction by an Atlanta businessman, who had it moved to a nearby community, where he restored it to use as a weekend home.

The most distinctive feature of Iris Court is the colonnade of sixteen pillars that wraps almost completely around the house, creating a two-

The home on which this plan is based is a private home and is not open to the public.

•

story portico. The square wooden pillars are in a modified Doric style, decorated with vertical paneling.

Both the original and our version also feature a low-pitched hip roof topped with a windowed cupola and three tall chimneys. The front facade has a second-floor wrought-iron balcony above a Federal-style paneled door with sidelights and transom. Tall windows on the first floor use a six-over-nine configuration, while on the second-floor they are six-over-six.

This grand exterior encloses a spacious two-story floor plan with a center hall. There are six fireplaces—look for them in the living room, dining room, family room, family bedroom, master bedroom and master bath. First-floor views of the rear grounds are enjoyed from the family room and the sun-filled nook. The spacious kitchen boasts a large work island/snack bar, a pantry and easy access to the laundry room and back service entrance. The second floor contains two family bedrooms, each with its own bath, and a lavish master suite with a balcony and a pampering bath. A study/bedroom with its own balcony completes the upstairs. Plans for a detached garage with an enclosed lap pool are included with the blueprints.

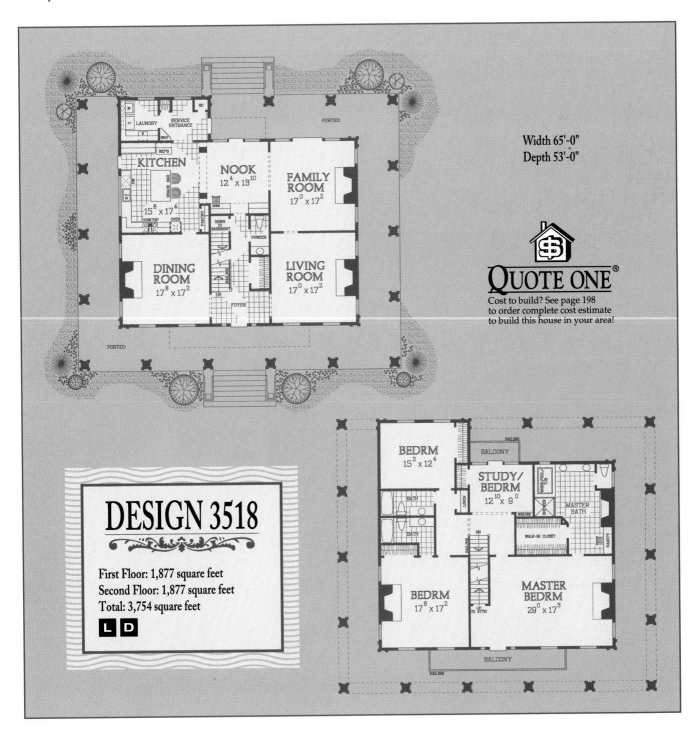

Width 65'-0"
Depth 53'-0"

QUOTE ONE®
Cost to build? See page 198
to order complete cost estimate
to build this house in your area!

DESIGN 3518

First Floor: 1,877 square feet
Second Floor: 1,877 square feet
Total: 3,754 square feet

L D

This home, as shown in the photographs, may differ from the actual blueprints. For more detailed information, please check the floor plans carefully.
Photos by Laszlo Regos

THIS DIGNIFIED BRICK home is reminiscent of Tulip Hill, an 18th-Century manor in Arundel County, Maryland. It features the symmetrical facade and classical details of the Georgian era. Notice also the round window in the pediment and the slender-columned portico. The two-story center section is perfectly complemented by the 1½-story wings, one of which is filled by the elegant step-down gathering room, equally appropriate for family activities or for entertaining on a grand scale. A study and the formal dining room flank the foyer. Each of these rooms is warmed by a fireplace.

Oak paneling and a planked floor are the right touches to reflect the glow of a cozy fire in the first-floor study.

The breakfast room and the kitchen are drenched in sunlight from the sliding glass door and the triple window above the sink. Sleeping quarters on the second floor include three family bedrooms sharing a full bath. The luxurious master suite provides a quiet retreat featuring a fireplace, a pampering master bath, a dressing room with a huge walk-in closet, and a spacious lounge.

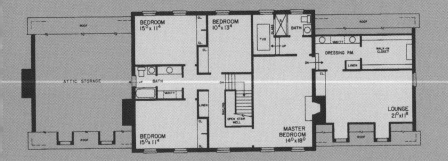

An efficient island kitchen with an adjacent breakfast nook feeds hungry family and friends.

The elegant gathering room is perfect for formal or informal occasions.

Width 92'-0"
Depth 32'-8"

DESIGN 2683

First Floor: 2,126 square feet
Second Floor: 1,882 square feet
Total: 4,008 square feet

L **D**

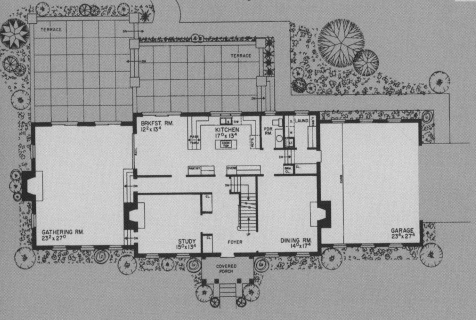

QUOTE ONE®

Cost to build? See page 198
to order complete cost estimate
to build this house in your area!

This home, as shown in the photographs, may differ from the actual blueprints. For more detailed information, please check the floor plans carefully.
Photos by Andrew D. Lautman

T HIS TRADITIONAL CAPE COD COTTAGE is updated with an open floor plan that invites easy living. True to tradition, the formal living room is located in the front of the plan, just off the foyer. Comfortable living will surely be centered around the fireplace in the family room and will spread into the

(Far left) A casual elegance springs from the marble-tiled foyer, which reflects sunlight from an abundance of windows.

The master suite is cozy yet spacious, a perfect homeowners' retreat.

adjoining kitchen. Enjoy casual dining at the snack bar or sit down for a meal in the formal dining room with its bumped-out bay window. A study on the main level would also make a nice guest room, thanks to the full hall bath nearby. Up the central stairs, you will find the master bedroom with a private bath and two secondary bedrooms that have private access to a shared bath.

DESIGN 2571

First Floor: 1,137 square feet
Second Floor: 795 square feet
Total: 1,932 square feet

L D

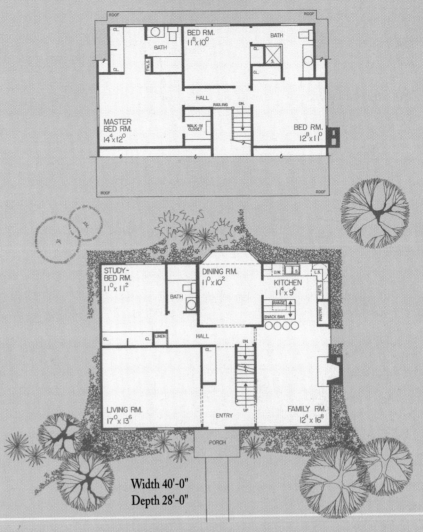

Width 40'-0"
Depth 28'-0"

Removing a kitchen wall changed a peninsula into an island and created an open space with the formal dining room.

This home, as shown in the photographs, may differ from the actual blueprints. For more detailed information, please check the floor plans carefully.
Photos by William G. Kumpf

A slight change in the floor plan puts the fireplace, topped with a wonderful mantel, in the center of the brick wall instead of in a corner.

T HE BRUSH-EVERARD House was built in Williamsburg, Virginia, in 1717. The historic adaptation shown in these photographs includes the steeply pitched roof, gabled dormers and shuttered double-hung windows that were common features of the period. The center entrance leads to the formal areas at the front of the plan and to the family room in back. Both the formal living room and the cozy family room have fireplaces.

The U-shaped kitchen is convenient to both the formal dining room and the breakfast room. A large utility room is located nearby. The sleeping zone is located upstairs for privacy. Three bedrooms include two secondary bedrooms and a lavish master suite.

Earthtone tiles add the finishing touch to the master bath.

A snack bar and a breakfast area provide two options for casual meals.

DESIGN 2520

First Floor: 1,419 square feet
Second Floor: 1,040 square feet
Total: 2,459 square feet

L **D**

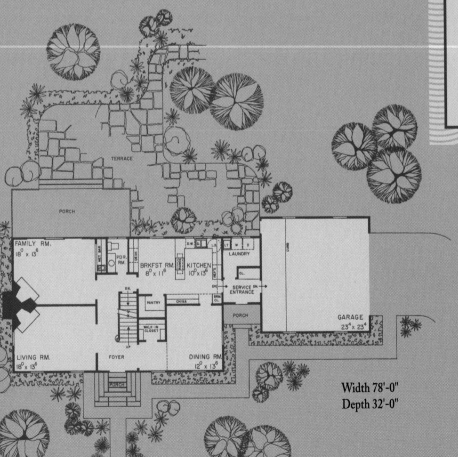

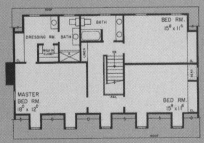

Width 78'-0"
Depth 32'-0"

This home, as shown in the photographs, may differ from the actual blueprints. For more detailed information, please check the floor plans carefully.
Photos by Andrew D. Lautman

THIS CLASSIC GEORGIAN DESIGN CONTAINS a variety of features that make it outstanding: a pediment gable with cornice work and dentils, beautifully proportioned columns, the front-door detailing and the window treatment. Behind the facade is an equally elegant interior. Imagine greeting your friends in the large receiving hall. It is graced by two curving staircases and opens to the formal living and dining rooms. Beyond the living room is the study, which provides access to the rear terrace. The gathering room boasts a fireplace flanked by windows, access to the terrace and a handy wet bar. The work center includes a kitchen with an island cooktop, a break-

A sweeping double stairway highlights an elegant receiving hall.

Built-in bookcases added to any room make a cozy corner for reading.

fast room, a washroom and a laundry. The second-floor sleeping zone is also outstanding. An extension over the garage allows for a huge walk-in closet in the master suite and a full bath with tub in the left front bedroom.

A fireplace flanked by bookcases is the focal point for this comfortable living room.

There's ample space for a sitting area in the sumptuous master bedroom.

DESIGN 2889

First Floor: 2,349 square feet
Second Floor: 1,918 square feet
Total: 4,267 square feet

L D

Width 90'-4"
Depth 44'-8"

QUOTE ONE®

Cost to build? See page 198
to order complete cost estimate
to build this house in your area!

This home, as shown in the photographs, may differ from the actual blueprints. For more detailed information, please check the floor plans carefully.
Photos by Andrew D. Lautman

THE EXTERIOR DETAILING OF THIS RAMBLING CAPE COD RECALLS 18TH-CENTURY NEW ENGLAND architecture. The narrow clapboards and shuttered, multi-pane windows add to the effect. Inside, the wide entry foyer leads to a study or an optional bedroom on the right and a formal living room on the left. A fireplace and sliding glass doors to the solarium enhance this living space. The master bedroom also provides access to the out-of-doors, as well as a private bath with His and Hers vanities and walk-in closets. A sensational family room features a beam ceiling, a full-fledged bar, a built-in desk and a fireplace. Two family bedrooms on the second floor share a full bath with a double vanity.

A deck stretching across the back of the home encourages a variety of outdoor activities.

DESIGN 2615

First Floor: 2,563 square feet
Second Floor: 552 square feet
Total: 3,115 square feet

L D

Width 87'-8"
Depth 68'-8"

QUOTE ONE®

Cost to build? See page 198
to order complete cost estimate
to build this house in your area!

*The large island
kitchen makes food
preparation a breeze.
Furnishings reinforce
the Colonial feel of the
exterior.*

ABOUT THE DESIGNERS

Larry E. Belk Designs

The design philosophy of Larry E. Belk combines traditional exteriors with upscale interiors. Flowing, open spaces and interesting angles define the interiors and provide views that showcase the natural environment. Dynamic exteriors reflect Larry's painstaking research and talent as a fine artist.

Frank Betz Associates, Inc.

Celebrating over twenty years as a leader in the home design industry, Frank Betz Associates touches every point of the homebuilding market with innovative plans. Frank and his associates develop quality, versatile home plans that meet many homebuilding needs.

Chatham Home Planning, Inc.

Based in Mobile, Alabama, Chatham Home Planning was founded over fifteen years ago. Surrounded by beautiful historical homes, the company specializes in designs that have a strong historical look, including Southern cottages, Georgian classics, French Colonials and traditionals. Chatham's first priority is to design a home that is aesthetically pleasing and fits with its surroundings.

Design Basics, Inc.

For over a decade, Design Basics has been developing plans for custom home builders. The firm has consistently appeared in Builder magazine as the top-selling designer. Their Houston-based affiliate, Carmichael & Dame Designs, has brought a fresh, new approach to luxury homes across a broad spectrum of price ranges.

Design Profile, Inc.

With more than twenty years in the design and construction industry, Steve Butcher directs operations for clients in the United States and abroad. The firm specializes in traditional and Southwest home designs with open, flexible floor plans and innovative exteriors. Design Profile, Inc. offers custom design and will modify its stock plans using computer drafting technology

Design Traditions

Design Traditions was established with the tenets of innovation, quality, originality and uncompromising architectural techniques in traditional and European homes. Their plans are known for extensive detail and thoughtful design and are particularly popular throughout the Southeast.

James Fahy Design

James Fahy Design is a full-service architectural engineering firm, providing consulting and principal design services in the residential and light commercial industries. His firm is committed to continual development of fresh, innovative designs through a residential service group.

Fillmore Design Group

The Fillmore Design Group's designs are characterized by European influence, by massive brick gables and high-flowing, graceful rooflines. Each plan is created by an experienced designer and checked and rechecked for accuracy. Attention to detail has paid off in plans that exhibit both quality and appeal.

Donald A. Gardner Architects, Inc.

The firm of Donald A. Gardner was established in response to a demand for designs that reflect constantly changing lifestyles. Don's specialty is providing homes with refined, custom details and open floor plans. Trouble-free construction documents place the firm at the leading edge of the home-plan industry.

Home Planners

Home Planners is one of the longest-running and most successful home design firms in the United States. All of Home Planners designs are created with the care and professional experience that over fifty years in the home-planning business affords. This company's homes are designed to be built, lived in and enjoyed.

Homes For Living, Inc.

Homes For Living was founded by Samuel Paul in the early 1950s. His son David joined the company in 1963. The recipient of many professional awards for outstanding design, the firm follows the tenet that good house design starts with an effective plan, one that is well thought out and efficiently executed to meet its objective.

The Housing Associates

In the old-fashioned manner, R.L. Pfotenhauer believes in the personal approach. Sensitivity to clients' needs brought his efforts to the attention of the public; his special focus on each project has endeared him to clients and allowed him to maintain a national and international presence in the home plans market.

Living Concepts Home Planning

Innovative and versatile, the diversified staff of Living Concepts shows unlimited wealth in both the architectural styles of its designs and its talent. The company's plans range from classical to European with a flair that has helped establish the firm's reputation. Each design is created with an eye toward function and livability.

Greg Marquis and Associates

Incorporating the various features of Southern architecture, the designs of Greg Marquis include emphasis on accurate, detailed drawings and functional floor plans. Greg's designs focus on utilizing space without sacrificing the unique and appealing floor plans which have made his designs so popular.

Alan Mascord Design Associates, Inc.

Mascord Design Associates has a reputation for designing homes that are easy to build, yet meet the rigorous demands of the buyer's market, winning local and national awards. The company's trademark is creating floor plans that work well and exhibit excellent traffic patterns.

Mark Stewart and Associates, Inc.

The strengths of Mark Stewart and Associates include producing popular elevations that give home builders the best value for their money with attractive exteriors and space that is wisely designed for optimum use. The result is a portfolio of practical designs with timeless character.

EARLY NEW ENGLAND STYLES

THE FIRST HOUSES BUILT IN NEW ENGLAND REFLECTED the medieval styles still popular in Europe. They were almost always of wood and employed little ornamentation. Generally two stories high, they were essentially compact boxes, with straightforward lines and simple facades clad in shingles or clapboards.

As warmth was a priority during the bitter New England winters, most had a massive central chimney. Windows were small—usually either fixed in place (night air was believed to be noxious) or casements that swung on hinges. In the early years, when glass was especially hard to come by, the openings were covered with boards or with paper coated in linseed oil.

There were usually just two rooms on the first floor. The "hall" held an enormous cooking fireplace and was used for cooking, eating, sleeping and work. The parlor, or "best room," generally contained the family's finest furnishings, including the master bed—the most elaborate, expensive and important piece of furniture in a household. The upstairs contained a loft or children's bedrooms.

Today's garrison-style home had its beginnings in this era. The overhanging second story, often embellished with carved pendants, was characteristic of 16th-Century houses in England, where it added extra floor space to the top stories of row houses and offered protection to pedestrians below.

Some houses had a rear lean-to, either part of the original house or a later addition. This lean-to, another holdover from medieval England, provided space for a separate kitchen. Its sloping roofline, sweeping almost to the ground in back, echoed the profile of the boxes used to store salt, producing the familiar term "saltbox."

DESIGN 2101

First Floor: 1,338 square feet
Second Floor: 1,114 square feet
Total: 2,452 square feet

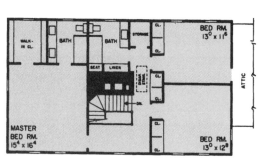

Width 80'-0"
Depth 28'-0"

This design is an adaptation of one of America's most famous Colonial dwellings, built in 1682 by the Reverend Joseph Capen, minister of the church in Topsfield, Massachusetts. Known as the Parson Capen House, it demonstrates many features that are representative of medieval English houses, including the bracketed second-floor overhang, pendant drops at the corners, massive pilastered chimney, narrow clapboards and cedar-shake roof. The floor plan, of course, has been updated and its dimensions enlarged to cater to today's living requirements. Exposed beams and fireplaces in the family and living rooms add to the Colonial theme, while the U-shaped kitchen, breakfast nook and powder room are definitely 20th-Century additions. The second floor offers three bedrooms, including a master suite with a large walk-in closet and double sinks in the bathroom.

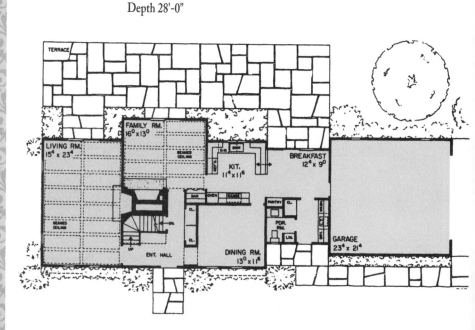

Design by R. L. Pfotenhauer

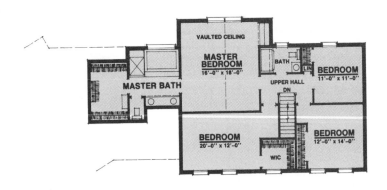

VAULTED CEILING

MASTER
BEDROOM
16'-0" x 18'-0"

BATH

LIN

MASTER BATH

BEDROOM
11'-0" x 11'-0"

UPPER HALL

DN

BEDROOM
20'-0" x 12'-0"

BEDROOM
12'-0" x 14'-0"

WIC

Width 92'-9"
Depth 36'-1"

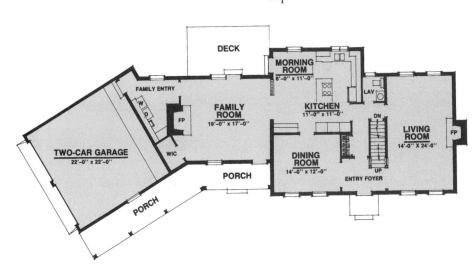

DECK

MORNING
ROOM
8'-0" x 11'-0"

FAMILY ENTRY

W
D

FP

FAMILY
ROOM
19'-0" x 17'-0"

KITCHEN
11'-0" x 11'-0"

LAV

DN

LIVING
ROOM
14'-0" X 24'-0"

FP

WIC

TWO-CAR GARAGE
22'-0" x 22'-0"

DINING
ROOM
14'-0" x 12'-0"

UP

PORCH

ENTRY FOYER

PORCH

DESIGN F124

First Floor: 1,527 square feet
Second Floor: 1,301 square feet
Total: 2,828 square feet

This is a wonderful four-bedroom family home with an angled side-entry garage and a porch with ranch-style trim. Lots of windows brighten the foyer from the adjoining formal dining room and living room, which has a fireplace. The large island kitchen contains a morning room with access to the rear deck. The family room has a walk-in closet next to a second fireplace, and access to the front porch and the rear deck. Upstairs, the master bedroom features a vaulted ceiling and a private bath with a garden tub and a compartmented toilet. Three family bedrooms and a full bath complete the plan.

DESIGN 2692

First Floor: 1,818 square feet
Second Floor: 1,395 square feet
Total: 3,213 square feet
Greenhouse: 147 square feet

The clapboarded saltbox exterior, diamond-pane windows and second-floor overhang were common features of 17th-Century New England homes. This adaptation is based on the Hyland House in Guilford, Connecticut. The original house was built in 1660; the saltbox shape was created in 1720 when a lean-to was added by Ebenezer Parmalee. In this house, Parmalee made the first town clock in America. The greenhouse is certain to be a focal point in this comfortable home. An adjacent clutter room offers endless possibilities with its potting area, space for a freezer, and ample space for hobbies, sewing and other activities. The country kitchen incorporates a cozy fireplace and U-shaped work area with built-ins. Formal areas are across the front of the house, with a quiet study in back. A large master suite is located upstairs, along with three other bedrooms.

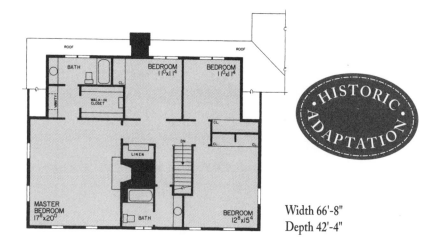

· HISTORIC ·
ADAPTATION

Width 66'-8"
Depth 42'-4"

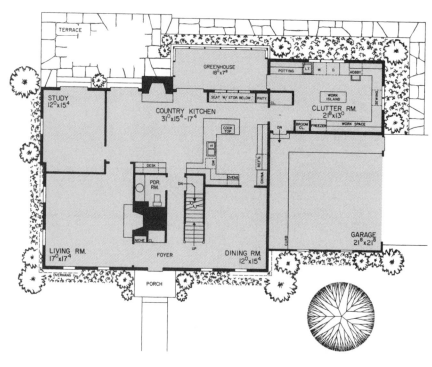

A. J. YOUNG
FUQUAY VARINA, N.C.

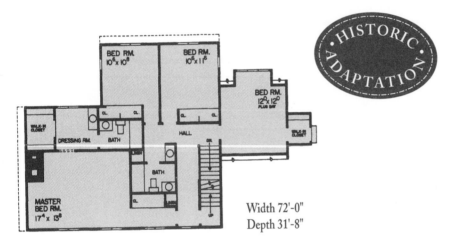

BED RM.
10⁶ x 10⁶

BED RM.
10⁶ x 11⁶

BED RM.
12⁰ x 12⁰
PLUS BAY

WALK-IN CLOSET

DRESSING RM.

BATH

HALL

WALK-IN CLOSET

BATH

MASTER BED RM.
17⁴ x 13⁸

·HISTORIC·
ADAPTATION

Width 72'-0"
Depth 31'-8"

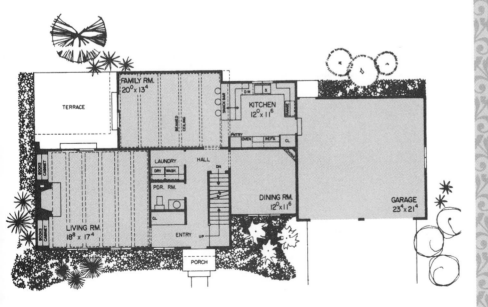

TERRACE

FAMILY RM.
20⁰ x 13⁴

SNACK BAR

KITCHEN
12⁰ x 11⁶

DW

BEAMED CEILING

PANTRY

OVEN

REFR.

BOOKS CABINET

LAUNDRY
DRY WASH

HALL

DN

LIVING RM.
18⁸ x 17⁴

PDR. RM.

DINING RM.
12⁰ x 11⁶

GARAGE
23⁴ x 21⁴

BOOKS CABINET

ENTRY

UP

PORCH

DESIGN 2642

First Floor: 1,222 square feet
Second Floor: 1,233 square feet
Total: 2,455 square feet

This design is based on one of the foremost examples of early Colonial style, Boston's Paul Revere House, built around 1676. The oldest house in Boston, it was the home of the great patriot from 1770 until 1800. The exterior reflects the medieval influence through design elements such as the bracketed second-floor overhang, pendant drops and weatherboarding. Colonial details include exposed beams in the living room and family room, wood-paneled walls in the entry and a built-in corner china cabinet in the dining room. Today's family will appreciate the U-shaped kitchen, where a work peninsula with a snack counter opens to the family room. Sliding glass doors open to a rear terrace from the family room and the living room. A simple stairway ascends to four bedrooms and two baths. Storage space over the garage is reached through a walk-in closet in one of the bedrooms.

DESIGN 2978

First Floor: 1,451 square feet
Second Floor: 1,268 square feet
Third Floor: 746 square feet
Total: 3,465 square feet

The birthplace of author Nathaniel Hawthorne, built in Salem, Massachusetts around 1730, was the inspiration for this three-story design. Both the original and this modern version feature a center chimney, gambrel roof and clapboard sheathing. The living space includes a family-pleasing country kitchen with an island cooktop and built-in desk, a library and front-facing living and dining rooms. Notice the 12-over-12-pane windows in the formal rooms. The highlight of the second floor is the luxurious master bedroom with His and Hers closets and a heavenly whirlpool spa. One of the two family bedrooms has a study alcove with a built-in desk. The third floor consists of a guest suite and a decidedly modern exercise room/studio.

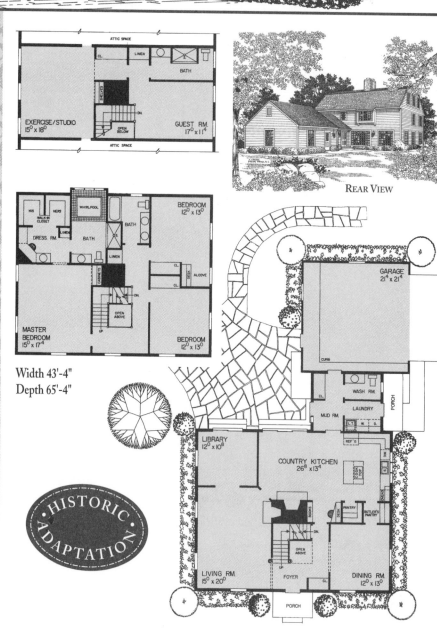

Width 43'-4"
Depth 65'-4"

REAR VIEW

HISTORIC ADAPTATION

Width 72'-0"
Depth 33'-7"

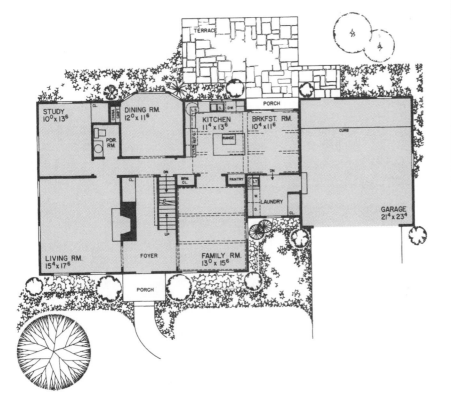

DESIGN 2649

First Floor: 1,501 square feet
Second Floor: 1,280 square feet
Total: 2,781 square feet

This design's front exterior is highlighted by four pedimented nine-over-nine windows, five second-story "eyebrow" windows and a massive central chimney. Beam ceilings give a Colonial look to the kitchen, breakfast room and family room, while the cooktop island, large laundry room and sliding glass doors to the rear porch are features that appeal to today's homeowners. A powder room is placed between the living and dining rooms for the convenience of family members and guests. The nearby study will provide a quiet retreat. Upstairs, the master suite has its own fireplace and a deluxe bath with a dressing area and dual vanities. An adjoining lounge, two good-sized family bedrooms and a compartmented bath complete the second floor.

Design by Home Planners

DESIGN 3506

First Floor: 1,609 square feet
Second Floor: 1,633 square feet
Total: 3,242 square feet

L D

If you share a passion for Americana, you might select this home, based on an 18th-Century New Jersey frame house. Historic touches include a paneled front door with carriage lamps on each side and a rear saltbox roof. The central foyer is flanked by formal living and dining rooms. A butler's pantry leads to the kitchen, which includes an island work counter and space for informal meals. The family room features a beam ceiling and a centered fireplace, which can also be enjoyed from the kitchen. A significant highlight is the first-floor bedroom. It is accompanied by a full bath, making it ideal as a guest suite or a home office. The upstairs holds four large bedrooms and three baths. The master suite is truly exceptional, including a sitting room (with an outdoor balcony) which looks over a railing and down to the sunken master bedroom.

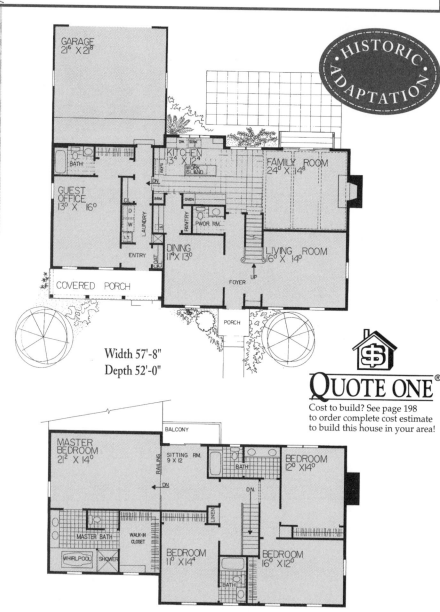

Width 57'-8"
Depth 52'-0"

HISTORIC ADAPTATION

QUOTE ONE®

Cost to build? See page 198 to order complete cost estimate to build this house in your area!

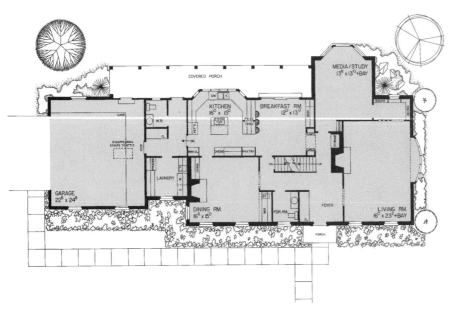

Width 87'-4"
Depth 42'-0"

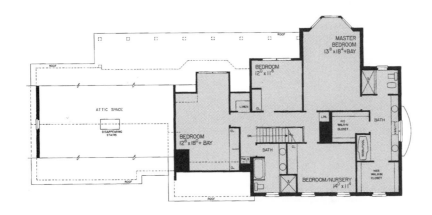

DESIGN 2963

First Floor: 2,046 square feet
Second Floor: 1,644 square feet
Total: 3,690 square feet

Featuring a gracious foyer and stairway at the off-center entry, this rambling home reflects the tendency of its Colonial ancestors to grow as families increased in size. Both the living and dining rooms boast large fireplaces for elegant entertaining and cozy relaxing. Family meals are likely to be served in the sunny breakfast room attached to the efficient U-shaped kitchen. To retreat from the clamor of an active household, family members can curl up with a good book—or watch a movie—in the media/study with its shelf-lined library nook. Upstairs, four bedrooms include a master suite with a bay window, twin walk-in closets and a luxurious bath.

Design by Design Basics, Inc.

DESIGN 7207

First Floor: 998 square feet
Second Floor: 1,206 square feet
Total: 2,204 square feet

A touch of New England characterizes this comfortable family home. A bright entry opens to a formal living room to the left and, to the right, a formal dining room with space for a hutch. A warming fireplace with built-in bookcases provides the focal point for the generous family room, perfect for informal gatherings. The U-shaped kitchen is a cook's delight, combining with the sunlit breakfast room to provide an airy, spacious feeling. The second floor houses the sleeping zone. Sure to please is the master suite—the bedroom highlighted by a vaulted ceiling and the private bath featuring a skylit dressing area, a whirlpool tub and a walk-in closet. Three family bedrooms, a full bath and a convenient laundry room complete the upstairs.

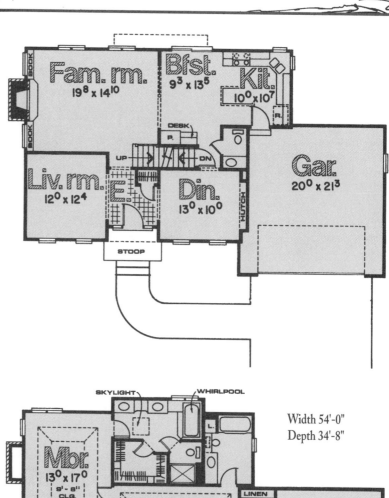

Fam. rm. 19⁸ x 14¹⁰

Bfst. 9³ x 13⁵

Kit. 10⁰ x 10⁷

Liv. rm. 12⁰ x 12⁴

Din. 13⁰ x 10⁰

Gar. 20⁰ x 21³

STOOP

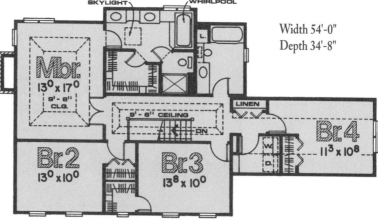

SKYLIGHT WHIRLPOOL

Mbr. 13⁰ x 17⁰ 9'-8" CLG.

9'-8" CEILING

LINEN

Br. 4 11³ x 10⁸

Br. 2 13⁰ x 10⁰

Br. 3 13⁸ x 10⁰

Width 54'-0"
Depth 34'-8"

Design by Mark Stewart and Associates, Inc.

DESIGN J134

First Floor: 1,082 square feet
Second Floor: 1,104 square feet
Total: 2,186 square feet
Bonus Room: 270 square feet

This modern adaptation starts with a symmetrical Colonial exterior featuring dormers, small-paned windows with shutters, and a simple front door outlined with sidelights. The interior is spacious, with a minimum of walls. Formal rooms flank the tiled entry hall, providing a large open area for entertaining. The family room, kitchen and nook are also open to each other, with a fireplace to warm the entire area. The second floor holds four bedrooms, including a master suite with a walk-in closet, a corner whirlpool tub and a dual-bowl vanity. A bonus room over the garage offers a walk-in closet and plenty of natural light.

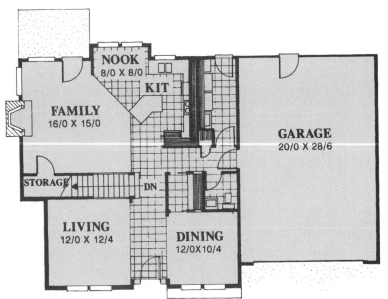

NOOK
8/0 X 8/0

KIT

FAMILY
16/0 X 15/0

GARAGE
20/0 X 28/6

STORAGE

DN

LIVING
12/0 X 12/4

DINING
12/0 X 10/4

Width 54'-6"
Depth 36'-8"

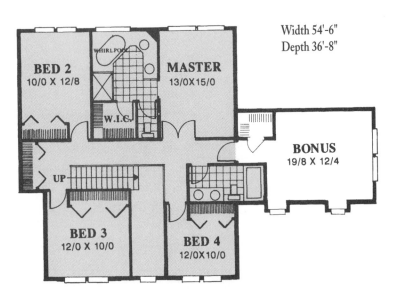

WHIRLPOOL

BED 2
10/0 X 12/8

MASTER
13/0 X 15/0

W.I.C.

BONUS
19/8 X 12/4

UP

BED 3
12/0 X 10/0

BED 4
12/0 X 10/0

DESIGN 2622

First Floor: 700 square feet
Second Floor: 700 square feet
Total: 1,400 square feet
Bonus Room: 247 square feet

L **D**

This Colonial adaptation provides a functional design that allows for expansion in the future. A cozy fireplace in the living room adds warmth to this space as well as the adjacent dining area. A powder room and a coat closet are nearby for the convenience of guests and family. The roomy L-shaped kitchen features a breakfast nook and an over-the-sink window. Upstairs, two family bedrooms share a full bath with a double vanity. The master bedroom is on this floor as well. Its private bath provides access to the attic. An additional storage area over the garage could be made into a bedroom, an office or a study.

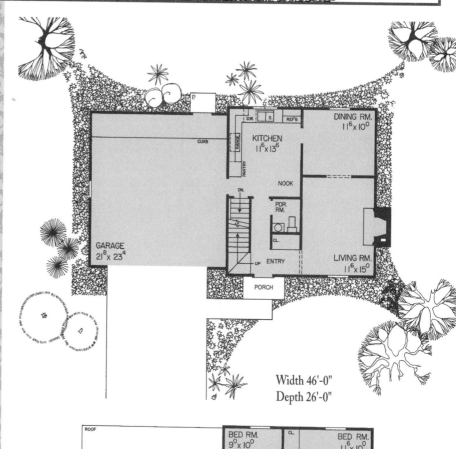

Width 46'-0"
Depth 26'-0"

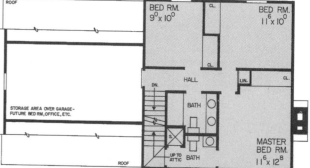

Design by Donald A. Gardner Architects, Inc.

© 1992 Donald A. Gardner Architects, Inc.

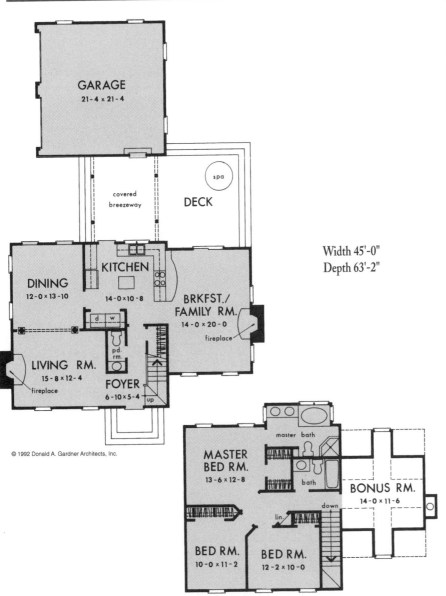

Width 45'-0"
Depth 63'-2"

© 1992 Donald A. Gardner Architects, Inc.

DESIGN 9691

First Floor: 1,044 square feet
Second Floor: 719 square feet
Total: 1,763 square feet
Bonus Room: 206 square feet

Here is a home that is Colonial through and through, but with something extra—an addition containing a breakfast/family room with a fireplace and access to a rear deck and spa. There is also a covered breezeway leading to the two-car garage. The formal living room has a second fireplace and opens through pillars to a formal dining room for ease in entertaining. An L-shaped island kitchen is centrally located, with space for a washer and dryer. Upstairs, three bedrooms include a master suite with a pampering bath and a walk-in closet. A bonus room with two dormers is available for future expansion.

DESIGN 2191

First Floor: 1,553 square feet
Second Floor: 1,197 square feet
Total: 2,750 square feet

L

This exquisite house reproduces such medieval and Tudor architectural details as cross gables, overhanging second and third stories, a saltbox roof and diamond-paned leaded-glass windows. It is based on the Witch House in Salem, Massachusetts, completed in 1675 by Judge Jonathan Corwin, who interrogated suspects in a second-floor chamber during the witch trials of 1692. Inside, rooms are more spacious than in the original, with a large living room for formal entertaining and a family room for informal gatherings. Colonial features include beam ceilings and fireplaces in both of these rooms and corner china cabinets in the dining room. Balusters and squared posts along the stairway are typical 17th-Century details. A handy pass-through separates the breakfast nook from the U-shaped kitchen.

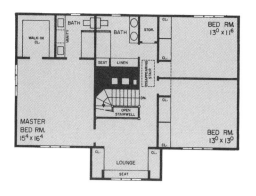

Width 80'-0"
Depth 38'-0"

HISTORIC ADAPTATION

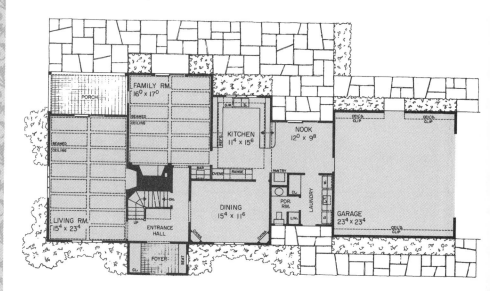

CAPE COD HOUSES

THE ORIGINAL CAPE COD WAS A "HALF HOUSE," ONE-and-a-half stories high, with a doorway at one end of the long side and two windows illuminating the single large room inside. Heat was provided by a fireplace at the same end as the door. Stairs led up to the children's sleeping quarters.

Variations were generally simple expansions of the design. The three-quarter Cape Cod added a room and one window on the opposite side of the door, usually a downstairs bedroom that could be entered from the front vestibule. Its fireplace was located off the central chimney, like others in the house.

The full Cape doubled the half house, and resembled the popular Cape Cod cottage that survives today. The typical first-floor plan included a parlor, master bedroom and kitchen, plus a small borning room, a buttery and one or more additional bedrooms. The attic was finished for additional sleeping quarters as needed. The compactness of Cape Cod cottages maximized living space by minimizing hallways. Inherent in the design was the necessity to walk through one room to reach another.

While 17th-Century Cape Cods had gabled roofs, some later variations had bowed roofs, made by bending green wood over a large rock and leaving it to dry in an arch shape. Gambrel-roofed Capes were popular in the Cape Ann area of Massachusetts.

As families grew in size or farming activities increased, additions were made to the original house, often resulting in a long row of connected buildings that might include a summer kitchen, a tool shed, a milk room and a barn.

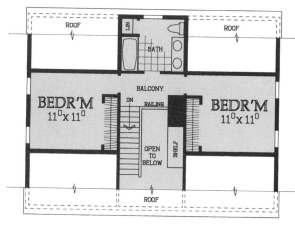

QUOTE ONE®

Cost to build? See page 198
to order complete cost estimate
to build this house in your area!

Width 38'-0"
Depth 28'-0"

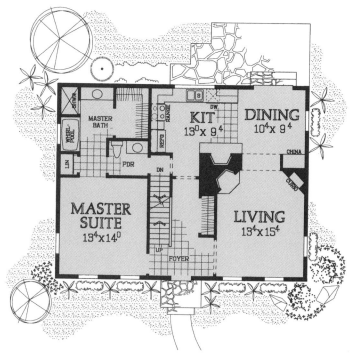

DESIGN 3511

First Floor: 1,064 square feet
Second Floor: 582 square feet
Total: 1,646 square feet

This charming Cape Cod is based on a home in East Dennis, Massachusetts, built in 1795. The front door framed by louvered blinds is an authentic exterior detail. The living room features a corner fireplace and a built-in curio cabinet. Nearby, the dining room is highlighted with a built-in china closet and access to the rear grounds. A warming fireplace shares space with the efficient kitchen and the dining area. First-floor master suites are rarely found in today's Cape Cod-style homes, and this one is exceptional. The master bedroom combines with a master bath complete with a whirlpool tub, a separate shower and a walk-in closet. The second floor is comprised of two family bedrooms sharing a full bath.

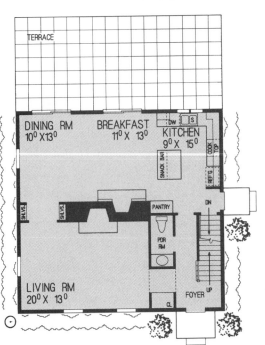

QUOTE ONE®

Cost to build? See page 198
to order complete cost estimate
to build this house in your area!

Width 32'-0"
Depth 30'-0"

DESIGN 3501

First Floor: 960 square feet
Second Floor: 733 square feet
Total: 1,693 square feet

L D

This Cape Cod half house is small, but complete, with three bedrooms and two baths upstairs and plenty of living space on the first floor. Although half-houses usually placed the chimney at the door end, this one has it in the center, supporting fireplaces in both the living room and the breakfast room. The rear of the home is left open, from the dining room with outdoor access to the efficient kitchen with an island snack bar. Be sure to notice the built-in bookshelves, pantry and handy coat closet. If you wish, use the breakfast area as an all-purpose dining room and turn the dining room into a library or sitting room.

DESIGN 2657

First Floor: 1,217 square feet
Second Floor: 868 square feet
Total: 2,085 square feet

L

What could be more classic than this full Cape with its delightful symmetry? The exterior has clapboard siding, muntined double-hung windows and a transom-lit entrance flanked by shutters and carriage lamps. The massive, corbelled chimney serves two fireplaces—one in the living room, the other in the kitchen. The white picket fence and resulting entrance court complete a picture of charm. Flanking the foyer are the formal dining and living rooms, the latter with a bay window and access to a covered porch. Dominating the back of the first floor is the enormous country kitchen. The U-shaped work area here is enhanced by an exposed-beam ceiling, a bay window and built-in shelves. A washroom and a laundry are close by. The cozy second floor holds three bedrooms and two full baths. Window seats in the dormers hide small storage areas.

Width 49'-8"
Depth 44'-0"

QUOTE ONE®
Cost to build? See page 198 to order complete cost estimate to build this house in your area!

· HISTORIC · ADAPTATION

REAR VIEW

Design by Home Planners

ENHANCED PLAN

Basic Plan:
Width 40'-0"
Depth 28'-0"

Expanded Plan:
Width 68'-0"
Depth 34'-0"

DESIGN 3715

First Floor: 1,312 square feet
Second Floor: 795 square feet
Total: 2,107 square feet

The design of this expandable Cape Cod provides plenty of room for all your family's needs. The kitchen extends as one large room over the snack bar into an expansive family room. Both the family room and the living room open from the center hall, which also leads to the dining room at the back of the house. The downstairs study could be converted into a fourth bedroom with an adjacent full bath. The upstairs bedrooms include a master suite with a walk-in closet and a private bath. The house may be enhanced by the addition of a fireplace, a bay window, a two-car garage, a laundry room and a rear deck. The blueprints show how to build both the basic and the enhanced versions of this home.

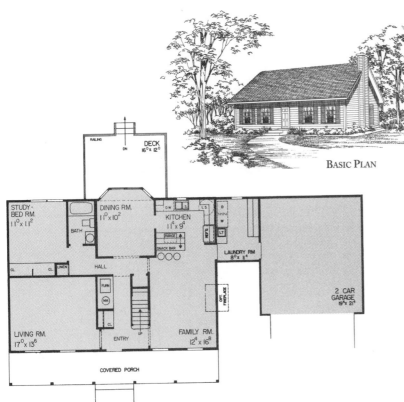

BASIC PLAN

Design by Home Planners

DESIGN 2145

First Floor: 1,182 square feet
Second Floor: 708 square feet
Total: 1,890 square feet

L

Historically referred to as a "half house," this authentic adaptation has its roots in the heritage of New England. Usually, these homes were developed in stages—a concept that works as well today as it did in the 17th Century. With completion of the second floor, the growing family doubles its sleeping capacity. There is also ample room for entertaining. The large living and family rooms offer fireplaces and built-ins, while a pass-through in the kitchen encourages meals at the snack bar on the covered porch. Everyone will enjoy the bay window overlooking the flower court to the rear of the house. The deluxe master bedroom is highlighted by a walk-in closet and a built-in desk and shelves. With an overall width of just 44 feet, this house will work well on a narrow or a corner building site.

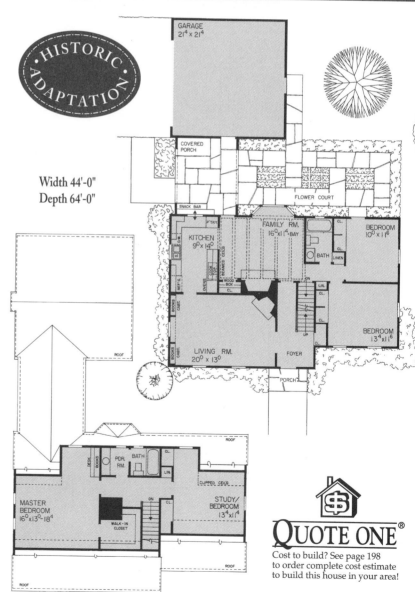

Width 44'-0"
Depth 64'-0"

QUOTE ONE®

Cost to build? See page 198
to order complete cost estimate
to build this house in your area!

HISTORIC ADAPTATION

Width 88'-0"
Depth 39'-0"

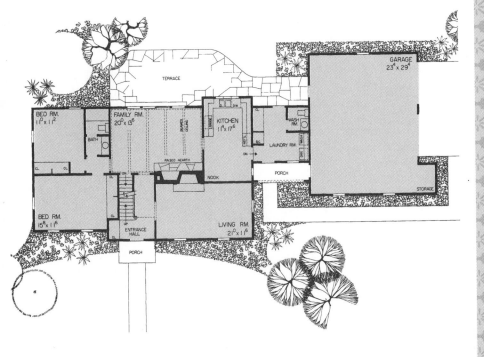

DESIGN 2395

First Floor: 1,481 square feet
Second Floor: 861 square feet
Total: 2,342 square feet

L

The central part of this design is a New England-style "half house," with an appeal that is ageless. The living quarters include two fireplaces, served by the large central chimney. The living room opens off the entrance hall, making entertaining easy. At the back of the house, the family room features an exposed-beam ceiling and access to a terrace. The spacious U-shaped kitchen offers the dishwasher a view of the terrace, plenty of counter space and an eating nook. The laundry room leads to the garage, and provides access to a front covered porch and the rear terrace. With two bedrooms downstairs, you could wait and finish the second floor at a later date. Or, one first-floor bedroom could serve as a guest suite while the other provides space for an office. The two second-floor bedrooms include a master suite with a private bath and an alcove.

DESIGN 2699

First Floor: 2,188 square feet
Second Floor: 858 square feet
Total: 3,046 square feet

L

This handsome Cape Cod brings to mind a Colonial farmhouse with its attached outbuildings, which might have included a summer kitchen, a tool shed, a milk room and a barn. Inside, the house is definitely up-to-date. To the left of the foyer, a spacious master suite invites relaxation with its pampering private bath and an adjacent lounge that could easily be converted into a study. A large living room with access to the rear terrace is warmed by a cheerful fireplace. The right side of the plan is comprised of a media room, a dining room and a country kitchen that is a cook's delight. A conveniently located mud room and laundry room complete the first floor. The second floor contains two secondary bedrooms, each with its own full bath, and a spacious lounge.

Width 106'-8"
Depth 32'-0"

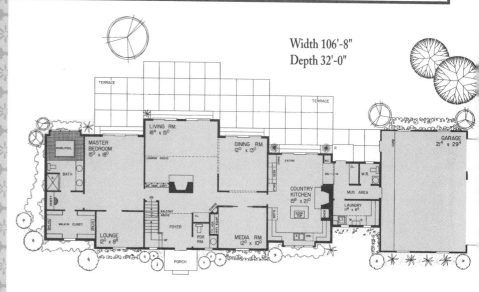

HISTORIC ADAPTATION

QUOTE ONE®

Cost to build? See page 198
to order complete cost estimate
to build this house in your area!

REAR VIEW

QUOTE ONE®

Cost to build? See page 198 to order complete cost estimate to build this house in your area!

HISTORIC · ADAPTATION

BEDROOM 11² X 17⁴

BEDROOM 11² X 15⁰

BATH

DESIGN 2995

First Floor: 2,465 square feet
Second Floor: 617 square feet
Total: 3,082 square feet

L **D**

From the weathervane on the three-car garage to the massive chimney and beyond, this New England Colonial delivers beautiful proportions and great livability. The central foyer is flanked by the formal dining and living rooms. The living room is free from cross-room traffic and includes a central fireplace. The well-equipped kitchen features a preparation island and shares a snack bar with the family room, which has a second fireplace, an eating area and access to the terrace. The library, with its twin bookcases and a projecting bay window, is conveniently located next to the master suite. The master bedroom has a front-facing bay window and access to the rear terrace, which stretches the full width of the house. The master bath features a whirlpool tub and a sloped ceiling. Upstairs, two bedrooms share a full bath; each has a built-in desk.

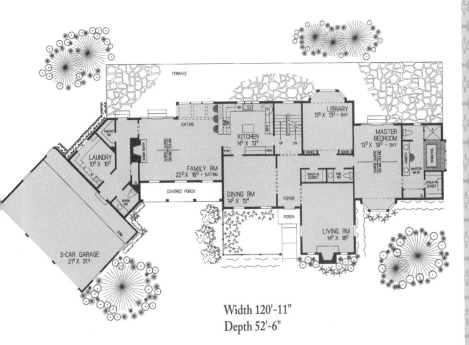

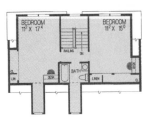

Width 120'-11"
Depth 52'-6"

DESIGN 3336

Square Footage: 2,022

L

Compact and comfortable, you'll love this three-bedroom plan! It is a good building candidate for a small family or for empty-nesters. The rustic facade is highlighted by stone detailing, a cupola and a dovecote in the garage gable. Sliding glass doors across the back of the house encourage outdoor relaxing on the terrace. Outdoor eating is easy with access to a covered porch from both the dining room and the breakfast room. The foyer leads into a large gathering room with a sloped ceiling and a fireplace. The nearby kitchen offers new angles on your favorite amenities and convenient service to all eating areas. The master bedroom is spacious, with a sloped ceiling and a bayed sitting area. Its private bath pampers with a whirlpool tub, dual lavatories and a compartmented toilet. Two family bedrooms offer views of the front yard and share a full hall bath.

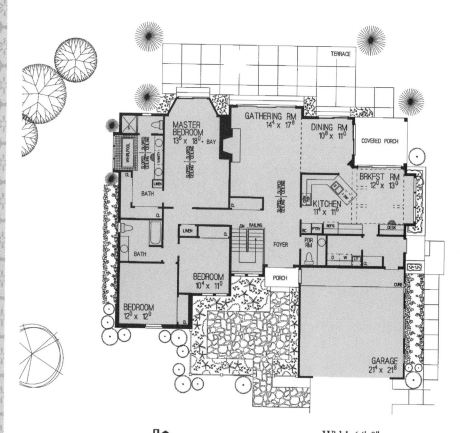

Width 64'-0"
Depth 55'-4"

QUOTE ONE®

Cost to build? See page 198
to order complete cost estimate
to build this house in your area!

Design by Home Planners

DESIGN 3340

Square Footage: 1,689

Width 58'-0"
Depth 52'-6"

QUOTE ONE®

Cost to build? See page 198
to order complete cost estimate
to build this house in your area!

A skylit covered patio extends an invitation to enjoy all seasons in comfort. The interior provides its own special appeal. Bedrooms are effectively arranged to the front of the plan, out of the traffic flow of the house. One bedroom offers a comfortable window seat, while a second could double nicely as a study or a home office. The adjacent master suite includes a walk-in closet and a private bath with dual sinks. The living room/dining area is highlighted by a fireplace, sliding glass doors to the patio and an open staircase with a built-in planter. The breakfast room provides a built-in desk—making it a breeze to get organized—and also accesses the patio for outdoor dining. An efficient U-shaped kitchen with a snack bar, a laundry room and a garage with extra storage complete the plan.

DESIGN 2636

First Floor: 1,211 square feet
Second Floor: 747 square feet
Total: 1,958 square feet

This version of a Nantucket Island saltbox is adapted from a cottage built around 1820 by Captain Alexander Bunker. The exterior includes many of the details of the original, including the shuttered front door and the classic entablature over the front doorway. Although the garage is a modern addition, the location of the kitchen—in the attached lean-to at the back of the house—is the same. The kitchen itself is totally up-to-date, with spaces for today's appliances and a large U-shaped work area. Down a step from the main hall, the kitchen offers sliding glass doors to a flagstone-paved terrace, as does the nearby dining room. A living room with a fireplace, a family bedroom and a laundry room complete the first floor. Upstairs, the master bedroom has a large walk-in closet and a separate vanity area in a bath shared with a third bedroom.

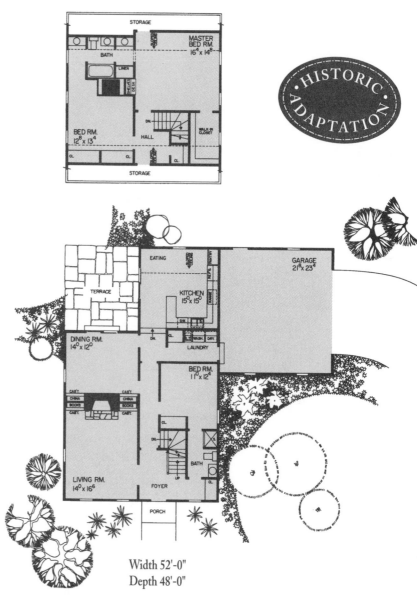

Width 52'-0"
Depth 48'-0"

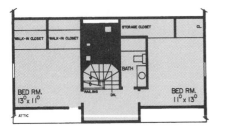

BED RM.
13⁰ x 11⁰

BED RM.
11⁰ x 13⁰

WALK-IN CLOSET | WALK-IN CLOSET

STORAGE CLOSET | CL.

BATH

RAILING | DN.

ATTIC

HISTORIC ADAPTATION

Width 59'-8"
Depth 37'-8"

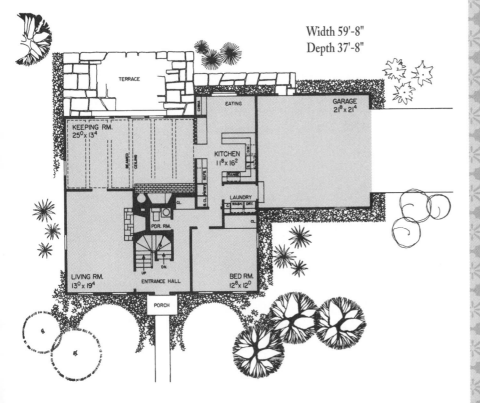

TERRACE

KEEPING RM.
25⁰ x 13⁴

EATING

GARAGE
21⁸ x 21⁴

KITCHEN
11⁸ x 16²

LAUNDRY
WASH DRY

PDR. RM.

LIVING RM.
13⁰ x 19⁴

ENTRANCE HALL

BED RM.
12⁸ x 12⁰

PORCH

DESIGN 2635

First Floor: 1,317 square feet
Second Floor: 681 square feet
Total: 1,998 square feet

This Cape Cod-style house adds the sloped rear roof, tall front facade and shingled exterior of a traditional Nantucket cottage. It is based on the 1763 Edward Allen House. Random-width wood paneling, exposed beams in the keeping room and a simple balustrade along the curving staircase add rustic appeal to the interior. The large center chimney supports fireplaces in the keeping and living rooms. As in its Colonial predecessors, this plan places the kitchen in the lean-to section of the house. The U-shaped work area includes a pass-through to the eating area. A first-floor bedroom could also serve as a study or a home office. Plenty of storage space is available to two upstairs bedrooms sharing a full bath.

DESIGN 9430

First Floor: 1,150 square feet
Second Floor: 543 square feet
Total: 1,693 square feet

While fitting on the smallest of lots, this great 1½-story Cape still encompasses some dynamic features. A dramatic, two-story hearth room serves as the main living area in the home. Tall windows flank the fireplace and a glass door leads to the outdoor area. A section of the upper hallway overlooks the hearth room, integrating the upper floor with the lower. The formal living and dining rooms are open to each other, creating a great space for entertaining. The master bedroom is conveniently located on the first floor, overlooking the backyard and offering direct access to the full bath serving the lower floor. Large family bedrooms and a bath round out the upstairs.

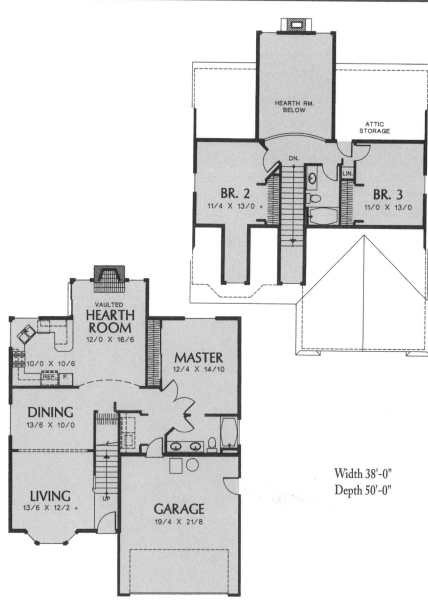

Width 38'-0"
Depth 50'-0"

Design by Home Planners

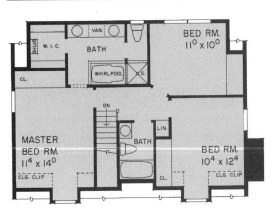

Width 48'-0"
Depth 32'-0"

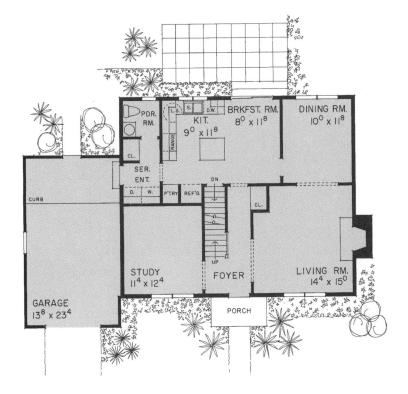

DESIGN 3571

First Floor: 964 square feet
Second Floor: 783 square feet
Total: 1,747 square feet

L **D**

For those interested in both traditional charm and modern convenience, this Cape Cod fits the bill. Enter the foyer and find a quiet study to the left and a living room with a fireplace to the right. Straight ahead is the kitchen, with an island countertop adding lots of room for meal preparation. The adjoining breakfast room has sliding glass doors to the back patio. The formal dining room is just beyond. The service entry, flanked by the laundry area and a powder room, leads to a sizeable storage area in the garage. Upstairs, two family bedrooms share a full bath, while the master suite includes a private bath with a whirlpool tub, separate shower, double vanity and walk-in closet.

DESIGN 2631

First Floor: 1,634 square feet
Second Floor: 1,011 square feet
Total: 2,645 square feet

L D

This Cape Cod-style house is based on those built by early Colonial settlers along the Maryland coast. The main part of the exterior is symmetrical, with two small-paned and shuttered windows on either side of the simple front door and three dormers providing light to the second floor. The entry is flanked by a good-sized living room with a fireplace and a formal dining room. The addition of an ell makes possible the inclusion of a large family room. There is also space for a breakfast nook as well as the work areas of the home—the U-shaped kitchen, a laundry room and a washroom. A first-floor study has access to a full bath, making it ideal as a guest suite. The second floor offers two bedrooms with walk-in closets and a master suite with a private bath.

HISTORIC ADAPTATION

Width 80'-0"
Depth 32'-0"

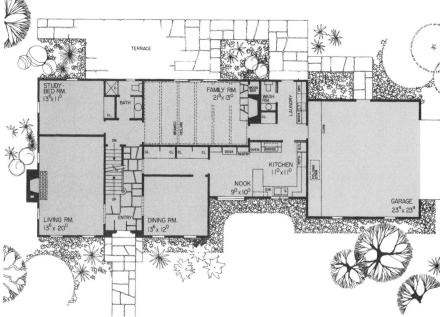

Design by Donald A. Gardner Architects, Inc.

© 1989 Donald A. Gardner Architects, Inc.

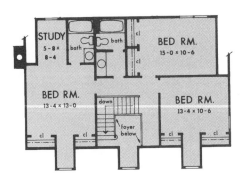

Width 85'-10"
Depth 37'-8"

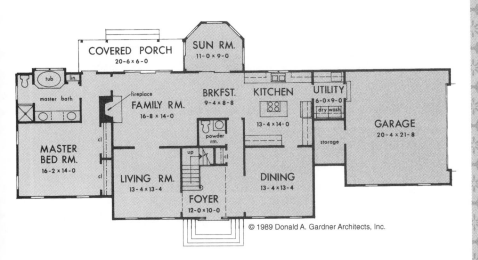

© 1989 Donald A. Gardner Architects, Inc.

DESIGN 9675

First Floor: 1,750 square feet
Second Floor: 977 square feet
Total: 2,727 square feet

Traditional charm complements a contemporary interior. A central entrance foyer allows direct access to formal living in the front of the house and casual living in the rear, where family room, breakfast room and kitchen form a continuous open area. A passive-solar sun room offers a new dimension to this four-bedroom plan. The master bedroom is located on the first floor for convenience and privacy—and easy access to the covered back porch. A spacious master bath provides a double-bowl vanity, shower and whirlpool tub. Two generously proportioned bedrooms on the second floor share a hall bath, while the third has its own bath and a study nook.

DESIGN B129

First Floor: 1,229 square feet
Second Floor: 551 square feet
Total: 1,780 square feet

The recessed entry of this Cape Cod design opens onto a large family room with a fireplace and a pass-through to the kitchen. The L-shaped kitchen also has an island work area and a snack bar for meals on the go. The kitchen opens to the dining area, which provides access to a rear deck and to the laundry room. The first-floor master suite includes a large bedroom and a deluxe bath with a walk-in closet, double-bowl vanity, garden tub and separate shower. Two bedrooms, a full bath and lots of attic storage are on the second floor. Please specify basement, crawlspace or slab foundation when ordering.

Width 63'-0"
Depth 32'-0"

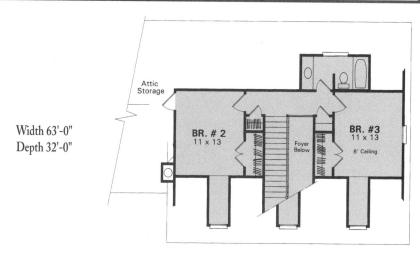

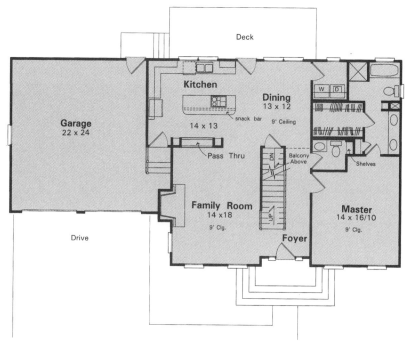

Design by Donald A. Gardner Architects, Inc.

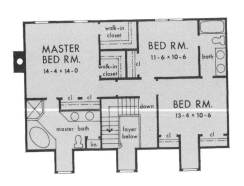

MASTER BED RM.
14-4 × 14-0

walk-in closet

walk-in closet

cl

BED RM.
11-6 × 10-6

bath

cl cl

down

master bath

foyer below

lin.

BED RM.
13-4 × 10-6

cl cl

Width 79'-4"
Depth 31'-10"

DESIGN 9649

First Floor: 1,401 square feet
Second Floor: 949 square feet
Total: 2,350 square feet

With Cape Cod styling, this lovely design has the best in livable floor plans. The attractive front door opens to a central foyer flanked by the formal living and dining rooms. To the rear is the informal area—a family room with a fireplace and the kitchen with its bayed breakfast nook. A bright sun room is located just off the family room, while at the other end of the plan, a utility room leads to the garage. The rear deck, with built-in seating, is reached by sliding glass doors in the sun room and the family room. Three bedrooms are found upstairs—a master suite with two walk-in closets and a pampering bath, and two family bedrooms sharing a full bath with dual lavatories.

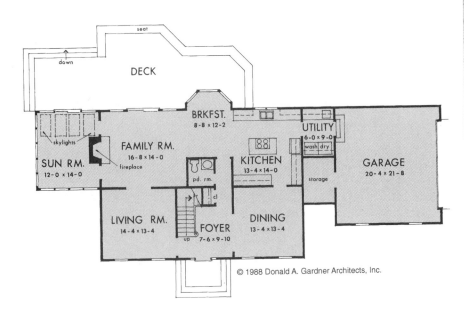

seat

down

DECK

BRKFST.
8-8 × 12-2

UTILITY
6-0 × 9-0

wash dry

skylights

FAMILY RM.
16-8 × 14-0

fireplace

SUN RM.
12-0 × 14-0

KITCHEN
13-4 × 14-0

storage

GARAGE
20-4 × 21-8

pd. rm.

cl

LIVING RM.
14-4 × 13-4

FOYER
7-6 × 9-10

UP

DINING
13-4 × 13-4

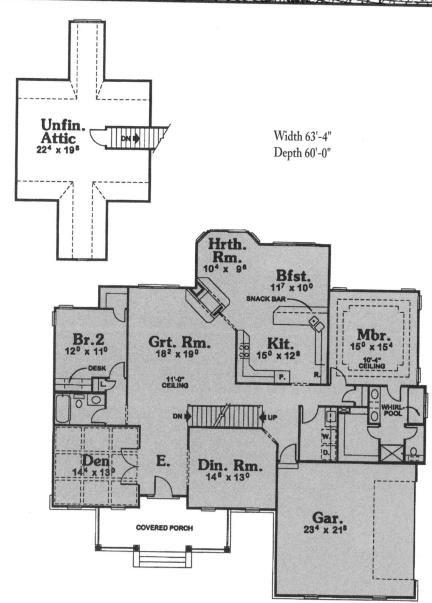

DESIGN 7015

Square Footage: 2,242

A covered porch with Colonial detailing, small-paned windows and twin gables create an attractive exterior for this compact design. Double doors allow the beam-ceilinged den to be closed off from the rest of the house, providing a quiet retreat. Across the entry hall is the dining room, with easy access from the front door as well as a door leading to the kitchen. The great room opens directly off the entry and shares a through-fireplace with the hearth room, resulting in comfortable areas for both large and small gatherings. Windows across the back of the house provide natural light for the kitchen, which offers a snack bar to the breakfast room for casual meals. The master suite includes a bedroom with a tray ceiling and a sumptuous bath with a walk-in closet, a whirlpool tub and a dual-bowl vanity. A second bedroom has a built-in desk and access to a full bath and linen closet.

Width 63'-4"
Depth 60'-0"

Design by James Fahy Design

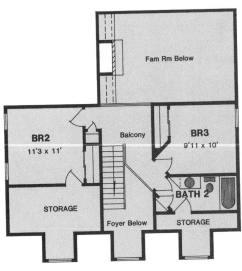

BR2
11'3 x 11'

Balcony

BR3
9'11 x 10'

Fam Rm Below

STORAGE

BATH 2

Foyer Below

STORAGE

Width 63'-0"
Depth 42'-0"

DESIGN C100

First Floor: 1,228 square feet
Second Floor: 483 square feet
Total: 1,711 square feet

This quaint Cape Cod offers loads of charm. The corner wrapping porch, dormers and Victorian gable decoration help create its appeal. A rear covered porch and a deck add plenty of space for outdoor living. The large formal dining room will be a showpiece as you enter. The U-shaped kitchen and octagonal dinette open to the vaulted family room, where built-in bookcases flank the fireplace. A snack bar separates the family room from the kitchen, while the dinette leads to a laundry/mud room and lavatory. The master suite and its private porch are on the first floor, making this plan a good choice for empty-nesters. The second floor provides two more bedrooms, a full bath and a balcony with views of the family room and foyer.

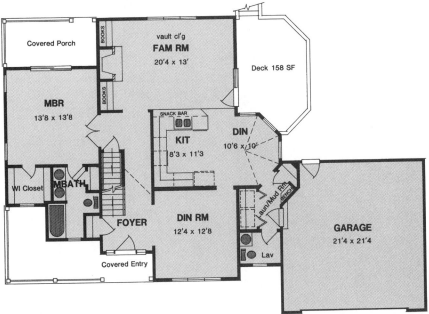

Covered Porch

vault cl'g
FAM RM
20'4 x 13'

Deck 158 SF

BOOKS

BOOKS

MBR
13'8 x 13'8

SNACK BAR

KIT
8'3 x 11'3

DIN
10'6 x 10'

WI Closet

MBATH

FOYER

DIN RM
12'4 x 12'8

Laun/Mud Rm
BENCH

GARAGE
21'4 x 21'4

Covered Entry

Lav

DESIGN 9486

First Floor: 1,368 square feet
Second Floor: 972 square feet
Total: 2,340 square feet
Bonus Room: 344 square feet

Special details, such as the two dormer windows and double-columned front entry, add great charm to this well-designed home. Inside, it features formal living and dining rooms, a tucked-away den and a large family room with a vaulted ceiling and a fireplace. The island kitchen is adjacent to a breakfast nook and has a wonderful walk-in pantry and a built-in desk. Upstairs, there are three bedrooms including a lovely master suite with a whirlpool spa, a compartmented toilet and loads of closet space. A bonus room over the garage can be developed later into a fourth bedroom, office space or a playroom.

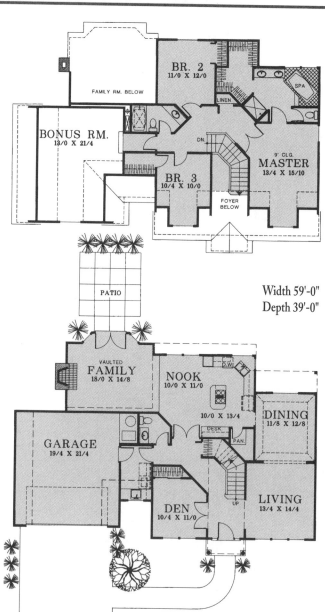

Width 59'-0"
Depth 39'-0"

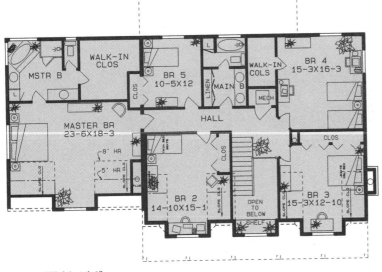

Width 64'-0"
Depth 39'-0"

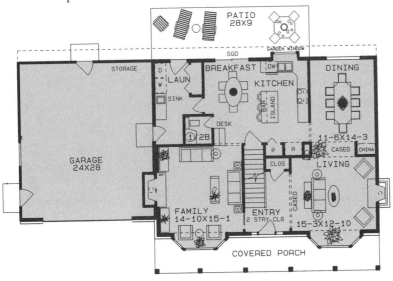

DESIGN K104

First Floor: 1,274 square feet
Second Floor: 1,920 square feet
Total: 3,194 square feet
Unfinished Basement: 1,240 square feet

This Cape Cod-style home boasts five bedrooms for the large family. The spacious master suite provides a wonderful retreat for parents, with a dormer sitting area, a huge walk-in closet and a compartmented bath with twin vanities and a corner garden tub. The eat-in kitchen includes an island bar and a built-in desk as well as sliding doors to the patio. The formal living and dining rooms fill the right side of the plan and include a bay window, a fireplace and a built-in china closet. The family room also features a fireplace and a bay window. The laundry room catches kids coming and going, with access to the rear yard and the garage. A full basement offers a future game room, a bath and one or two bedrooms with lots of extra storage space.

DESIGN 2643

First Floor: 1,446 square feet
Second Floor: 1,281 square feet
Total: 2,727 square feet

This design is based on the historic Moore House, where in 1781, General George Washington and Lord Cornwallis signed an agreement ending the siege at Yorktown, Virginia, and marking the beginning of the end of the American Revolution. The gambrel roof is broken by five gables on both the front and the rear of the home, providing all of the second-floor bedrooms with natural light. The interior of the home is also symmetrical—four rooms, each with a corner fireplace, are on the first floor and four bedrooms, including the master suite, are on the second. The formal living and dining rooms are on either side of the front entry for easy entertaining, while the family room is secluded to the rear of the plan. A large laundry room leads from the breakfast room to the terrace and to the two-car garage.

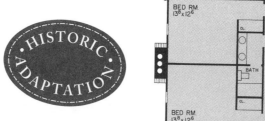

HISTORIC ADAPTATION

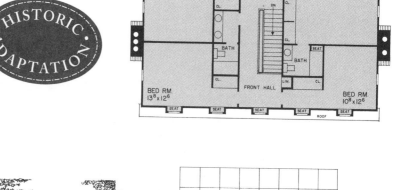

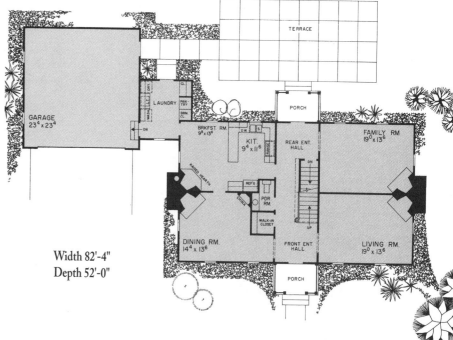

Width 82'-4"
Depth 52'-0"

HISTORIC ADAPTATION

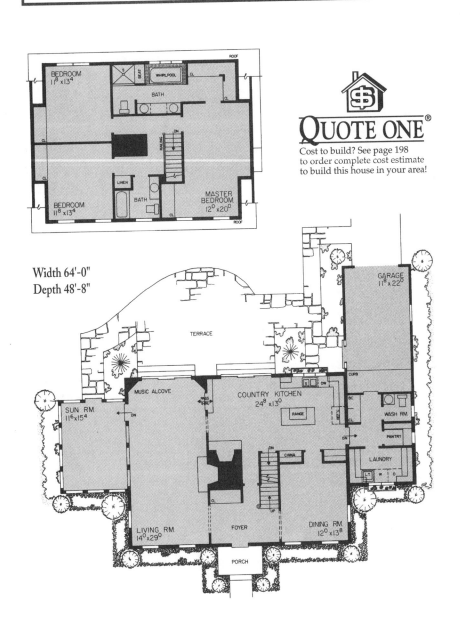

Width 64'-0"
Depth 48'-8"

QUOTE ONE®

Cost to build? See page 198
to order complete cost estimate
to build this house in your area!

DESIGN 2986

First Floor: 1,592 square feet
Second Floor: 1,054 square feet
Total: 2,646 square feet

This Colonial home has all the exterior charm of its ancestors—paired windows flank the entry while shed dormers add headroom to the second story. A modern interior makes it perfect for today. To the immediate left of the entry is a living room with a music alcove and a fireplace. To the right is the formal dining room. In its own wing, a few steps down from the living room is a cheery sun room. The country kitchen, with an island range, built-in china cabinets and a fireplace, offers plenty of space for informal eating. Both it and the music alcove have sliding doors to the rear terrace. A spacious laundry room and a washroom complete this level. Upstairs, two family bedrooms share a full bath, while the master suite pampers with a whirlpool tub, twin vanities and plenty of closet space.

DESIGN 2131

First Floor: 1,214 square feet
Second Floor: 1,097 square feet
Total: 2,311 square feet

L D

The gambrel roof, the vertical siding and a hayloft door on the garage are inspired by Colonial cottages still popular in New England. The contemporary interior makes good use of the available space and retains an Early American flavor through such details as exposed beams in the family room, two fireplaces (one with a wood box), corner china cabinets and decorative moldings and chair rails. The formal living and dining rooms are placed together for easy entertaining and for easy access from the U-shaped kitchen. A sliding door can be closed to keep out kitchen sounds when the meal is in progress. A breakfast nook provides a cozy corner for informal dining. The second floor holds four bedrooms, including a master suite with a dressing room and a private bath.

HISTORIC ADAPTATION

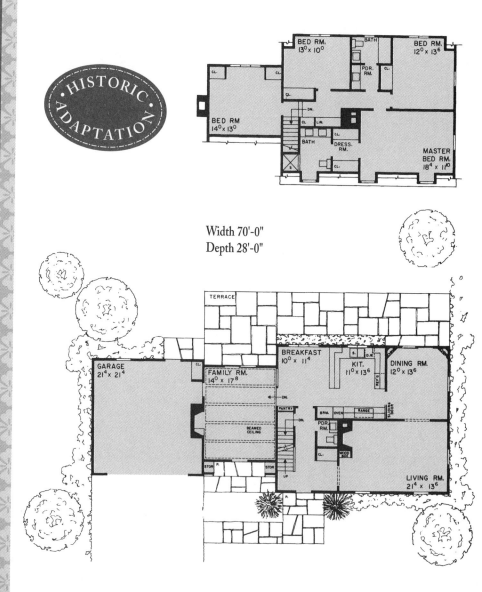

Width 70'-0"
Depth 28'-0"

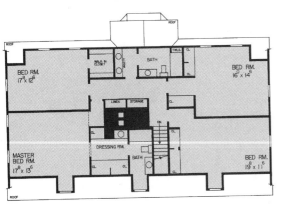

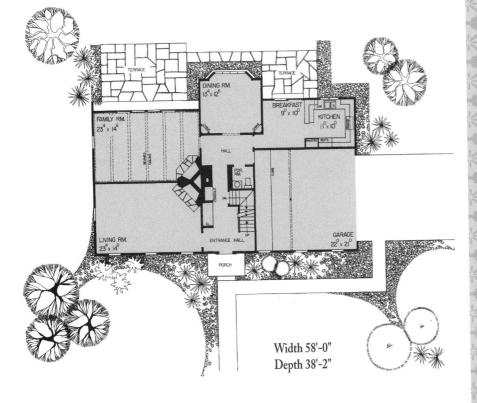

Width 58'-0"
Depth 38'-2"

DESIGN 2397

First Floor: 1,405 square feet
Second Floor: 1,580 square feet
Total: 2,985 square feet

Built in 1677, the Harlow Old Fort House of Plymouth, Massachusetts, is the inspiration for this design. Sergeant William Harlow, a town selectman, used the timbers from the Old Fort on Burial Hill in one of the first wooden gambrel-roofed houses in the colonies. Narrow clapboards, shutters and a transom-lit front door are also authentic details. Exposed beams, random-width siding and other decorative details continue the theme inside. The center chimney supports back-to-back corner fireplaces in the living and family rooms, providing warmth for formal entertaining and informal relaxation. The dining room is a showplace, with its wall of windows and built-in china closets. A pass-through counter in the kitchen permits easy service to the adjoining breakfast room. The master suite features a private bath with a dressing room. A shed dormer adds space to two bedrooms across the rear of the house.

DESIGN 2656

First Floor: 1,122 square feet
Second Floor: 884 square feet
Total: 2,006 square feet

L D

A gambrel roof provides volume and authenticity to this charming Cape Cod reproduction. Individual dormers in the front and a shed dormer across the rear allow in plenty of natural light. The shutter-trimmed front door opens to a central foyer that leads to all areas of the house. Family and guests will all delight in the massive corner fireplace in the living room. A beam ceiling contributes to the rustic atmosphere. Mealtime options include a dining room, breakfast room and snack bar. The U-shaped kitchen easily serves them all. With both a covered porch and a terrace, outdoor dining is another possibility. A front study has built-in bookshelves and would make a fine home office. Upstairs, three bedrooms include a master suite with a dressing room and twin vanities.

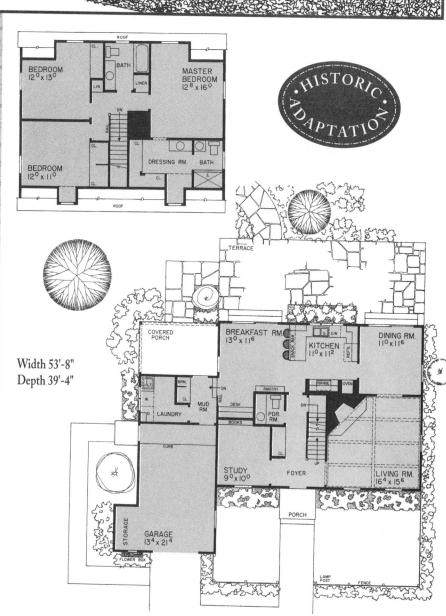

Width 53'-8"
Depth 39'-4"

ENHANCED PLAN

HISTORIC ADAPTATION

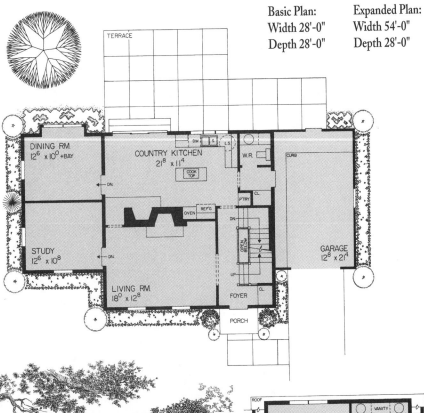

Basic Plan:
Width 28'-0"
Depth 28'-0"

Expanded Plan:
Width 54'-0"
Depth 28'-0"

TERRACE

DINING RM.
12⁶ x 10⁰ +BAY

COUNTRY KITCHEN
21⁸ x 11⁴

COOK TOP

W.R.

CURB

STUDY
12⁶ x 10⁸

OVEN REF'G

P'TRY

CL.

DN.

OPEN BELOW

GARAGE
12⁸ x 21⁴

LIVING RM.
18⁰ x 12⁸

UP

FOYER

PORCH

DESIGN 2983

First Floor (Basic Plan): 776 sq. ft.
First Floor (Expanded Plan): 1,072 sq. ft.
Second Floor (Both Plans): 652 sq. ft.
Total (Basic Plan): 1,428 sq. ft.
Total (Expanded Plan): 1,724 sq. ft.

This charming gambrel-roofed Colonial cottage is reminiscent of the simple houses built and occupied by seafarers on Cape Ann, Massachusetts, in the 17th and 18th Centuries. This adaptation offers a new twist—it is designed to expand as your need and/or budget grows. The basic house offers the necessities—and more. The living room and the large country kitchen each have a fireplace. The kitchen is well equipped, with a pantry, an island cooktop and sliding doors to the terrace. A washroom is nearby. The expanded version adds a bay-windowed dining room and a study on one side and a garage with extra storage space on the other. In both versions, the second floor contains two good-sized bedrooms, each with a private bath.

BASIC PLAN

ROOF

MASTER BEDROOM
15⁴ x 11⁴

BATH

VANITY

LINEN

WALK-IN CLOSET

LINEN

DN.

OPEN BELOW

BEDROOM
13⁸ x 10⁴ +DORMER

BATH

ROOF

DESIGN 2689

First Floor: 1,385 square feet
Second Floor: 982 square feet
Total: 2,367 square feet

This cozy three-bedroom Cape Cod design draws its inspiration from the Joseph Atwood House, the oldest house in Chatham, Massachusetts. It was built in 1752 by a sea captain who made long voyages to all parts of the globe. A century later it was the home of Joseph C. Lincoln, author of stories about Cape Cod. Although Capes usually had single-pitch roofs, the builder of the Atwood House used the gambrel roof to increase the amount of headroom on the second floor. Updated floor plans give this full-sized cottage a large country kitchen with a bay window and a work island/snack bar. Formal living and dining rooms are across the front of the house. The ell holds a mud room with a pantry and a washroom, a laundry room and a garage. There are three bedrooms upstairs, including a master suite with a deluxe bath.

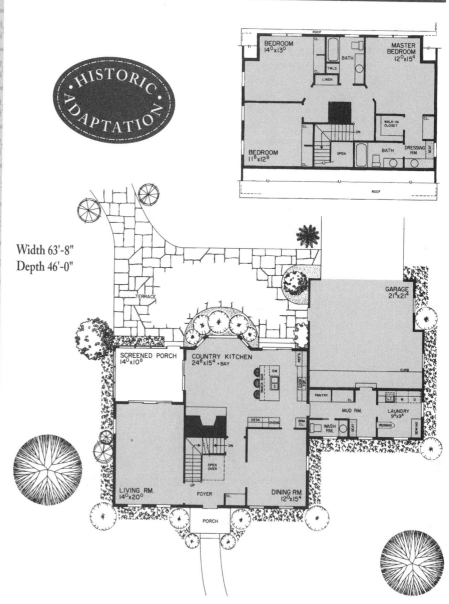

Width 63'-8"
Depth 46'-0"

Design by Home Planners

A. J. YOUNG
FUQUAY VIRGINIA NC

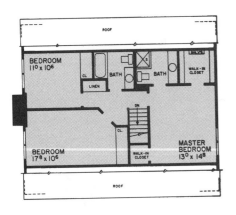

BEDROOM
11⁰ x 10⁶

BATH · BATH

WALK-IN CLOSET

CL

LINEN

DN

CL

BEDROOM
17⁸ x 10⁶

WALK-IN CLOSET

MASTER BEDROOM
13⁰ x 14⁸

ROOF

· HISTORIC ·
ADAPTATION

DESIGN 2644

First Floor: 1,349 square feet
Second Floor: 836 square feet
Total: 2,185 square feet

This unusual bowed-roof Cape is based on a cottage from the 17th Century. The curved roof was also known as a ship's bottom or rainbow roof. Otherwise, the house is a typical Cape, with two multi-pane windows on either side of the front door, all with full-length shutters. Inside is an outstanding plan with loads of livability. One raised-hearth fireplace warms the family room, while a second fireplace serves the sitting room. The kitchen area includes a work island, a pantry and a breakfast nook with access to the terrace and a pass-through to the family room. The master suite boasts two walk-in closets and a private bath with an extended vanity.

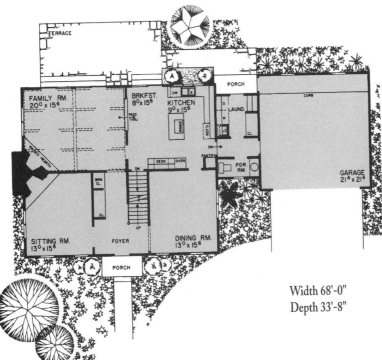

TERRACE

FAMILY RM.
20⁰ x 15⁶

PASS-THRU

BRKFST.
8⁰ x 15⁶

KITCHEN
9⁰ x 15⁶

PORCH

LAUND.

REF'S

CURB

RAISED HEARTH

DW

RANGE

DESK · OVEN

PANTRY

DN

PDR. RM.

GARAGE
21⁴ x 21⁴

DRM. CL.

CL

DN

UP

SITTING RM.
13⁰ x 15⁶

FOYER

DINING RM.
13⁰ x 15⁶

PORCH

Width 68'-0"
Depth 33'-8"

DESIGN 2632

First Floor: 1,460 square feet
Second Floor: 912 square feet
Total: 2,372 square feet

This historical house is based on dwellings built on Cape Ann, a rocky peninsula jutting out into the Atlantic Ocean just north of Boston. Gloucester is one of its better-known communities. By the 17th Century, residents of Cape Ann had developed their own style of architecture—houses were asymmetrical, often with gambrel roofs and usually covered with clapboards. Often starting out as fishermen's cottages, the structures grew in size as wings were added. This interior is as interesting as its exterior. Long raised hearths in the family and living rooms support a see-through fireplace and a connecting wood box. Both rooms have beam ceilings. The U-shaped kitchen shares a snack bar and a desk with the breakfast room. A butler's pantry leads to the dining room, which features a built-in china closet. The second floor houses three bedrooms, two baths and ample storage.

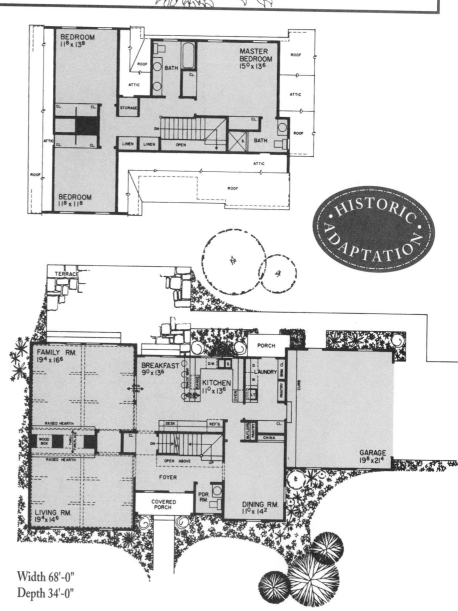

Width 68'-0"
Depth 34'-0"

GEORGIANS FROM THE NORTH

DURING THE 18TH CENTURY, GEORGIAN ARCHITECTURE became a favorite style for a growing middle class of homeowners in New England and surrounding regions. The exteriors of these homes were most often either clapboard or shingles, whereas the preferred materials in the South were bricks and stones. The basic Georgian house was a simple two-story box, two rooms deep, with symmetrical windows and doors.

Georgian roofs were lower pitched than their earlier counterparts and their cornices were more decorative. Cupolas and roof decks were common, as were widow's walks. Although end-gabled roofs are associated with Northern Georgian style and hip roofs with the South, both styles were used freely in both areas. Also popular was the use of a triangular gable pediment centered on the front facade.

The emphasis placed on the front door in Georgian architecture heralded a departure from the unadorned past of New England. Taking advantage of the skills of Yankee carpenters and shipwrights, homebuilders ornamented their doors with a variety of pilasters and pediments. The pilasters were sometimes plain, sometimes fluted, either full height or raised on pedestals, and eventually evolved into columns. A simple triangular pediment over the door was the most common topping, but this ornamentation also included curved moldings decorated with small dentil blocks. The center window on the second story was often a Palladian window, characterized by a central arch rising above elongated rectangular sidelights.

DESIGN 2653

First Floor: 2,016 square feet
Second Floor: 1,656 square feet
Total: 3,672 square feet

L

This design is based on a home built in 1715 by Thomas Barnard, a minister in Andover, Massachusetts. It demonstrates the introduction of Georgian symmetry and classical elegance to the simplicity of the medieval saltbox. Colonial detailing inside includes beam ceilings, wainscoting and china closets in the dining room—early Americans would have displayed fine pewter and earthenware there. Modern amenities include sliding glass doors from the family room to the terrace, a large laundry room, a well-equipped island kitchen and a quiet library. The master suite pampers with two walk-in closets with built-in shelves and a bath with twin vanities and a dressing room. A second bath with two vanities is shared by three bedrooms, one of which could serve as a study.

· HISTORIC · ADAPTATION

Width 71'-8"
Depth 50'-0"

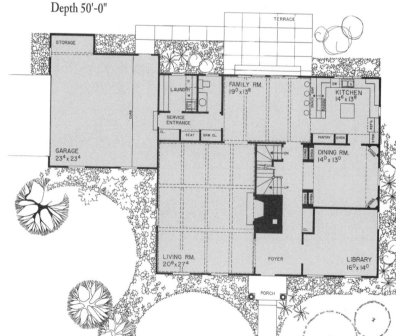

GARAGE
23⁴ x 23⁴

VERANDA

FAMILY ROOM
17⁸ x 18

KITCHEN/
BRKFST
15⁴ x 29²

LIBRARY
12⁸ x 13² BAY

LIVING ROOM
18⁴ x 15⁶

FOYER

DINING ROOM
15⁰ x 13²

·HISTORIC·
ADAPTATION

Width 53'-0"
Depth 75'-6"

ATTIC

MASTER
BATH

WALK-IN CLOSET

WALK-IN CLOSET

BEDROOM
12⁰ x 14⁴ BAY

BATH

LINEN

UP
TO ATTIC

OPEN
TO BELOW

RAILING

BEDROOM
14¹⁰ x 12⁰

READING AREA

MASTER
BEDROOM
15⁹ x 21⁸

QUOTE ONE®

Cost to build? See page 198
to order complete cost estimate
to build this house in your area!

DESIGN 3504

First Floor: 2,124 square feet
Second Floor: 1,658 square feet
Total: 3,782 square feet

L

Following the Revolutionary War, many New Englanders settled in New York near the Catskill Mountains. In Rensselaerville, a number of quietly dignified Georgian houses were built, with clapboard siding, symmetrically placed windows and a central motif of wide pedimented doorways below Palladian windows. The dramatic foyer of this present-day version has a curving, open staircase to the second floor, where a sumptuous master suite and two other bedrooms await family members and guests. The living room, separated from the foyer by two columns, has a fireplace and is near the dining room for easy entertaining. A U-shaped kitchen features an island cooktop and a snack bar shared with the breakfast area. The sunken family room boasts a second fireplace and sliding doors to the veranda. A bay-windowed library offers a quiet retreat from the bustle of family activities.

Design by Home Planners

DESIGN 2687

First Floor: 1,819 square feet
Second Floor: 1,431 square feet
Total: 3,250 square feet

L D

The Mission House in Stockbridge, Massachusetts, was built in 1739 by the Rev. John Sergeant, the first missionary to the Housatonic Indians. This adaptation replicates its plain clapboard exterior, embellished only by the elaborate doorway with a scroll or "swan's neck" pediment and fluted pilasters. The twin chimneys and window placement exemplify Georgian symmetry. Inside, the foyer opens to the living room with its commanding fireplace. A china cabinet marks the entrance to the bay-windowed dining room. A quiet study or media room is placed to the left of the foyer. The family living center is the country kitchen, which offers plenty of room for informal dining and lounging in front of the fireplace. Note the attached greenhouse. The second floor offers four bedrooms, including the master suite with its whirlpool tub, two lavatories and a walk-in closet.

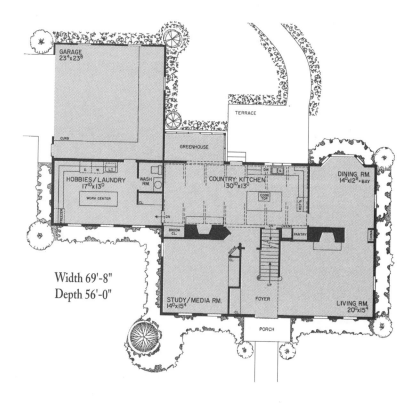

Width 69'-8"
Depth 56'-0"

Design by R.L. Pfotenhauer

DESIGN F106

First Floor: 1,805 square feet
Second Floor: 1,652 square feet
Total: 3,457 square feet
Optional Lower Level: 1,660 square feet

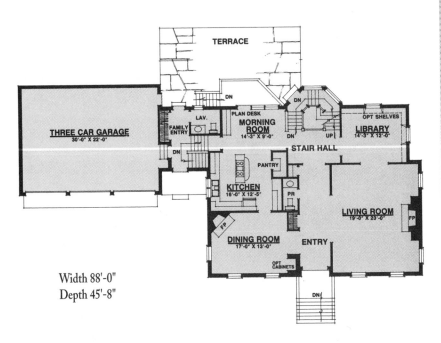

Width 88'-0"
Depth 45'-8"

TERRACE

DN

THREE CAR GARAGE
30'-0" X 22'-0"

FAMILY ENTRY   LAV.   PLAN DESK   DN   OPT SHELVES
MORNING ROOM
14'-3" X 9'-0"   LIBRARY
14'-3" X 12'-0"
DN   UP

STAIR HALL
DN

PANTRY
KITCHEN
16'-0" X 12'-5"   PR

LIVING ROOM
19'-0" X 23'-0"   FP

FP
DINING ROOM
17'-0" X 13'-0"   ENTRY

OPT CABINETS

DN

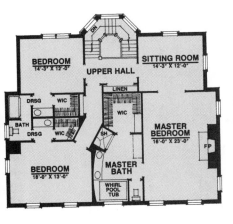

DN

BEDROOM
14'-3" X 12'-0"   UPPER HALL   SITTING ROOM
14'-3" X 12'-0"

DRSG   WIC   LINEN

BATH   WIC

DRSG   WIC   MASTER BEDROOM
16'-0" X 23'-0"   FP

BEDROOM
18'-0" X 13'-0"   SH

MASTER BATH

WHIRL POOL TUB

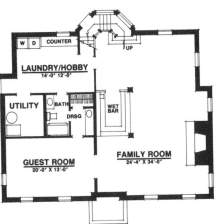

W   D   COUNTER   UP

LAUNDRY/HOBBY
14'-0" 12'-0"

UTILITY   BATH   WET BAR

DRSG

GUEST ROOM
20'-0" X 13'-0"   FAMILY ROOM
24'-4" X 34'-0"

OPTIONAL LOWER LEVEL

Twin chimneys adorn the gable ends of this dignified Georgian, while louvered shutters and a detailed entry with wrought-iron railings hint at the elegance to be found within. The view from the entry is of a unique rear stair and hall. Fireplaces highlight the formal dining and living rooms, which flank the entry. The library is nestled in a quiet corner in back. The island kitchen opens to a morning room with a planning desk and stairs to the rear terrace. A family entry passes by a lavatory and a coat closet. On the second floor, two family bedrooms each have a walk-in closet and a private dressing area and vanity. The master suite boasts a fireplace, a sitting room and a private bath with a whirlpool tub and a walk-in closet. The lower level can be finished to include a family room, laundry/hobby room and guest suite at a later date.

Design by R.L. Pfotenhauer

DESIGN F132

First Floor: 1,890 square feet
Second Floor: 1,874 square feet
Total: 3,764 square feet

This attractive Georgian house is based on the Dyer House on Nantucket Island. It is typical of wood-frame houses built there by 18th-Century whalers and is named for descendants of Captain William Dyer, who came to the colonies from England in the early 1600s. It is not known whether the Connecticut patriot Eliphalant Dyer ever occupied the house, but if he did he would feel quite at home in this modern reproduction. Formal entertaining is easy in the living and dining rooms, which share a through-fireplace. A second fireplace connects the family room and the morning room, which overlooks the terrace and provides a sunny area for relaxing. A planning desk in the kitchen and a walk-in pantry are nice touches, as are optional built-ins throughout the first floor. Four upstairs bedrooms include a sumptuous master suite.

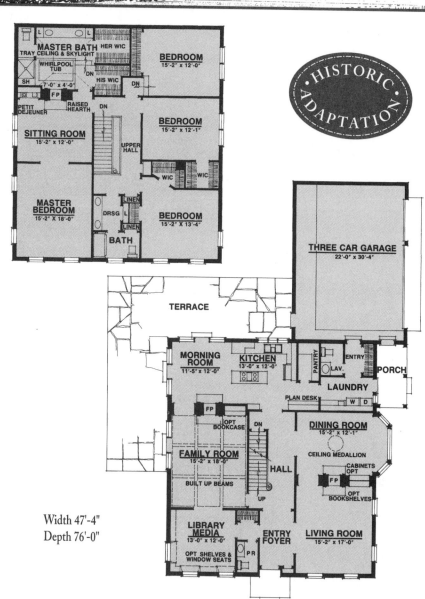

Width 47'-4"
Depth 76'-0"

Design by Home Planners

DESIGN 2659

First Floor: 1,023 square feet
Second Floor: 1,008 square feet
Third Floor: 476 square feet
Total: 2,507 square feet

L D

In 1770, Nathanael Greene, a young Quaker, moved to Anthony, Rhode Island, to manage a branch of his father's iron foundry. During the Revolution he rose through the ranks to became George Washington's second-in-command. Modeled after Greene's homestead, this design exhibits Georgian symmetry, from the shuttered windows to the central entrance, with its pilasters, bracketed pediment and twin carriage lamps. Indoors, the compact plan is practical and efficient. The study may serve instead as a media room or home office. The U-shaped kitchen works well with the breakfast room and the formal dining room. A mud room with laundry equipment and a closet leads to the garage. The master suite and two family bedrooms fill the second floor, while two rooms on the third floor provide areas for hobbies and studying.

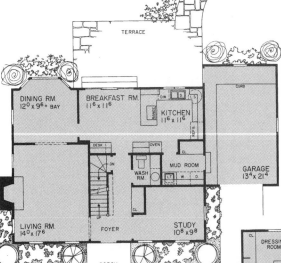

HISTORIC ADAPTATION

Width 49'-8"
Depth 32'-0"

QUOTE ONE®

Cost to build? See page 198
to order complete cost estimate
to build this house in your area!

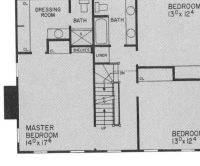

REAR VIEW

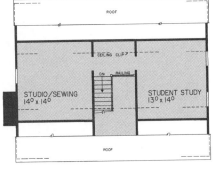

Design by R.L. Pfotenhauer

DESIGN F107

First Floor: 1,830 square feet
Second Floor: 1,723 square feet
Total: 3,553 square feet
Bonus Room: 534 square feet

Traditional Georgian symmetry sets the tone for this elegant home. A wraparound porch is a welcome addition to the sunken family room. The kitchen provides plenty of counter space for the family chef and a snack bar for casual meals in the morning room. The bay-windowed dining room shares a through-fireplace with the living room. Built-in cabinets and bookcases are optional. The room to the left of the foyer can be used as a quiet study or library, or a home office. The highlight of the second floor is the master suite, featuring a morning kitchen, a fireplace and a luxurious bath with twin walk-in closets and dressing areas. Three other bedrooms share a full bath with a double-bowl vanity. A rear stairway allows for private access from the first floor.

Width 72'-1"
Depth 74'-8"

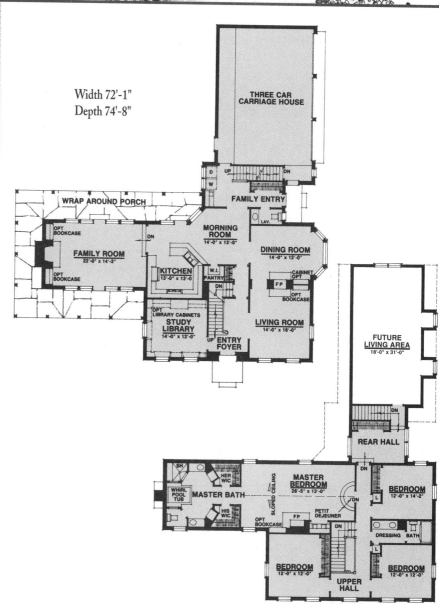

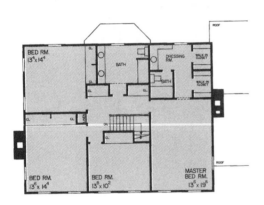

BED RM.
13⁵ x 14⁴

BED RM.
13⁶ x 14⁴

BED RM.
13⁸ x 10⁰

MASTER
BED RM.
13⁸ x 19⁸

BATH DRESSING RM. WALK-IN CLOSET BATH WALK-IN CLOSET

QUOTE ONE®

Cost to build? See page 198
to order complete cost estimate
to build this house in your area!

Width 66'-0"
Depth 36'-0"

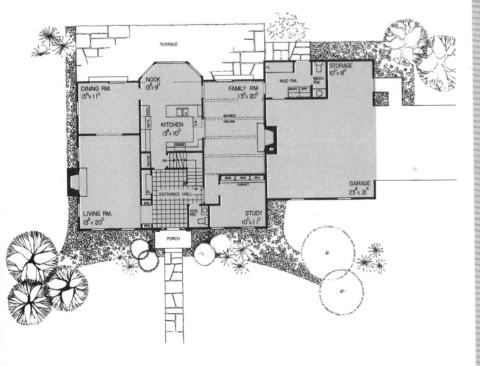

DINING RM.
13⁶ x 11⁰

NOOK
13⁶ x 9⁰

FAMILY RM.
13⁶ x 20⁰

STORAGE
10⁶ x 8⁰

MUD RM.

KITCHEN
13⁶ x 10⁰

BEAMED CEILING

TERRACE

GARAGE
23⁸ x 21⁴

ENTRANCE HALL

LIVING RM.
13⁶ x 20⁰

STUDY
10⁶ x 11⁰

PORCH

DESIGN 2610

First Floor: 1,505 square feet
Second Floor: 1,344 square feet
Total: 2,849 square feet

L D

This full two-story traditional
will be noteworthy wherever
it is built. It strongly recalls
images of a New England of yester-
year—and well it should, for the
window treatment and front
entrance detail are authentic. The
narrow horizontal siding and the
corner boards are appealing, as are
the two massive chimneys. Inside, a
large entrance hall, powder room
and coat closet welcome guests and
family. Formal rooms are to the left
of the hall, and a study with built-
in bookshelves is to the right. The
U-shaped kitchen benefits from all
that natural light from the bay window of the nook. A beam ceiling, a
fireplace and sliding glass doors are
features of the family room. The
mud room area includes a closet,
laundry equipment and an extra
washroom. Upstairs, there are four
bedrooms, two full baths and plenty
of closets.

DESIGN 9344

First Floor: 1,000 square feet
Second Floor: 1,345 square feet
Total: 2,345 square feet

Repeating window detailing, an arched entry and a brick facade highlight the exterior of this modern, two-story Colonial home. Formal rooms at the front provide entertaining ease. The dining room is served by a convenient passageway for quick kitchen service, while bright windows and French doors add appeal to the living room. A relaxing family room has a bayed conversation area plus a clear view through the sunny breakfast room into the gourmet kitchen. Features include wrapping counters, a snack bar, two lazy Susans and a pantry. Upstairs, a U-shaped hall with a view to below leads to four bedrooms. Bedroom 2 has its own bath. Homeowners will love the expansive master retreat. This oasis features a private sitting room, two walk-in closets, compartmented bath, separate vanities and a whirlpool tub.

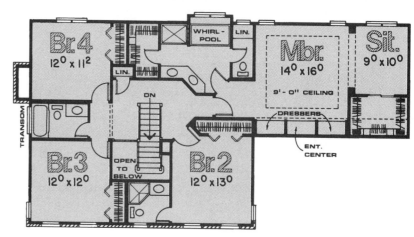

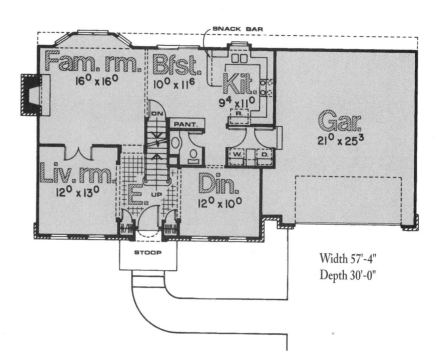

Width 57'-4"
Depth 30'-0"

Design by Design Basics, Inc.

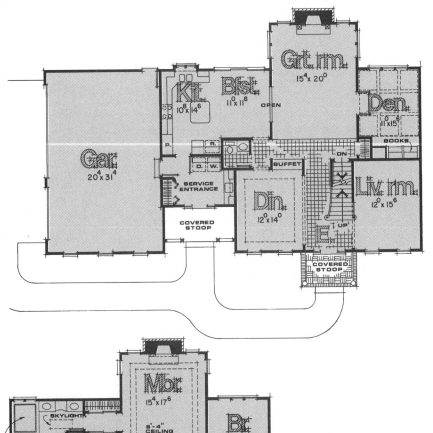

Width 68'-0"
Depth 40'-0"

DESIGN 9302

First Floor: 1,536 square feet
Second Floor: 1,343 square feet
Total: 2,879 square feet

This delightful elevation will be appreciated by anyone aspiring to live in Colonial style. A pedimented stoop with columns welcomes guests to the attractive front door, while three arches decorate the covered porch at the service entry to the mud/laundry room. Inside, the formal dining room, with a serving buffet, and the formal living room flank an elegant two-story entry. The great room is perfect for informal gatherings around the fireplace. Folks looking for a quieter spot might prefer the den with its beam ceiling and built-in bookcases. In the roomy island kitchen, cooks will appreciate the pantry and the attached breakfast area. Upstairs, the spacious master suite has its own fireplace, as well as three closets and a built-in dresser. A sophisticated skylit master bath has a two-person whirlpool and plant shelf. A second bath has twin vanities, a linen closet and a separate tub and shower.

DESIGN 9299

First Floor: 2,063 square feet
Second Floor: 894 square feet
Total: 2,967 square feet

An elegant brick elevation and rows of shuttered windows lend timeless beauty to this two-story Colonial design. The volume entry surveys formal dining and living rooms and the magnificent great room. Sparkling floor-to-ceiling windows flank the fireplace in the great room, which also boasts a cathedral ceiling. French doors, bayed windows, a wet bar and a decorative ceiling highlight the private den. Special lifestyle amenities in the kitchen and bayed breakfast area include a built-in desk, wrapping counters and a preparation island. A boxed ceiling adds elegance to the master suite. In the master bath/dressing area, note the large walk-in closet, His and Hers vanities, oval whirlpool tub and compartmented toilet. Each of the three family bedrooms upstairs has a roomy closet and a private bath.

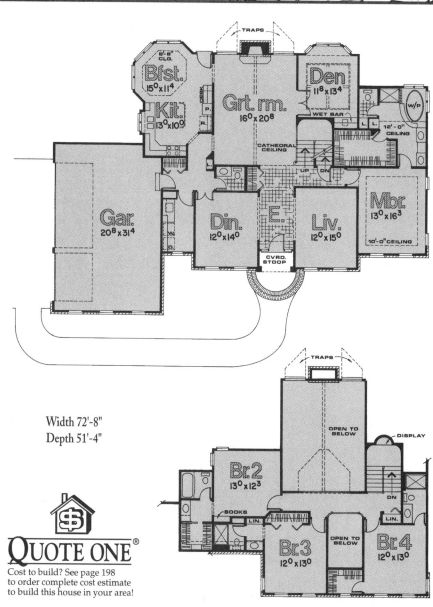

Width 72'-8"
Depth 51'-4"

QUOTE ONE®

Cost to build? See page 198 to order complete cost estimate to build this house in your area!

Design by James Fahy Design

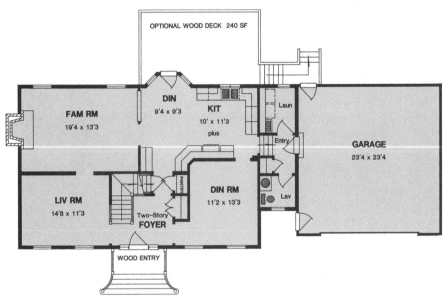

OPTIONAL WOOD DECK 240 SF

FAM RM
19'4 x 13'3

DIN
9'4 x 9'3

KIT
10' x 11'3
plus

Laun

Entry

GARAGE
23'4 x 23'4

LIV RM
14'8 x 11'3

PANTRY

DIN RM
11'2 x 13'3

Lav

Two-Story
FOYER

WOOD ENTRY

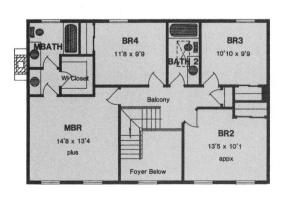

MBATH

BR4
11'8 x 9'9

BR3
10'10 x 9'9

BATH 2

W/ Closet

Balcony

MBR
14'8 x 13'4
plus

BR2
13'5 x 10'1
appx

Foyer Below

Width 70'-0"
Depth 35'-4"

DESIGN C106

First Floor: 1,179 square feet
Second Floor: 971 square feet
Total: 2,150 square feet

This stately Georgian-style Colonial will fit well in any neighborhood. Wide casings, heavy molding and louvered vents add to the classic look of this impressive facade. Inside, a two-story foyer with an L-shaped stairway welcomes visitors. Large living and dining rooms are accented by oversized double-hung windows. The kitchen offers maximum cupboard space and is open to a bay window in the dinette. A masonry fireplace draws you into the well-sized family room. The second floor takes full advantage of available space: four bedrooms, including a master suite, and an open balcony overlooking the first floor.

DESIGN J135

First Floor: 1,203 square feet
Second Floor: 1,029 square feet
Total: 2,232 square feet
Bonus Room: 223 square feet

In this design, the classic symmetry of the Georgian era has been given a definitely modern look. Small-paned windows, shutters and gables remind us of its heritage. Inside, the tile of the foyer continues back to the kitchen and divides the formal rooms from the family living areas. The den has French doors, allowing it to be closed off for privacy, peace and quiet. The family room, featuring a fireplace, a built-in desk and sliding doors to the backyard, is open to the breakfast nook. A powder room is nearby. The kitchen offers the option of a cooktop island or an L-shaped counter with a snack bar. The second story consists of a deluxe master suite, three family bedrooms with a shared compartmented bath, a balcony overlook and a bonus room.

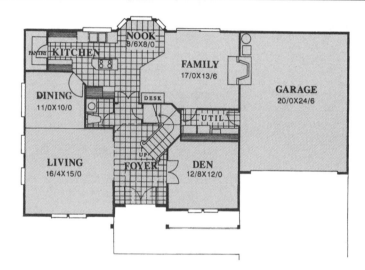

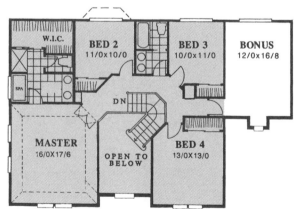

Width 60'-0"
Depth 35'-0"

Design by Alan Mascord Design Associates, Inc.

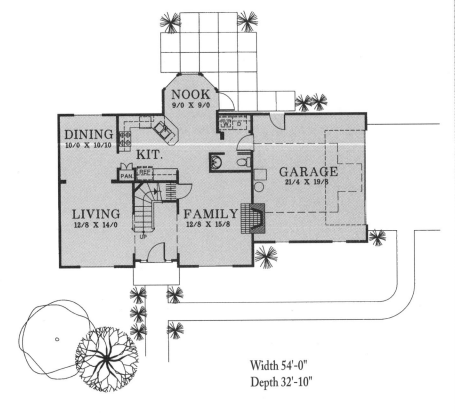

Width 54'-0"
Depth 32'-10"

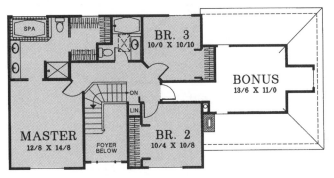

DESIGN 9462

First Floor: 935 square feet
Second Floor: 772 square feet
Total: 1,707 square feet
Bonus Room: 177 square feet

Colonial styling gives a classic form to this popular design. The dramatic two-story foyer, with its angled stairway, forms the circulation hub for this comfortable family home. The formal living room and adjacent dining room have easy access to the kitchen—perfect for entertaining. The cook-friendly kitchen overlooks the bay-windowed breakfast nook, and is close to the service entrance and the family room. Upstairs is a master bedroom with a spa tub, large shower, double vanity and walk-in closet. Two additional bedrooms are provided, along with a bonus room over the garage, which could be the fourth bedroom. A flexible rear-, front- or side-entry garage works well for corner lots or lots served by a lane.

DESIGN P119

First Floor: 1,424 square feet
Second Floor: 1,256 square feet
Total: 2,680 square feet

An elegant arch-top clerestory and a box-bay window set off this understated Colonial adaption and introduce an interior blessed with a wealth of amenities. Formal rooms feature boxed columns with shelves for curios and books, while the family room boasts a vaulted ceiling and an extended-hearth fireplace. A cozy den (or make it a fifth bedroom) is entered through double doors and has its own entrance to the full bath/powder room. The U-shaped kitchen offers a large pantry and easy access to both the formal dining room and the casual breakfast area. An elegant master suite shares the second floor with three family bedrooms and a convenient laundry. Please specify basement or crawl-space foundation when ordering.

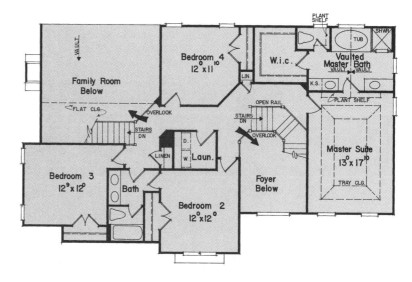

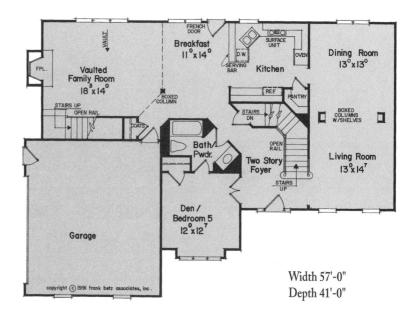

Width 57'-0"
Depth 41'-0"

Design by Frank Betz Associates, Inc.

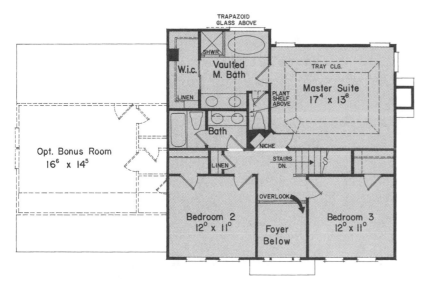

TRAPAZOID GLASS ABOVE

W.i.c.

LINEN

SHWR

Vaulted M. Bath

TRAY CLG.

Master Suite
17⁴ x 13⁶

PLANT SHELF ABOVE

Bath

NICHE

Opt. Bonus Room
16⁶ x 14⁵

LINEN

STAIRS DN.

OVERLOOK

Bedroom 2
12⁰ x 11⁰

Foyer Below

Bedroom 3
12⁰ x 11⁰

Storage

D.

W.

Pdr.

Laund.

NICHE

Breakfast

FRENCH DOOR

PANTRY

SERVING BAR

Family Room
19² x 13⁸

FPL.

RANGE

DW.

Kitchen

REF.

STAIRS UP

Garage

COATS

STAIRS DN.

copyright © 1993 frank betz associates, inc.

Dining Room
12⁰ x 11⁰

Two Story Foyer

Living Room
12⁰ x 11⁰

Width 55'-4"
Depth 33'-0"

DESIGN P131

First Floor: 1,028 square feet
Second Floor: 878 square feet
Total: 1,906 square feet
Optional Bonus Room: 315 square feet

Colonial symmetry is accented by fine detailing on the exterior of this elegant three-bedroom home. Inside, cross-room traffic is non-existent in the formal living room to the right of the two-story foyer, while the formal dining room offers direct access to the efficient kitchen. Family living takes place at the rear of the home in the spacious family room, which is enhanced by a warming fireplace and a French door to the rear yard. A nearby sunny breakfast nook is convenient for those early-morning coffee breaks. Upstairs, two family bedrooms—each with a walk-in closet—share a full hall bath. The lavish master bedroom suite is rife with amenities, including a large walk-in closet, a separate shower and tub, a compartmented toilet and a dual-bowled vanity. Please specify basement, crawlspace or slab foundation when ordering.

Design by Frank Betz Associates, Inc.

DESIGN P134

First Floor: 1,068 square feet

Second Floor: 977 square feet

Total: 2,045 square feet

Optional Bonus Room: 412 square feet

Two upper-level floor plan options are included with this delightful Georgian-inspired design. Both options include a deluxe master suite—a bedroom with a tray ceiling and a private bath with a bay-windowed tub, dual vanities and a walk-in closet with a plant shelf. There are also two family bedrooms, a full bath and a balcony overlook. The second option includes an upper-level laundry room and a bonus room with a walk-in closet. Downstairs, the large family room with a fireplace, a bayed breakfast room and an efficient kitchen cater to comfort. Formal dining and living rooms flank the two-story foyer, which leads to a powder room and a coat closet. Please specify basement or crawl-space foundation when ordering.

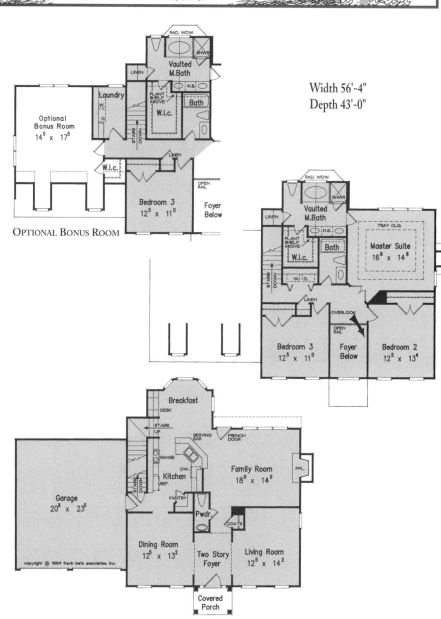

Width 56'-4"
Depth 43'-0"

OPTIONAL BONUS ROOM

Design by Frank Betz Associates, Inc.

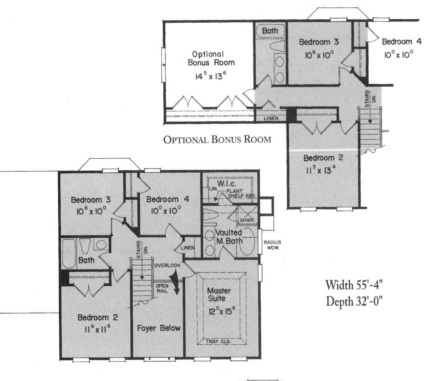

OPTIONAL BONUS ROOM

Optional Bonus Room
14.5 x 13.6

Bath

Bedroom 3
10.6 x 10.0

Bedroom 4
10.0 x 10.0

STAIRS DN.

LINEN

Bedroom 2
11.3 x 13.4

Bedroom 3
10.6 x 10.0

Bedroom 4
10.0 x 10.0

W.i.c.
LIN. PLANT SHELF ABV.

SHWR.

Vaulted M. Bath

RADIUS WDW.

LINEN

STAIRS DN.

OVERLOOK

OPEN RAIL

Bath

Bedroom 2
11.6 x 11.6

Foyer Below

Master Suite
12.0 x 15.6

TRAY CLG.

Width 55'-4"
Depth 32'-0"

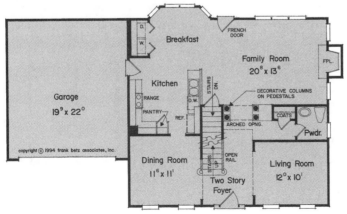

Garage
19.9 x 22.0

D.
W.

Breakfast

FRENCH DOOR

Family Room
20.8 x 13.6

FPL.

Kitchen

RANGE

PANTRY

REF.

D.W.

STAIRS DN.

DECORATIVE COLUMNS ON PEDESTALS

ARCHED OPNG.

COATS

Pwdr.

Dining Room
11.6 x 11'

STAIRS UP

OPEN RAIL

Two Story Foyer

Living Room
12.0 x 10'

copyright © 1994 frank betz associates, inc.

DESIGN P206

First Floor: 1,007 square feet
Second Floor: 877 square feet
Total: 1,884 square feet
Optional Bonus Room: 328 square feet

Colonial charm is highly evident in the facade of this stucco home—from the gabled roof to the classic symmetry of the windows and the decorative details of the front door. Inside, the two-story foyer is flanked by the formal dining room to the left and the formal living room to the right. Casual living takes place directly ahead through an arched hallway. Spaciousness is the theme here, perpetuated by the large family room, the open bayed breakfast area and the roomy kitchen, which all flow together to make entertaining a breeze. Upstairs, a lavish master suite includes a tray ceiling, a walk-in closet and a sumptuous bath. Three family bedrooms share a full hall bath. An optional second-floor plan is included, adding a bonus room over the garage. Please specify basement or crawlspace foundation when ordering.

Design by R.L. Pfotenhauer

DESIGN F137

First Floor: 1,807 square feet
Second Floor: 1,652 square feet
Total: 3,459 square feet
Optional Lower Level: 1,657 square feet

This design and the one on page 99 are based on a house built in 1758 in Portsmouth, New Hampshire, by Captain Gregory Purcell. Known also as the Samuel Lord House, for a later owner, it is most famous for twice being the residence of John Paul Jones—while he was fitting out his warship, Ranger, in 1777, and while building America in 1781-1782. The beautiful Georgian facade is typically called "five over four and a door," describing the arrangement of windows. An elegant stairway leads to the front door and an entry flanked by the formal dining and living rooms, both with distinctive fireplaces. The family chef will delight in the island kitchen, the pantry and the morning room with a built-in desk. The second floor offers three bedrooms, including a sumptuous master suite, while the optional lower level has space for future expansion.

Width 88'-0"
Depth 40'-8"

TERRACE

THREE CAR GARAGE
30'-0" X 22'-0"

FAMILY ENTRY
LAV.
PLAN DESK
MORNING ROOM
14'-3" X 9'-0"
OPT SHELVES
LIBRARY
14'-3" X 12'-0"

STAIR HALL
PANTRY
KITCHEN
16'-0" X 12'-5"
PR
LIVING ROOM
19'-0" X 23'-0"
FP

FP
DINING ROOM
17'-0" X 13'-0"
ENTRY
OPT CABINET

DN

HISTORIC ADAPTATION

BEDROOM
14'-3" X 12'-0"
UPPER HALL
SITTING ROOM
14'-3" X 12'-0"
DRSG
WIC
LINEN
BATH
WIC
DRSG
WIC
SH
MASTER BEDROOM
16'-0" X 23'-0"
FP
BEDROOM
18'-0" X 13'-0"
MASTER BATH
WHIRL POOL TUB

W   D   COUNTER   UP
LAUNDRY/HOBBY
14'-0" 12'-0"
UTILITY
BATH
WET BAR
DRSG
GUEST ROOM
20'-0" X 13'-0"
FAMILY ROOM
24'-4" X 34'-0"

OPTIONAL LOWER LEVEL

HISTORIC ADAPTATION

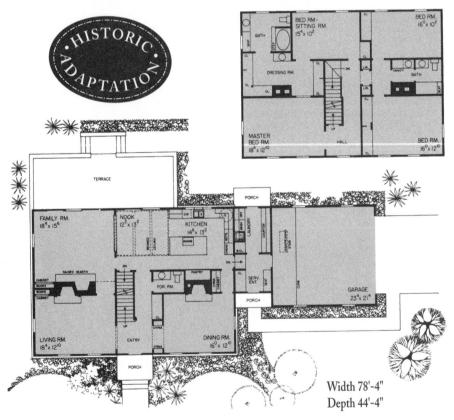

Width 78'-4"
Depth 44'-4"

REAR VIEW

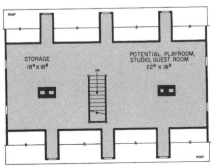

DESIGN 2556

First Floor: 1,675 square feet
Second Floor: 1,472 square feet
Third Floor: 1,016 square feet
Total: 4,163 square feet

D

This design, like the previous one, recalls a home built by sea captain Gregory Purcell in 1758. Following his death in 1776, his widow, Sarah, supported herself and seven children by taking in boarders, the most famous being John Paul Jones. This beautiful Georgian features a gambrel roof with pedimented dormers and corbelled chimneys, and a classical doorway with a segmented pediment and pilasters. The central hallway is also Georgian, as are many interior details included with the plan. The dining room works for sunlit holiday brunches and cozy firelit suppers. Back-to-back fireplaces and built-ins separate the living and family rooms. The L-shaped kitchen has an island cooking counter and opens into the breakfast nook. The second floor offers four bedrooms, one of which could serve as a sitting room for the master suite.

DESIGN 2980

First Floor: 1,648 square feet
Second Floor: 1,368 square feet
Third Floor: 567 square feet
Total: 3,583 square feet

This late-Georgian adaptation is reminiscent of the Cowles house built in Farmington, Connecticut around 1786. The projecting central pavilion, Ionic columns, Palladian window and pedimented gable are among the details that set the character of this historic house. Dentils, wooden quoins and bracketed cornices complete the picture of elegance. Inside, the foyer leads to the formal living room, the library and the U-shaped kitchen. The family room opens to the sun room and shares a snack bar and a desk with the kitchen. A through-fireplace warms the living and dining rooms, while individual fireplaces are also found in the library and the master bedroom. The master bath features a whirlpool tub, twin lavatories, a vanity and a walk-in closet. The third floor offers a private guest suite and a large area for hobbies and other activities.

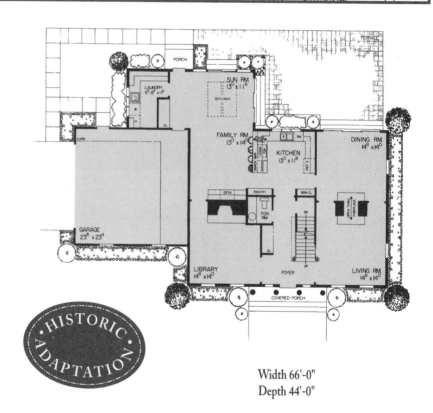

HISTORIC ADAPTATION

Width 66'-0"
Depth 44'-0"

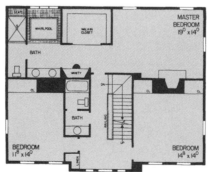

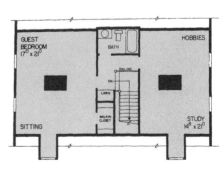

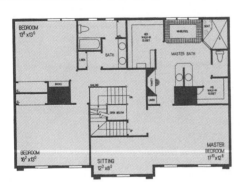

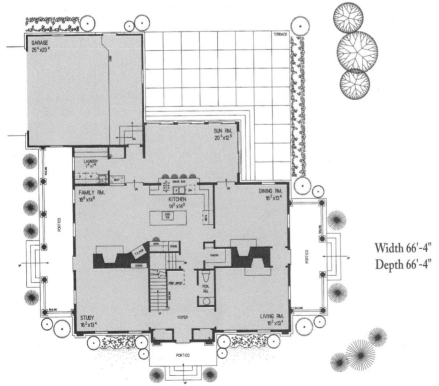

Quote One®

Cost to build? See page 198
to order complete cost estimate
to build this house in your area!

Width 66'-4"
Depth 66'-4"

DESIGN 2989

First Floor: 1,972 square feet
Second Floor: 1,533 square feet
Total: 3,505 square feet

L

This home recalls the Longfellow House in Cambridge, Massachusetts, residence of the poet for forty-five years. Featuring a hip roof with a widow's walk, it was built in 1759 by Major John Vassall, an ardent Tory who was driven out of the house in 1774. It served for a while as George Washington's command center. Longfellow's residency began in 1837, when he came to Harvard to teach English. Elegant two-story pilasters frame the front entrance and are repeated at the corners. Two porches retain the symmetry and add outdoor living space. On the first floor are the formal living and dining rooms, each with a fireplace. A front study connects to the family room, which offers built-ins and another fireplace. Upstairs are three bed-rooms, including a wonderful master suite with a sitting room and a deluxe private bath.

Design by R. L. Pfotenhauer

DESIGN F111

First Floor: 1,997 square feet
Second Floor: 1,687 square feet
Total: 3,684 square feet
Optional Lower Level: 960 square feet
Future Living Area: 582 square feet

Twin chimneys, a widow's walk, prominent dormers and a five-sided porch enhance the gracious exterior of this home—an adaptation of the Governor Langdon House, built in Portsmouth, New Hampshire, in 1784. John Langdon was known not only for serving three terms as governor, but also for contributing a warehouse full of Jamaican rum to the Continental Army. The entry foyer, featuring a grand staircase, is flanked by the formal living and dining rooms. Both have warming, welcoming fireplaces. An island kitchen includes a walk-in pantry and an adjacent morning room. The family room offers a raised-hearth fireplace and access to a wraparound porch. The huge master suite is filled with every amenity, including a small kitchenette. Two family bedrooms—with walk-in closets and separate dressing areas—share a full bath.

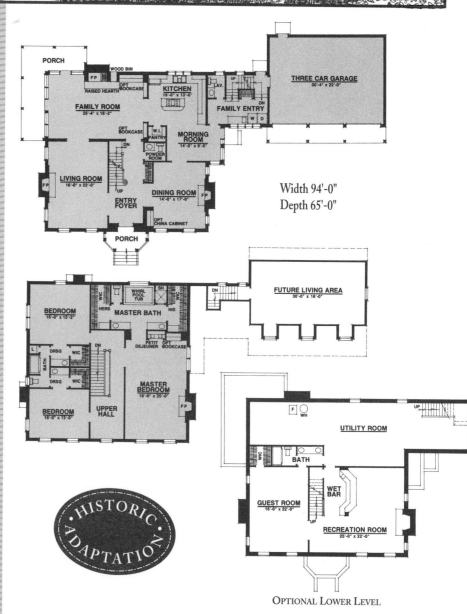

Width 94'-0"
Depth 65'-0"

HISTORIC · ADAPTATION

OPTIONAL LOWER LEVEL

Design by R. L. Pfotenhauer

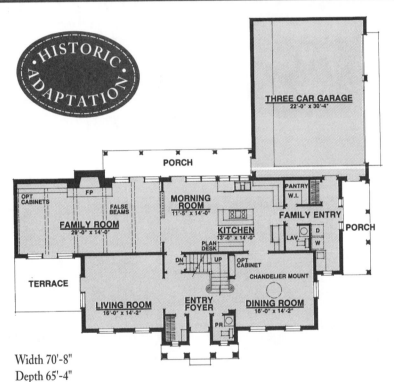

HISTORIC ADAPTATION

THREE CAR GARAGE
22'-0" x 30'-4"

PORCH

OPT CABINETS | FP | FALSE BEAMS

MORNING ROOM
11'-5" x 14'-0"

PANTRY W.I.

FAMILY ENTRY

FAMILY ROOM
29'-0" x 14'-0"

KITCHEN
13'-0" x 14'-0"

PORCH

LAV. | D | W

PLAN DESK

DN | UP | OPT CABINET

CHANDELIER MOUNT

TERRACE

LIVING ROOM
16'-0" x 14'-2"

ENTRY FOYER

DINING ROOM
16'-0" x 14'-2"

PR

Width 70'-8"
Depth 65'-4"

SH | HER WIC | OPT CABINETS | FP

DRESSING WIC

WHIRL POOL TUB | **MASTER BATH** | **MASTER BEDROOM**
23'-0" x 14'-0" | **BEDROOM**
11'-5" x 14'-0" | BATH

WIC

HIS WIC | PETIT DEJEUNER

DRESSING

BEDROOM
14'-2" x 14'-2"

BEDROOM
13'-0" x 14'-2"

UPPER HALL

WIC | BATH | LINEN

DESIGN F135

First Floor: 1,702 square feet
Second Floor: 1,733 square feet
Total: 3,435 square feet

Sheldon's Tavern, the model for this handsome exterior, can truthfully proclaim, "George Washington slept here." He spent one night in the northeast room, and mentioned it in his diary. Elisha Sheldon built the house in 1760. In 1779, his son converted it to a tavern. The thoroughly up-to-date floor plan of this adaptation places formal rooms at the front of the house and a wide open informal area across the back. A spacious family room features a fireplace and doors to a front terrace and a rear covered porch. Also offering access to the porch, the morning room shares a planning desk and a snack bar with the kitchen. A short hallway leads past a walk-in pantry and a washroom to a side porch. Upstairs, the master suite pampers with a fireplace, a kitchenette and a wonderful bath. Each of three family bedrooms has a walk-in closet.

DESIGN F133

First Floor: 1,789 square feet
Second Floor: 2,060 square feet
Total: 3,849 square feet
Future Living Area: 448 square feet
Optional Lower Level: 1,033 sq. ft.

The original of this house is in Litchfield, Connecticut, built in 1793 by Julious Deming. It was designed by Scottish architect William Spratt, who considered it his masterpiece. The exterior is grand, with three massive chimneys and a decorative balcony overlooking the pillared front entrance. Mantels, mirrors, hardware and interior fittings were imported from England by Deming. This home would be a proper setting for similar furnishings. On the first floor, fireplaces warm the three main rooms, while plenty of multi-pane windows let in natural light. Coffee breaks—and casual meals—will be a treat in the morning room, which opens off the kitchen. The second floor offers three bedrooms with private baths, one a sumptuous master suite, another lighted by the elegant Palladian window.

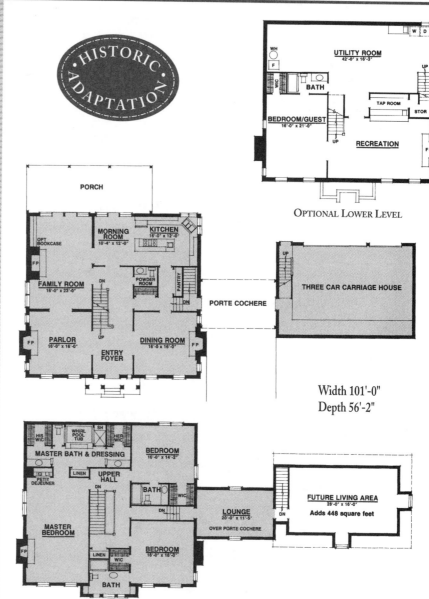

HISTORIC ADAPTATION

OPTIONAL LOWER LEVEL

Width 101'-0"
Depth 56'-2"

Design by Home Planners

HISTORIC · ADAPTATION

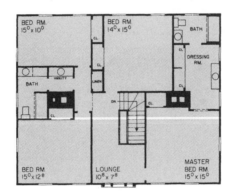

BED RM. 15⁰ x 10⁰

BED RM. 14⁰ x 15⁰

BATH

CL

CL

DRESSING RM.

BATH

VANITY

LINEN

CL

DN

CL

BED RM. 15⁰ x 12⁸

LOUNGE 10⁸ x 7⁸

MASTER BED RM. 15⁰ x 15⁰

Width 74'-0"
Depth 34'-0"

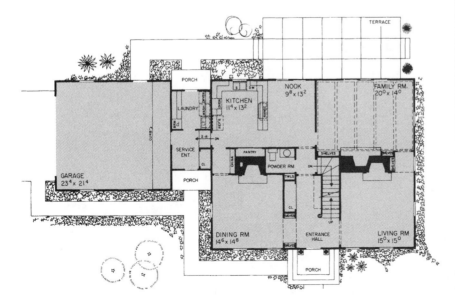

TERRACE

PORCH

LAUNDRY

KITCHEN 11⁴ x 13²

NOOK 9⁸ x 13²

FAMILY RM. 20⁰ x 14⁰

SERVICE ENT.

DN

PORCH

CHINA

PANTRY

POWDER RM.

SHELVES

SHELVES

TWLS

GARAGE 23⁴ x 21⁴

CL

SHELVES

UP

DINING RM. 14⁶ x 14⁸

ENTRANCE HALL

LIVING RM. 15⁰ x 15⁰

PORCH

DESIGN 2639

First Floor: 1,556 square feet
Second Floor: 1,428 square feet
Total: 2,984 square feet

L D

By the end of the 18th Century, prosperity had arrived in the New World. Based on the Alexander Field House in Longmeadow, Massachusetts, this design reflects the elegance and fine detailing that rich Yankee merchants demanded in their homes. A raised doorway, defined by pilasters and pediment, and a second-story Palladian window are capped by a fanlit pediment projecting from the hip roof. The interior is similarly elaborate and recalls the skills of New England woodworkers in many details included in the plans. The first floor is divided into fourths, with the formal living and dining rooms (each with a fireplace) at the front and casual areas across the back. A third fireplace and a beam ceiling add rustic charm to the family room. Upstairs, a lounge, naturally lit by the Palladian window, leads to four bedrooms, including a fine master suite.

DESIGN 2522

First Floor: 1,835 square feet
Second Floor: 1,625 square feet
Total: 3,460 square feet

Sir William Pepperrell is remembered for his victory at the siege of Louisburg, Nova Scotia, in 1745. This stately mansion is based on the Lady Pepperrell House, where his widow lived in style. Built in 1760 in Kittery Point, Maine, it captures the simple elegance of the period. It employs the frame construction characteristic of New England Georgian homes, with exquisite detailing indoors and out. Steps lead to a projected pavilion that is distinguished from the clapboard walls by smooth boards that simulate masonry. A grand entrance is framed by Ionic pilasters elevated on pedestals. The foyer opens to family and living rooms with fireplaces, and leads past an open stairway to the dining room. To the right, a study with a walk-in closet provides a quiet spot, while the U-shaped kitchen and eating nook are to the left. The master suite is luxurious, with a fireplace, sitting room and walk-in closet.

HISTORIC ADAPTATION

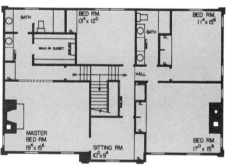

Width 61'-8"
Depth 36'-8"

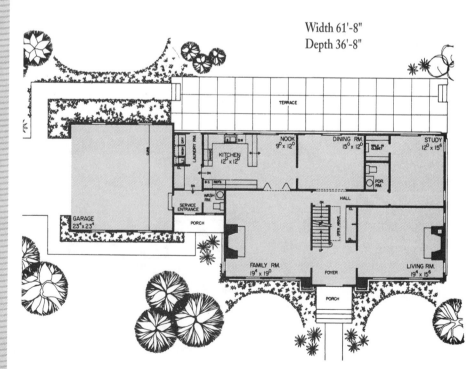

FARMHOUSES

FARMHOUSES WERE COMMON THROUGHOUT THE Colonies, and they were a varied lot. They had exteriors of wood, stone and brick. Some had gabled roofs; others had gambrel roofs. In New England, houses of this period were primarily one-and-a-half or two stories high, with white clapboard exteriors. While the main portion of the house was generally rectangular in shape, the overall structure frequently had an irregular configuration, due to the addition of various dependencies.

For German-style farmhouses, such as many built in Pennsylvania, stone was the favored building material, although clapboarding was used on later additions. Like those in New England, these homes had steep roofs to help shed the snow, but often with the addition of a pent roof between stories. An unsupported hood over the front entrance was traditional.

In addition to the country kitchen and prominent chimney, a popular characteristic of the farmhouse was the covered porch. Of course, not all farmhouses had front porches. Those that did followed no stringent rules concerning their size, style or location. Some were large, others small. Some had pillars and railings and wrapped around two or more sides of the house. Others were barely large enough to accommodate a couple of rocking chairs.

Southern farmhouses often had porches on two levels, with pillars across the front. As befitted the main house of a plantation, many of these dwellings featured the elegant symmetry and ornamentation of the Georgian period. Also popular was the "raised cottage" design, originally developed in flood-plain areas to protect the first floor from water damage, but used elsewhere for aesthetic reasons.

DESIGN 2542

First Floor: 2,025 square feet
Second Floor: 1,726 square feet
Total: 3,751 square feet

L

This fieldstone farmhouse has its roots in the rolling countryside of Pennsylvania. Based on the Pottsgrove home in Pottstown, which was built in 1752, it features the popular pent roof of that era and shows the types of additions that came as the family fortune increased. Two chimneys support five fireplaces. The simple elegance of Georgian design is evident in many interior details, such as the paneled dado and fireplace wall in the living room. The study is tucked away in a corner of the house, with sliding doors that open to a secluded porch. The spacious and versatile family room is a congenial place for everyday activities or informal get-togethers. The stone fireplace with built-in bookcases and a storage bin for firewood dominates the space. Wood paneling and a beam ceiling contribute to its cozy ambiance. The kitchen features a work island, ample storage and a large dining area.

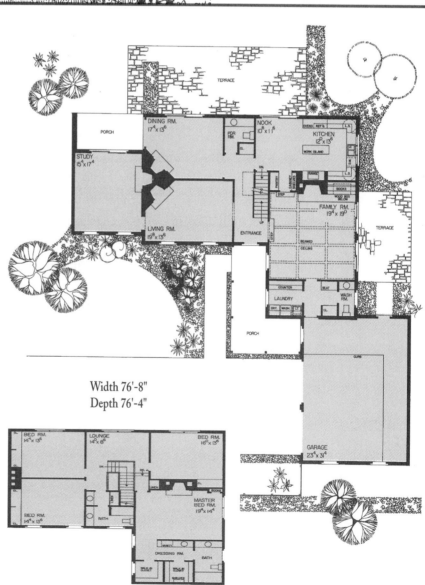

Width 76'-8"
Depth 76'-4"

Design by Home Planners

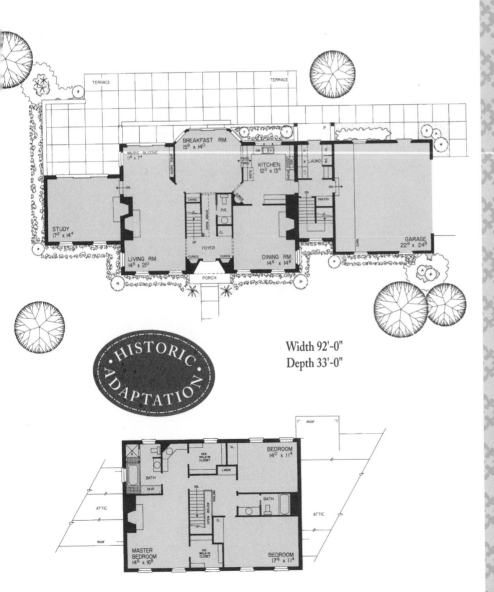

Width 92'-0"
Depth 33'-0"

HISTORIC · ADAPTATION

DESIGN 2976

First Floor: 1,787 square feet
Second Floor: 1,260 square feet
Total: 3,047 square feet

This two-story farmhouse brings to mind the stone houses of Bucks County, Pennsylvania. Notice the Georgian symmetry, the wood trim and the recessed center entrance, common traits of this rural genre. The foyer, featuring niches for curios, opens to the living room with its adjacent music alcove and to the dining room. Both rooms have fireplaces, as does the study, located at one end of the house for privacy. The U-shaped kitchen has a triple window over the sink and a pass-through to the large breakfast room. A good-sized laundry room and a pantry are nearby. A fourth fireplace is found upstairs in the master suite, which also boasts His and Hers walk-in closets and vanities. Two family bedrooms and a shared bath complete the plan.

DESIGN M118

Square Footage: 2,078

Colonial style meets farmhouse style, furnishing old-fashioned charisma with a flourish. The interior holds a contemporary floor plan filled with amenities. From the entry, double doors lead to the country dining room, which is open to the island kitchen. Taking center stage nearby is the spacious great room, warmed by a center fireplace and offering access to the covered patio. The secluded master suite is tucked behind the three-car garage, providing the homeowners with a private getaway. The bedroom features a vaulted ceiling and access to the patio, while the private bath contains a garden tub, double-bowl vanity, separate shower and compartmented toilet. Beyond the bath is a huge walk-in closet with two built-in chests. Three family bedrooms—one doubles as a study or home office—a full bath and a utility room complete the plan.

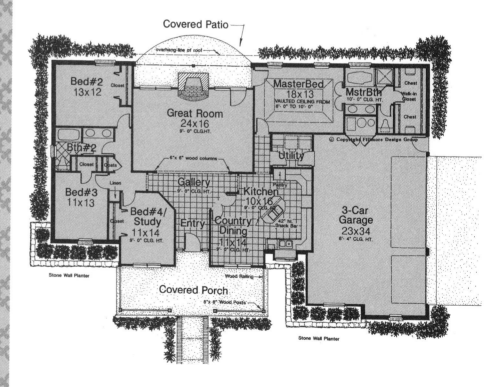

Width 75'-0"
Depth 47'-10"

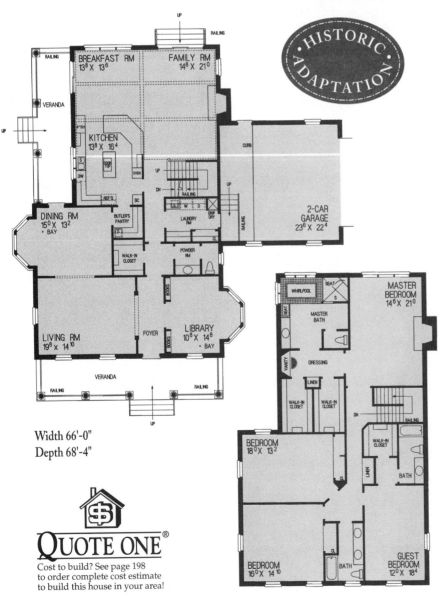

HISTORIC ADAPTATION

BREAKFAST RM 13⁸ X 13⁶

FAMILY RM 14⁸ X 21⁰

KITCHEN 13⁸ X 16⁴

2-CAR GARAGE 23⁸ X 22⁴

DINING RM 15⁰ X 13² • BAY

BUTLER'S PANTRY

LAUNDRY RM

POWDER RM

WALK-IN CLOSET

LIVING RM 19⁸ X 14¹⁰

FOYER

LIBRARY 10⁸ X 14⁸ • BAY

VERANDA

Width 66'-0"
Depth 68'-4"

MASTER BEDROOM 14⁶ X 21⁰

MASTER BATH

WHIRLPOOL   SEAT

DRESSING

WALK-IN CLOSET

WALK-IN CLOSET

BEDROOM 18⁰ X 13²

WALK-IN CLOSET

LINEN

BATH

BEDROOM 16⁰ X 14¹⁰

BATH

GUEST BEDROOM 12⁰ X 18⁴

$B
Quote One®

Cost to build? See page 198
to order complete cost estimate
to build this house in your area!

DESIGN 3502

First Floor: 2,086 square feet
Second Floor: 2,040 square feet
Total: 4,126 square feet

L D

This Pennsylvania farmhouse is reminiscent of the solid, comfortable homes once so prevalent on homesteads throughout America. The early 1800s saw stone cottages like this, as well as log ones, being built. The columned front porch leads to a formal foyer with living room on the left and library on the right. The formal dining room connects directly to the living room and indirectly to the island kitchen through a butler's pantry. The family room and breakfast room have beam ceilings and are both open to the kitchen. A covered veranda leads to a side yard. On the second floor are four bedrooms, including a guest room with a private bath. The master bedroom has a fireplace and a fine bath with a whirlpool tub. Two walk-in closets grace the dressing area. The two family bedrooms share a full bath with a double vanity.

DESIGN 2988

First Floor: 1,458 square feet
Second Floor: 1,075 square feet
Third Floor: 462 square feet
Total: 2,995 square feet

L D

The bell-shaped gambrel roof was a trademark of farmhouses in the 17th-Century Dutch colony of New Netherland. It is particularly charming on the garage added to this modernized version of the Guyen-Lake-Tyson House. Front and rear covered porches encourage outdoor activities, while second-story dormers provide natural light for the bedrooms. A formal dining room with corner cabinets leads through a butler's pantry to the wonderful country kitchen. With a large bay window, snack bar/work island, pantry and built-in desk, this will be the center of family life. A media room with built-ins and a living room with a fireplace fill the right side of the house. The master suite includes a whirlpool tub, twin vanities and a dressing room with stairs leading to a third-floor exercise room and study/sewing room.

QUOTE ONE®
Cost to build? See page 198
to order complete cost estimate
to build this house in your area!

Width 62'-0"
Depth 44'-0"

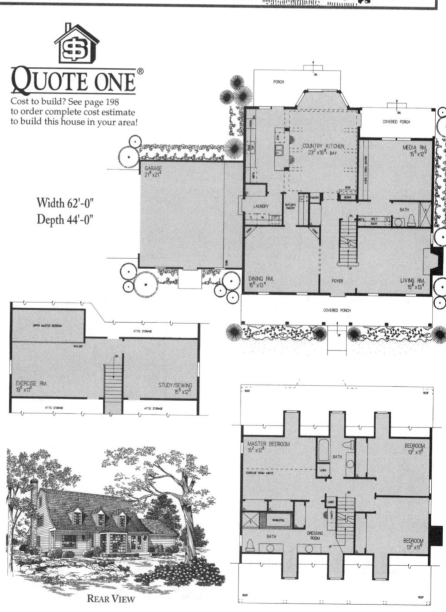

REAR VIEW

HISTORIC ADAPTATION

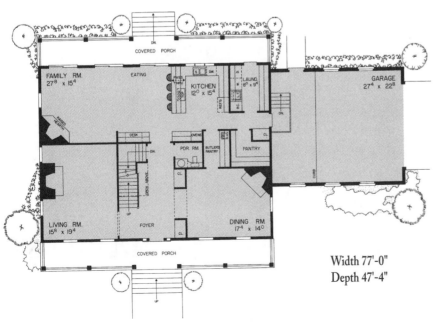

Width 77'-0"
Depth 47'-4"

DESIGN 2697

First Floor: 1,752 square feet
Second Floor: 1,486 square feet
Total: 3,238 square feet

This Dutch Colonial design recalls the Vreeland House, built near Englewood, New Jersey, in 1818. Characteristic of this pleasing style are the clapboard siding, the gambrel roof, the chimneys at both ends and the covered porches across the front and the rear of the house. The elliptical fanlight and classical detailing of the front doorway reflect the newly popular Federal style. Our updated floor plans include a large family room with a raised-hearth fireplace and a built-in desk, and a front living room with a fireplace. The kitchen offers a pass-through to an eating area off the family room. There is also a formal dining room, with a third fireplace and a butler's pantry with a wet bar. On the way to the garage are the laundry room and a walk-in pantry. The second floor has three family bedrooms sharing two full baths. The master suite includes a pampering bath with a dressing area and a walk-in closet.

HISTORIC ADAPTATION

DESIGN 2694

First Floor: 2,026 square feet
Second Floor: 1,386 square feet
Total: 3,412 square feet

L

This rambling farmhouse is based on the retirement home of John Jay, the first chief justice of the United States. Located in Katonah, New York, it dates from around 1800, and was built on land purchased by his grandfather from the Indians. The raised porches of this design were common in the Hudson River Valley. Notice the saltbox roof on the garage and the Federal detailing of the front door. The first floor includes a grand living room with a fireplace and a music alcove, a library with another fireplace and built-in bookshelves, a light-filled dining room, a large country kitchen with a third fireplace and a snack bar, and a utility room with laundry facilities and a work bench. Three upstairs bedrooms include a master suite with a walk-in closet, vanity seating, a whirlpool tub and double sinks. Each of two family bedrooms contains a double closet.

REAR VIEW

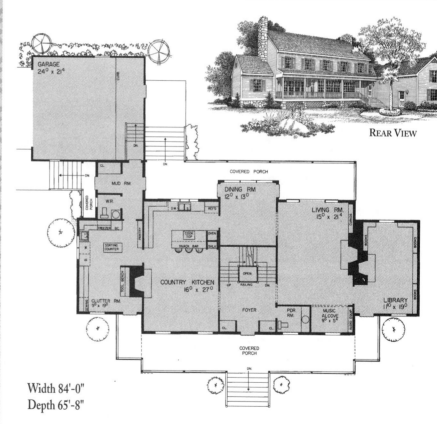

Width 84'-0"
Depth 65'-8"

QUOTE ONE®

Cost to build? See page 198
to order complete cost estimate
to build this house in your area!

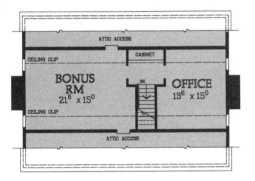

BONUS RM 21⁶ x 15⁰

CABINET

OFFICE 13⁶ x 15⁰

ATTIC ACCESS

CEILING CLIP

CEILING CLIP

ATTIC ACCESS

· HISTORIC · ADAPTATION

MASTER BATH

WHIRL-POOL

SHWR

BATH

LIN.

VANITY

WALK-IN CLOSET

BEDRM 13⁶ x 12²

MASTER SUITE 17² x 13⁴

BEDRM 13⁶ x 12²

Width 40'-0"
Depth 40'-0"

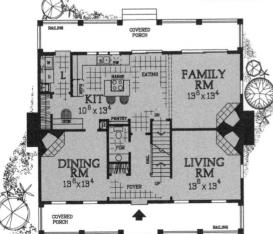

RAILING

COVERED PORCH

W D

L

S DW

RANGE

EATING

FAMILY RM 13⁶ x 13⁴

KIT 10⁶ x 13⁴

DESK

PANTRY

PDR

DINING RM 13⁶ x 13⁴

RAIL

FOYER

UP

LIVING RM 13⁶ x 13⁴

COVERED PORCH

RAILING

$ QUOTE ONE ®

Cost to build? See page 198
to order complete cost estimate
to build this house in your area!

DESIGN 3510

First Floor: 1,120 square feet
Second Floor: 1,083 square feet
Third Floor: 597 square feet
Total: 2,800 square feet

Sweeping front and rear raised porches with columns, detailed railings and centered stairs characterize this Southern farmhouse. It is based on a home built by Philip Alston, who came from Nova Scotia to North Carolina in 1772. He became justice of the peace and clerk of the court, but fled the area in 1790 when he was accused of murdering one man and ordering the murder of another. Designed to accommodate a narrow building site, the floor plan delivers outstanding livability. The kitchen features an island cooktop, an eating nook and a planning desk. Sliding glass doors provide access to the rear porch. Corner fireplaces add a hospitable glow to the family, living and dining rooms. In the master suite, a fourth fireplace and a dressing area with a walk-in closet and separate vanity set the tone. Third-floor possibilities include a home office, a hobby area or a studio.

DESIGN 3507

First Floor: 1,360 square feet
Second Floor: 1,172 square feet
Total: 2,532 square feet

L

A gambrel roof and a covered porch highlight the exterior of this raised cottage, based on the Booth House, built around 1756 in Edenton, North Carolina. An elevated front entrance features two sets of steps, a patterned railing and a muntined door flanked by carriage lamps. Named for Robert H. Booth, a wealthy merchant who owned it in the 19th Century, the original home had just two rooms and a hall downstairs and three bedrooms upstairs. This version has a far more complete floor plan, with formal living and dining rooms across the front and a large informal area in the back. The kitchen boasts a cooking island, snack bar, planning desk and access to the veranda through a breakfast area. Twin pillars support an archway opening to the large family room, which is enhanced by one of four fireplaces. The master suite includes a sitting area and a luxurious master bath.

Cost to build? See page 198
to order complete cost estimate
to build this house in your area!

Width 44'-0"
Depth 42'-0"

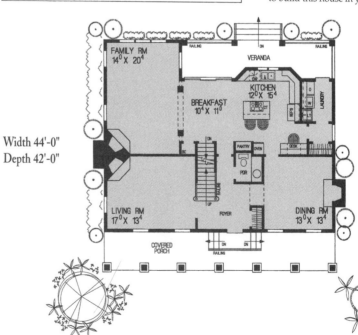

Design by Homes for Living, Inc.

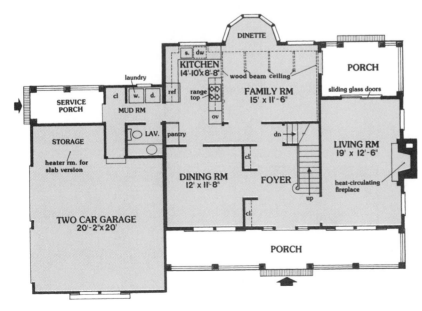

Width 58'-0"
Depth 37'-6"

2x6 studs
for added insulation

BED RM 2
12' x 11'-6"

BATH

BATH

W.I.C.

cl

cl

cab

lin.

BALCONY

cl cl

H

dn

railing

MASTER
BED RM
18'-8" x 12'-6"

BED RM 3
13'-4" x 10'

BED RM 4
12' x 9'-8"

cl

DINETTE

KITCHEN
14'-10" x 8'-8"

s.

dw

laundry

wood beam ceiling

PORCH

cl

w.

d.

ref

range
top

FAMILY RM
15' x 11'-6"

sliding glass doors

SERVICE
PORCH

MUD RM

ov

LAV.

pantry

dn

LIVING RM
19' x 12'-6"

STORAGE

heater rm. for
slab version

cl

DINING RM
12' x 11'-8"

FOYER

up

heat-circulating
fireplace

TWO CAR GARAGE
20'-2" x 20'

cl

PORCH

DESIGN N100

First Floor: 1,082 square feet
Second Floor: 1,013 square feet
Total: 2,095 square feet

This attractive two-story Colonial farmhouse is highlighted by a shingled exterior, a welcoming front porch and shuttered small-paned windows. Inside, a center hall is enhanced by a decorative stairway leading to four bedrooms on the second floor. Flanking the foyer are the formal dining room and a large living room with a fireplace and sliding glass doors to a rear porch. Also accessible from the porch, the family room features a beam ceiling and a large bay-windowed dinette area. The family chef will appreciate the L-shaped kitchen with its cook-top island and pantry. The one-story left wing provides a mud room, a laundry and a lavatory in addition to the two-car garage and large storage area. The second-floor bedrooms include a master suite with a walk-in closet and a private bath. Three family bedrooms share a bath with a double-sink vanity.

DESIGN 8242

First Floor: 1,732 square feet
Second Floor: 818 square feet
Total: 2,550 square feet
Bonus Room: 592 square feet

Triple dormers, columns and balusters complement the high-pitched roof and lend Colonial charm to this country home. Interesting details include a dentiled roofline, arched windows, and pilasters and a transom decorating the front door. Twin arches and a focal-point fireplace define the great room, with two sets of doors to bring in the light. Meals will be a pleasure, whether in the formal dining room, the sunny breakfast nook or the kitchen, where a work island backs up to a snack bar. A secluded master suite offers separate dressing areas and walk-in closets, a knee-space vanity and a corner whirlpool tub. The second floor includes three family bedrooms and a full bath. An optional walk-out basement offers space for an additional bedroom or guest suite, a game room and a covered porch. Please specify slab, basement or crawlspace foundation when ordering.

Width 57'-10"
Depth 43'-7"

Design by Design Basics, Inc.

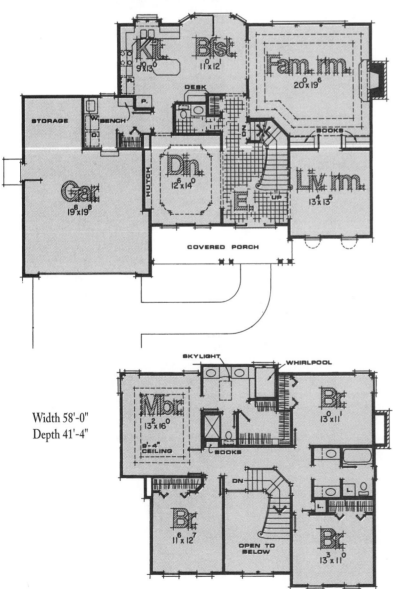

Width 58'-0"
Depth 41'-4"

DESIGN 9215

First Floor: 1,386 square feet
Second Floor: 1,171 square feet
Total: 2,557 square feet

Amenities for casual family living and entertaining abound in this attractive Colonial. A charming covered front porch makes for an inviting exterior. Inside, the two-story entry with a flared staircase opens into the formal dining and living rooms. French doors connect the living room with the more informal family room for expanded entertaining space. A spacious kitchen handily serves the family and dining rooms as well as the bay-windowed breakfast area. The first floor features nine-foot ceilings throughout. Built-ins include bookshelves in the family room, a hutch in the dining room, a desk in the kitchen and a bench in the laundry room. Upstairs are four bedrooms, one a master suite with a skylit bath offering a whirlpool tub and a large walk-in closet.

Design by Living Concepts Home Planning

DESIGN A154

First Floor: 1,669 square feet
Second Floor: 706 square feet
Total: 2,375 square feet
Bonus Room: 342 square feet

Skylights, an abundance of windows and five gable-roofed dormers flood this three-bedroom Colonial with natural light. A balcony connects two bedrooms and a bath on the second floor and overlooks the great room below. The great room will be the heart of this home, with its focal-point fireplace, built-in bookshelves and patio access. Wide views from the breakfast bay enhance the roomy kitchen, which offers a snack bar, a good-sized pantry and plenty of counter space. Double doors offer entry from the front porch to the dining room and to the master suite. The latter fills the left side of the plan with a large bedroom and a skylit bath boasting two lavatories, a corner garden tub, a step-down shower and two walk-in closets. Bonus space over the garage is reached by a back stairway.

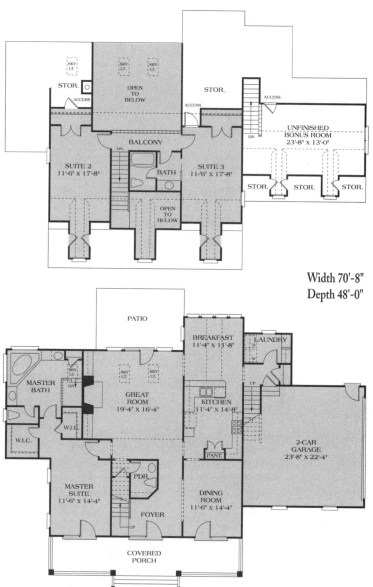

Width 70'-8"
Depth 48'-0"

Design by Donald A. Gardner Architects, Inc.

© 1990 Donald A. Gardner Architects, Inc.

B. NATHAN

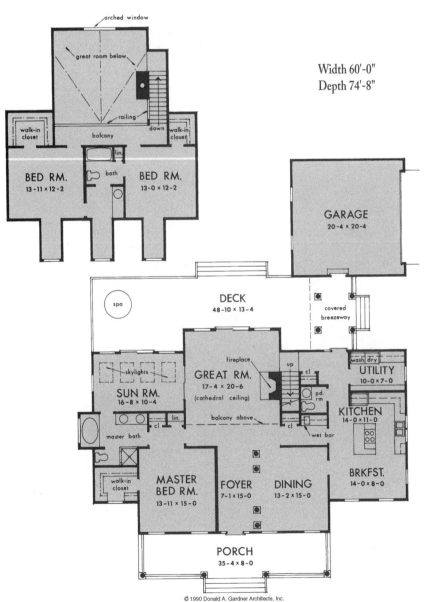

arched window

great room below

walk-in closet

balcony

railing

down

walk-in closet

lin.

bath

BED RM.
13-11 × 12-2

BED RM.
13-0 × 12-2

Width 60'-0"
Depth 74'-8"

GARAGE
20-4 × 20-4

spa

DECK
48-10 × 13-4

covered breezeway

skylights

fireplace

GREAT RM.
17-4 × 20-6
(cathedral ceiling)

up

cl

wash dry

UTILITY
10-0 × 7-0

SUN RM.
16-8 × 10-4

balcony above

lin.

cl

pd. rm.

KITCHEN
14-0 × 11-0

master bath

cl

wet bar

walk-in closet

MASTER BED RM.
13-11 × 15-0

FOYER
7-1 × 15-0

DINING
13-2 × 15-0

BRKFST.
14-0 × 8-0

PORCH
35-4 × 8-0

© 1990 Donald A. Gardner Architects, Inc.

DESIGN 9615

First Floor: 1,852 square feet
Second Floor: 735 square feet
Total: 2,587 square feet

This three-bedroom country home recalls the elegance of the past with its columned porch and triple dormers. Circle-head windows illuminate a contemporary floor plan inside. Columns define the foyer and dining room, adding architectural excitement to an already delightful design. A separate wing houses the roomy island kitchen, a breakfast area and the laundry room. The great room is enhanced by a cathedral ceiling, a fireplace, an arched window and a second-floor balcony overlooking the area. A sun room leads to a deck that graces the rear of the house. Notice the covered breezeway to the garage. The first-floor master suite offers private access to the sun room and features a deluxe bath with a bumped-out garden tub. Upstairs, two bedrooms with walk-in closets and a compartmented bath accommodate family or guests.

Design by Larry E. Belk Designs

DESIGN 8245

First Floor: 1,993 square feet
Second Floor: 894 square feet
Total: 2,887 square feet
Bonus Room: 176 square feet

Here's a country home that offers lots of down-home appeal, but steps out with upscale style inside. The front door is flanked by sidelights as well as by pairs of shuttered windows. Arch-topped dormers complement a Palladian window in the centered, front-facing gable. The grand foyer leads to a spacious great room featuring an extended-hearth fireplace and access to the rear covered porch. Open planning allows diners in the windowed breakfast nook to enjoy the glow of the fireplace; the secluded formal dining room has its own hearth. The master suite offers private access to the rear porch, and a spacious bath that boasts two walk-in closets, twin vanities and a windowed whirlpool tub. Two upstairs bedrooms share a full bath and a balcony hall that leads to a bonus room with a walk-in closet.

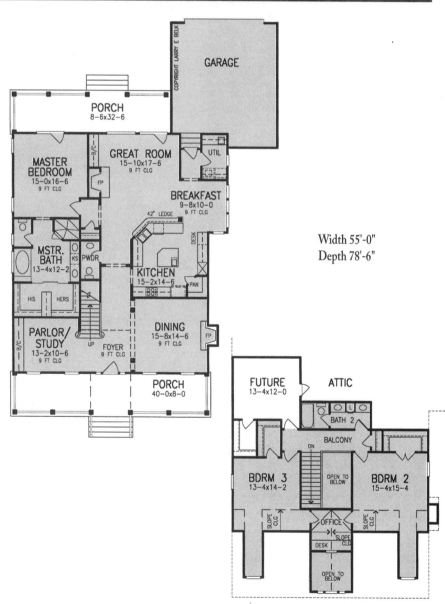

Width 55'-0"
Depth 78'-6"

Design by Donald A. Gardner Architects, Inc.

© 1993 Donald A. Gardner Architects, Inc.

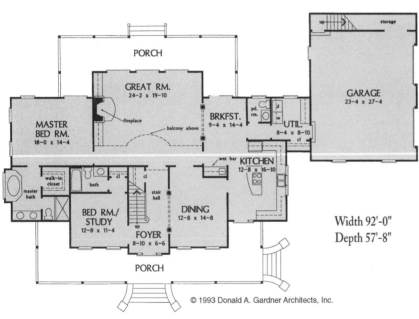

© 1993 Donald A. Gardner Architects, Inc.

Width 92'-0"
Depth 57'-8"

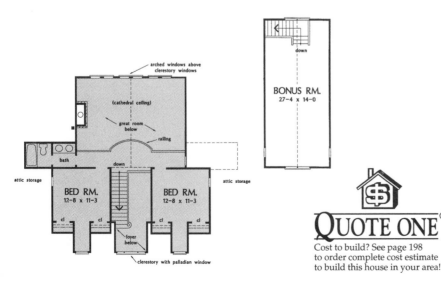

DESIGN 9723

First Floor: 2,064 square feet
Second Floor: 594 square feet
Total: 2,658 square feet
Bonus Room: 464 square feet

You'll find country living at its best with this spacious four-bedroom farmhouse, starting with a wraparound porch. A front Palladian window dormer and rear clerestory windows at the great room add exciting visual elements to the exterior while providing natural light to the interior. The large great room boasts a fireplace, bookshelves and a cathedral ceiling, allowing a curved balcony overlook above. The great room, master bedroom and breakfast room offer access to the rear porch for greater indoor/outdoor flow. The kitchen features a large cooktop island, windows over the sink, a wet bar and a convenient entrance from the front porch. Two first-floor bedrooms include a master suite with a walk-in closet and a private bath and a guest suite that could also serve as a study or home office. Two upstairs bedrooms, a compartmented bath and a generous bonus room complete the plan.

Quote One®

Cost to build? See page 198 to order complete cost estimate to build this house in your area!

Design by Donald A. Gardner Architects, Inc.

© 1994 Donald A. Gardner Architects, Inc.

B. NATHAN

DESIGN 9761

First Floor: 1,907 square feet
Second Floor: 656 square feet
Total: 2,563 square feet
Bonus Room: 467 square feet

Bay windows on three sides and a welcoming country porch in front dress up this fine farmhouse-style home. Inside, decorative columns lead from the foyer into the formal dining room, which is well lighted by one of the bay windows as well as two front-facing windows. The central hall opens to the expansive great room, which offers a fireplace, a cathedral ceiling and an overhead balcony. A screened porch with skylights is reached from the great room, the master bedroom and the breakfast area. A large cooktop island with a snack bar gives the kitchen an added measure of efficiency. The master suite features two bay windows, a large walk-in closet and a lavish bath with a whirlpool tub. Two family bedrooms share a full bath on the second floor.

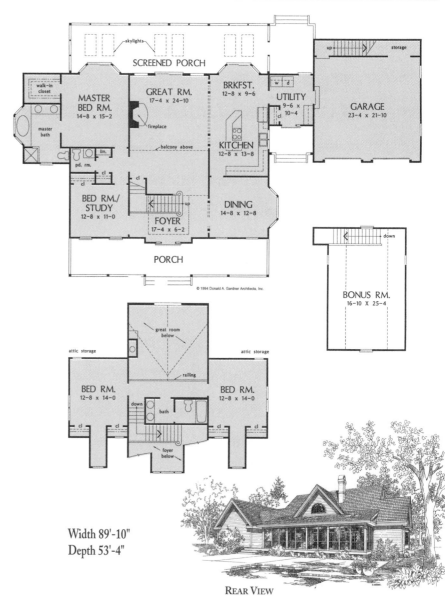

Width 89'-10"
Depth 53'-4"

REAR VIEW

Design by Donald A. Gardner Architects, Inc.

© 1991 Donald A. Gardner Architects, Inc.

B. NATHAN.

GARAGE
20 - 4 × 21 - 8

storage

DECK
34 - 8 × 12 - 0

seat   seat

DINING
13 - 0 × 12 - 0

KIT.
10 - 4 × 12 - 0

BRKFST.
10 - 8 × 9 - 8

pd. rm.

UTIL.

dry wash

down

walk-in closet

master bath

GREAT RM.
13 - 4 × 19 - 4

fireplace

FOYER

up

MASTER BED RM.
13 - 4 × 13 - 0

PORCH

Width 59'-0"
Depth 64'-0"

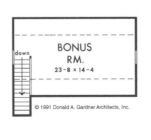

QUOTE ONE®

Cost to build? See page 198
to order complete cost estimate
to build this house in your area!

© 1991 Donald A. Gardner Architects, Inc.

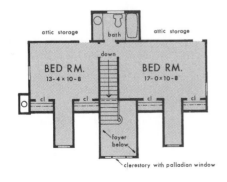

attic storage   attic storage

bath

down

BED RM.
13 - 4 × 10 - 8

cl   cl

BED RM.
17 - 0 × 10 - 8

cl   cl

foyer below

clerestory with palladian window

down

BONUS RM.
23 - 8 × 14 - 4

© 1991 Donald A. Gardner Architects, Inc.

DESIGN 9645

First Floor: 1,356 square feet
Second Floor: 542 square feet
Total: 1,898 square feet
Bonus Room: 393 square feet

The welcoming charm of this country farmhouse is expressed by its many windows and its covered wraparound porch. A two-story entrance foyer is enhanced by natural light from a Palladian window in the clerestory dormer. A first-floor master suite provides a private retreat for the homeowners, and includes a master bath with a large walk-in closet, a whirlpool tub, a separate shower and a double-bowl vanity. The first floor features nine-foot ceilings throughout, with the exception of the kitchen area, which offers an eight-foot ceiling. The second floor provides two additional bedrooms, a full bath and plenty of storage space. Please specify basement or crawl-space foundation when ordering.

Design by Donald A. Gardner Architects, Inc.

B. NATHAN

© 1990 Donald A. Gardner Architects, Inc.

DESIGN 9625

First Floor: 1,581 square feet
Second Floor: 549 square feet
Total: 2,130 square feet
Bonus Room: 334 square feet

Great flexibility is available in this plan—the great room/dining room can be reworked into one large great room with the dining room relocated across the hall. A sun room with a cathedral ceiling and a sliding glass door to the deck is accessible from both the breakfast and dining rooms. A large kitchen boasts a convenient cooking island. The master bedroom has a fireplace, a walk-in closet and a spacious master bath. Two second-floor bedrooms are equal in size and share a full bath with double-bowl vanity. Each bedroom has a dormer window and a walk-in closet. A large bonus room over the garage is accessible from the utility room below. Please specify basement or crawlspace foundation when ordering.

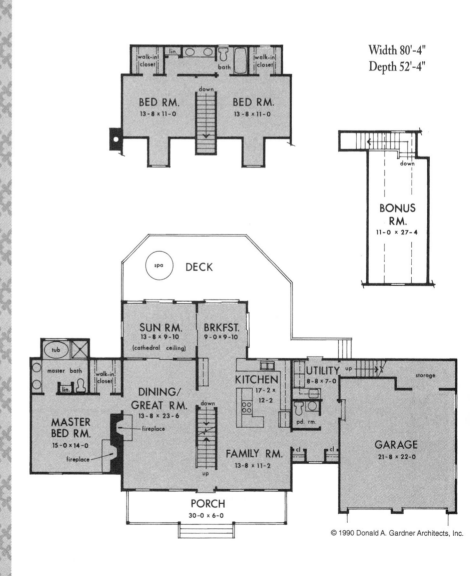

Width 80'-4"
Depth 52'-4"

© 1990 Donald A. Gardner Architects, Inc.

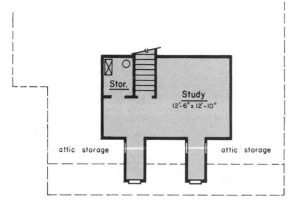

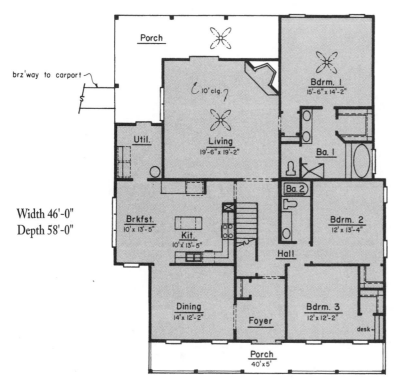

Width 46'-0"
Depth 58'-0"

DESIGN E105

First Floor: 2,020 square feet
Second Floor: 352 square feet
Total: 2,372 square feet

Eye-catching details provide a stylish exterior for this charming Southern cottage. Guests may want to stop a while on the attractive front porch, but eventually will make their way through the foyer and central hall to a magnificent living area with a corner fireplace, ten-foot ceiling and views of the side and rear yards. Or invite them out onto the L-shaped back porch and enjoy a quiet evening of conversation. The kitchen/breakfast area will appeal to the whole family—as views of the side yard tempt them to linger for just one more cup of coffee. A secluded master suite affords comfort to spare, with a walk-in closet, linen closet and twin-lavatory bath with a whirlpool tub and separate shower. A quiet study and lots of storage space are found upstairs. Please specify crawlspace or slab foundation when ordering.

Design by Donald A. Gardner Architects, Inc.

© 1995 Donald A. Gardner Architects, Inc.

DESIGN 9796

First Floor: 1,395 square feet
Second Floor: 489 square feet
Total: 1,884 square feet

Stylish rooms and a comfortable layout make this country home unique and inviting. The foyer opens from the wide covered porch and leads to the expansive great room, complete with a focal-point fireplace, a cathedral ceiling and access to the outdoors. The gourmet kitchen features a centered food-preparation island and offers views of the rear property through the formal dining room. A bayed breakfast nook is easily served by the kitchen and boasts a private screened porch—perfect for reading or casual meals. Family bedrooms, which share a full bath, are placed to the left of the first floor, while a lavish master suite offers room to ramble upstairs. A window dormer makes a cozy sitting nook, and a skylit bonus room offers the possibility of a nursery or a recreation room.

Width 54'-2"
Depth 53'-5"

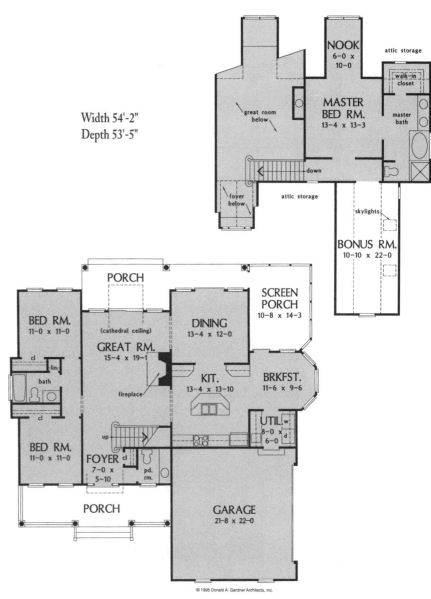

© 1995 Donald A. Gardner Architects, Inc.

Design by Donald A. Gardner Architects, Inc.

© 1990 Donald A. Gardner Architects, Inc.

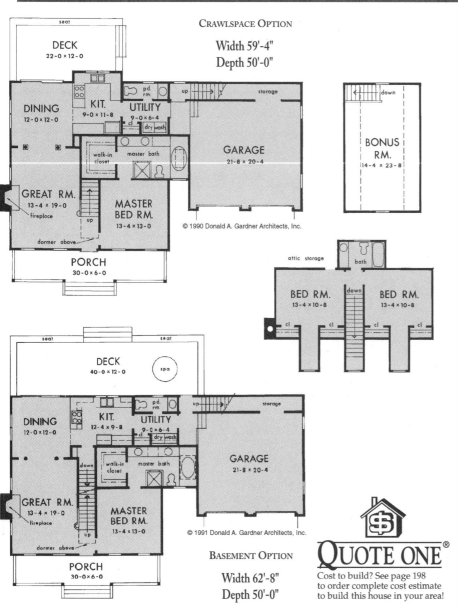

CRAWLSPACE OPTION

Width 59'-4"
Depth 50'-0"

DECK
22-0 × 12-0

DINING
12-0 × 12-0

KIT.
9-0 × 11-8

UTILITY
9-0 × 6-4
dry wash

p.d. rm.

up

storage

GARAGE
21-8 × 20-4

walk-in closet

master bath

GREAT RM.
13-4 × 19-0
fireplace

MASTER BED RM.
13-4 × 13-0

dormer above

PORCH
30-0 × 6-0

© 1990 Donald A. Gardner Architects, Inc.

BONUS RM.
14-4 × 23-8

down

attic storage

bath

BED RM.
13-4 × 10-8

down

BED RM.
13-4 × 10-8

cl

DECK
40-0 × 12-0
spa

seat

DINING
12-0 × 12-0

KIT.
12-4 × 9-8

UTILITY
9-0 × 6-4
dry wash

p.d. rm.

up

storage

GARAGE
21-8 × 20-4

down

walk-in closet

master bath

GREAT RM.
13-4 × 19-0
fireplace

MASTER BED RM.
13-4 × 13-0

dormer above

PORCH
30-0 × 6-0

© 1991 Donald A. Gardner Architects, Inc.

BASEMENT OPTION

Width 62'-8"
Depth 50'-0"

QUOTE ONE®
Cost to build? See page 198
to order complete cost estimate
to build this house in your area!

DESIGN 9626

First Floor (crawlspace foundation): **1,057 sq. ft.**
First Floor (basement foundation): **1,110 sq. ft.**
Second Floor: **500 sq. ft.**
Total (crawlspace foundation): **1,557 sq. ft.**
Total (basement foundation): **1,610 sq. ft.**
Bonus Room: **342 sq. ft.**

This compact two-story cottage is perfect for the economically conscious family. A covered front porch and a rear deck with built-in seats provide ample space for outdoor relaxing and entertaining. Indoor gatherings will benefit from the fireplace in the great room and the nearby dining room, with its access to the deck. The kitchen is offered in two versions, depending on whether the crawlspace or basement foundation option is selected. The master suite boasts a whirlpool tub with a skylight overhead, a separate shower and a double-bowl vanity. Second-floor bedrooms share a full bath, and there's a wealth of storage as well as a bonus room on this level. Please specify basement or crawlspace foundation when ordering.

DESIGN 8177

Square Footage: 1,834

Reminiscent of America's farmhouses, this home comes complete with covered front and rear porches, perfect for those warm summer evenings. Inside, the foyer opens to the great room, with a matching pair of double French doors flanking the fireplace and leading out to the rear porch. The dining room adds a formal flair, with square columns connected by arched openings. An angled L-shaped counter in the kitchen opens the area to the great room and provides a convenient pass-through. A snack bar and a sunny breakfast room provide space for casual dining. The master bedroom features a coffered ceiling and a walk-in closet. Amenities such as a double-bowl vanity, a corner whirlpool tub and a shower highlight the master bath. Two more bedrooms and a full bath complete the plan. Please specify crawlspace or slab foundation when ordering.

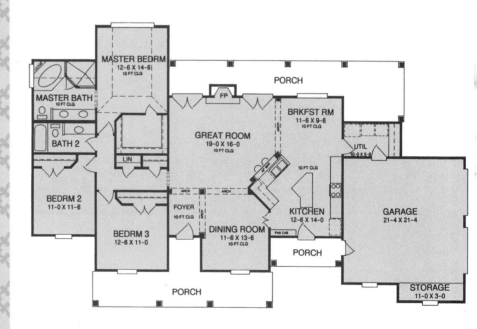

Width 78'-0"
Depth 48'-7"

Design by Donald A. Gardner Architects, Inc.

© 1991 Donald A. Gardner Architects, Inc.

B. NATHAN

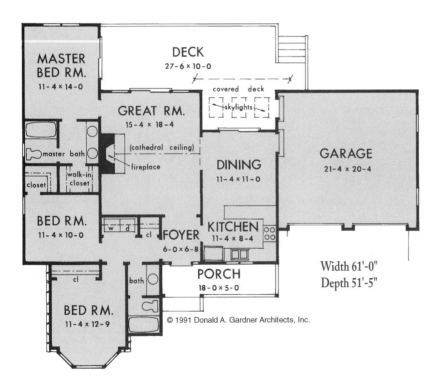

MASTER BED RM.
11-4 × 14-0

DECK
27-6 × 10-0

covered deck

skylights

GREAT RM.
15-4 × 18-4

(cathedral ceiling)

fireplace

master bath

walk-in closet

closet

DINING
11-4 × 11-0

GARAGE
21-4 × 20-4

BED RM.
11-4 × 10-0

w   d   cl

FOYER
6-0 × 6-8

KITCHEN
11-4 × 8-4

cl

bath

PORCH
18-0 × 5-0

BED RM.
11-4 × 12-9

© 1991 Donald A. Gardner Architects, Inc.

Width 61'-0"
Depth 51'-5"

DESIGN 9620

Square Footage: 1,310

A multi-paned bay window, dormers, a cupola, a covered porch and stone accents dress up this one-story cottage. The entrance foyer leads to an impressive great room with a cathedral ceiling and a fireplace. Located off the foyer, the U-shaped kitchen provides an ideal layout for food preparation and is open to the dining room for easy entertaining. An expansive deck offers shelter while admitting sunlight through skylights. A comfortable master bedroom located to the rear of the house takes advantage of the deck area and is assured privacy from two other bedrooms at the front of the house. The master bath includes a walk-in closet and a dual-bowl vanity. Laundry facilities are next to the family bedrooms, which share a full bath.

Design by Donald A. Gardner Architects, Inc.

© 1996 Donald A. Gardner Architects, Inc.   B. NATHAN

DESIGN 7616

Square Footage: 2,450
Bonus Room: 423 square feet

This elegant home's understated Early American country theme introduces an interior plan that represents the height of style—but never at the expense of comfort. The foyer opens on either side to quiet formal rooms—or make one a bedroom—and leads to a central gallery hall. Wide open living space with a cathedral ceiling is defined by back-to-back extended-hearth fireplaces. An L-shaped kitchen offers views of the outdoors while opening to the family room over an angled island counter. The nearby breakfast room leads to a private porch and to the two-car garage, which includes a workshop and additional storage space. Twin walk-in closets, a dressing area and a bumped-out tub highlight the master bath, which also offers a vaulted ceiling. A secondary bedroom has its own bath and shares access to linen storage.

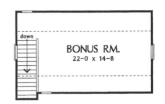

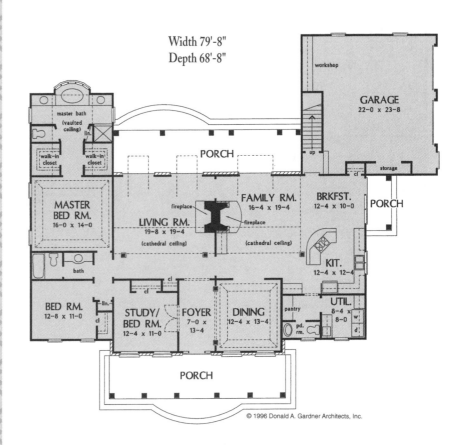

Width 79'-8"
Depth 68'-8"

© 1996 Donald A. Gardner Architects, Inc.

Width 56'-0"
Depth 52'-0"

QUOTE ONE®

Cost to build? See page 198
to order complete cost estimate
to build this house in your area!

DESIGN 3570

First Floor: 1,578 square feet
Second Floor: 1,546 square feet
Total: 3,124 square feet
Bonus Room: 380 square feet

L D

The unique design of this Southern Colonial will satisfy the most refined tastes. Well-designed traffic patterns define family and formal areas. But that doesn't mean all the amenities are left for company. The family room and its fireplace create a warm atmosphere for playing a board game with the kids or just relaxing, while the breakfast room includes a built-in desk and access to the rear porch. The kitchen features an island cooktop and a view onto the porch. The roomy first-floor laundry includes space for drip drying. If it's not laundry day, then take in the good weather from the second-floor balcony or slip into the master bath's whirlpool tub. With an additional three bedrooms, and two bathrooms as well as a large bonus room above the garage, your family will have plenty of room to grow.

DESIGN 3567

First Floor: 1,778 square feet
Second Floor: 1,663 square feet
Total: 3,441 square feet
Bonus Room: 442 square feet

L D

Spring breezes and summer nights will be a joy to take in on the verandas and balcony of this gorgeous Southern Colonial. Or, if you prefer, sit back and enjoy a good book in the library, or invite a friend over for a chat in the conversation room. The first floor also includes formal dining and living rooms, a service entry with a laundry, and a three-car garage. You'll find a bonus room over the garage, which you may decide to make into a media or exercise room. The master bedroom sports a fireplace, two walk-in closets, a double-bowl vanity, a shower and a whirlpool tub. Three other bedrooms occupy the second floor; one has its own full bath. Of course, the balcony is just a step away.

QUOTE ONE®

Cost to build? See page 198 to order complete cost estimate to build this house in your area!

Width 72'-0"
Depth 50'-0"

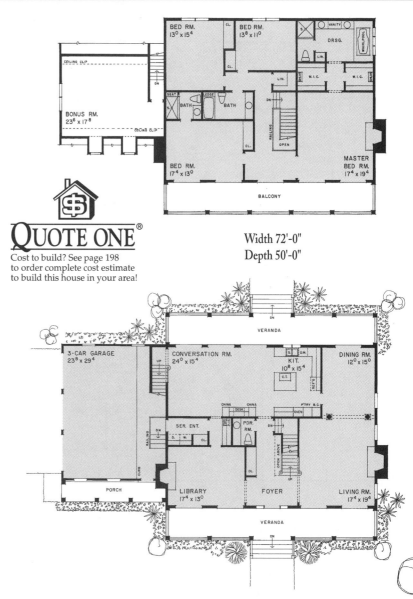

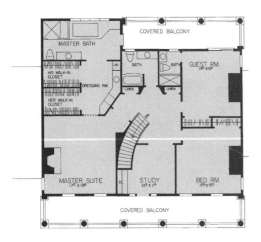

· HISTORIC ·
ADAPTATION

QUOTE ONE®

Cost to build? See page 198
to order complete cost estimate
to build this house in your area!

Width 95'-4"
Depth 48'-8"

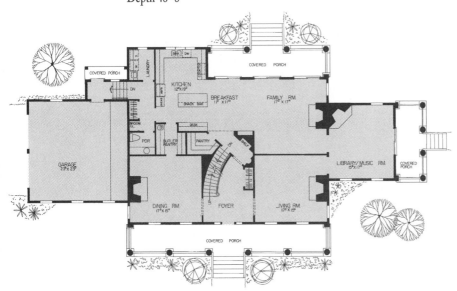

DESIGN 3508

First Floor: 2,098 square feet
Second Floor: 1,735 square feet
Total: 3,833 square feet

L

Make history with this modern version of Louisiana's "Rosedown House." Like its predecessor—built in the 1800s—the adaptation exhibits splendid Southern styling, but with today's amenities. The formal zone of the house is introduced by a foyer with a graceful, curving staircase. The dining and living rooms flank the foyer—each is highlighted by a fireplace. Off the living room, a library or music room offers comfort with a corner fireplace and a covered porch. This room also accesses the family room, where informal living is shared with a nearby breakfast room, kitchen and covered porch. Upstairs, the master suite encourages a romantic feeling with a fireplace. A large dressing room with two walk-in closets leads to the luxury bath. There are two more bedrooms (one with its own bath) and a study. Two covered balconies complete this superb plan.

DESIGN 2664

First Floor: 1,308 square feet
Second Floor: 1,262 square feet
Total: 2,570 square feet

D

A double porch extending across the front of this farmhouse recalls its antebellum Southern ancestry. Much of its charm is to be found in its symmetry—the center entrance, the spacing of the windows and the straightforward rectangular shape of the house. The break in the projecting roofline and the attractive columns and balustrade add extra interest. Inside, formal and informal living rooms flank the central foyer. The country kitchen has a commanding fireplace, an island cooktop and plenty of space for informal dining. It is but a step from the separate dining room and easily serves the terrace as well. Don't miss the beam ceilings, the bar, the laundry room and the strategically placed powder room. Upstairs, there are three family bedrooms and a full bath, plus a fine master suite.

HISTORIC ADAPTATION

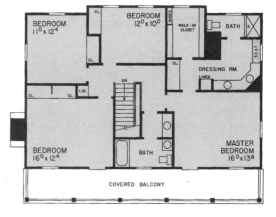

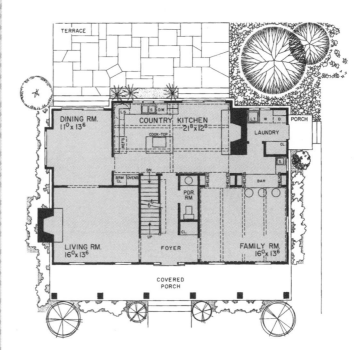

Width 44'-8"
Depth 36'-0"

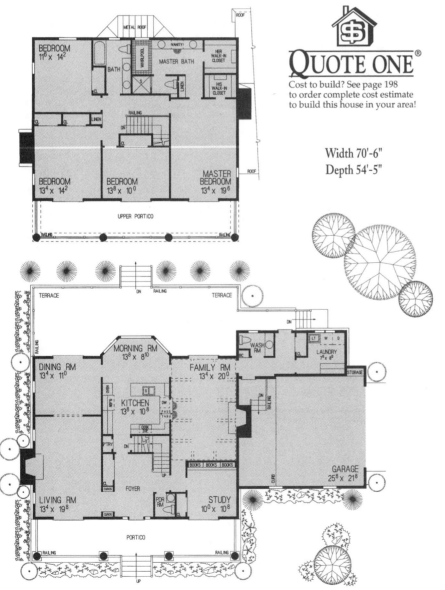

QUOTE ONE®

Cost to build? See page 198
to order complete cost estimate
to build this house in your area!

Width 70'-6"
Depth 54'-5"

DESIGN 3333

First Floor: 1,584 square feet
Second Floor: 1,344 square feet
Total: 2,928 square feet

L

A columned porch and balcony furnish a gracious entrance to this captivating Southern Colonial design. The foyer opens to a spacious living room with a centered fireplace and an adjoining dining room with access to the terrace. A U-shaped kitchen shares space with a sunny morning room and features a pass-through to the family room. A fireplace and a beam ceiling bid a warm welcome. The study provides a quiet spot and built-in bookshelves for the family's readers. The upstairs sleeping area includes three family bedrooms and a master suite. Relax and unwind in the master bedroom, or retreat to the private bath with its soothing whirlpool tub. A separate shower, a double-bowl vanity, and His and Hers walk-in closets round out the suite.

DESIGN 2996

First Floor: 2,191 square feet
Second Floor: 1,928 square feet
Total: 4,119 square feet

L D

In the early 19th Century, western New York's fertile Genesee River valley was dotted with prosperous farms. The Folger House, built around 1800 in Geneva, New York, looks ahead to a later trend of adding Greek Revival elements to the sensible frame manor houses. Covered porches upstairs and down, round columns and the triangular pediment are faithfully reproduced in this adaptation. Four chimney stacks decorate the ends of the house and herald four hearths inside—in the living room, dining room, family room and study. The traditional central hallway provides easy access to all areas of the house. Notice the powder room in the gallery, the bar in the study and the island snack bar and work center in the kitchen. The second floor holds four bedrooms, including a master suite with its own fireplace and a huge walk-in closet.

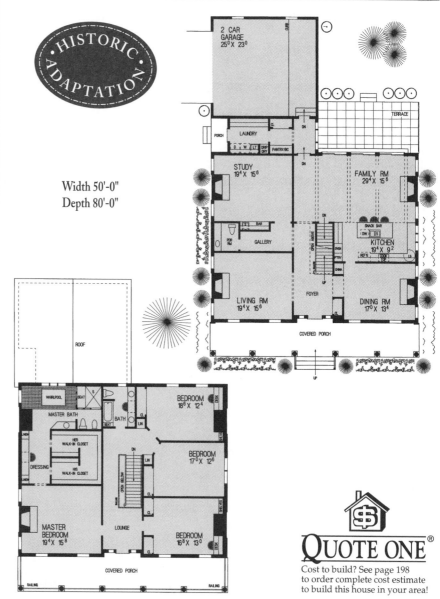

HISTORIC ADAPTATION

Width 50'-0"
Depth 80'-0"

QUOTE ONE®

Cost to build? See page 198
to order complete cost estimate
to build this house in your area!

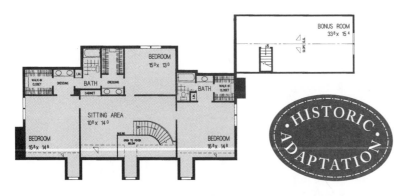

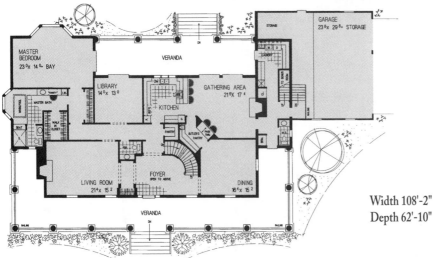

HISTORIC ADAPTATION

Width 108'-2"
Depth 62'-10"

QUOTE ONE®

Cost to build? See page 198
to order complete cost estimate
to build this house in your area!

REAR VIEW

DESIGN 3505

First Floor: 2,899 square feet
Second Floor: 1,519 square feet
Total: 4,418 square feet
Bonus Room: 540 square feet

L

Two verandas with tapered columns support this Southern raised cottage's low-pitched roof and its delicately detailed cornice work. The wood railing effectively complements the lattice-work below. Horizontal siding and double-hung windows with muntins and shutters enhance the historic appeal of this 1½-story home. Inside, the central foyer has a high ceiling and a dramatic curving staircase to the second floor. Formal living and dining rooms flank the foyer. The informal area includes a library, a U-shaped kitchen and a gathering area. The master suite offers a private bath and two closets. At the top of the dramatic staircase is a generous sitting area shared by three bedrooms. A bonus room further enhances this fabulous family home.

HISTORIC ADAPTATION

DESIGN 2698

Square Footage (Two-bedroom plan): **1,700**
Square Footage (One-bedroom plan): **1,436**

Here is the quintessential narrow-lot house, based on the "shotgun" house, a popular style found in 19th-Century New Orleans and many other Southern towns. Its origins go back to the West Indies and Africa and its name came from the fact that a bullet could travel through the front door and exit the rear without striking a partition. For the sake of contemporary planning, this version forsakes the rear door in favor of two full baths. (Note that a smaller one-bedroom, one-bath option is included in the blueprints.) The facade, although small, is charming, with its projecting gable and columned front porch. The interior offers plenty of living space—living and family rooms, each with a fireplace, an efficient kitchen with a snack bar, and a dining room. As a starter home or a retirement home, this unique house will serve its occupants well.

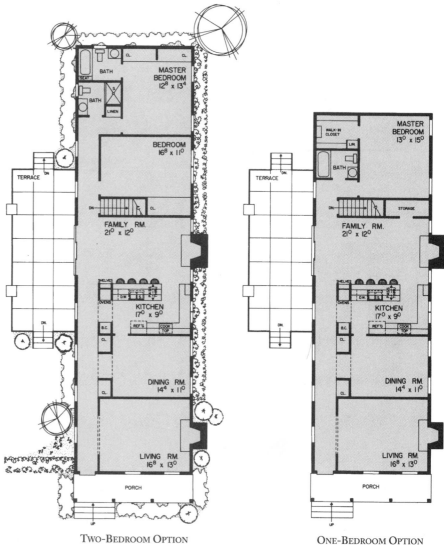

Two-Bedroom Option

Width 22'-0"
Depth 77'-4"

One-Bedroom Option

Width 22'-0"
Depth 65'-4"

Design by Donald A. Gardner Architects, Inc.

© 1997 Donald A. Gardner Architects, Inc.

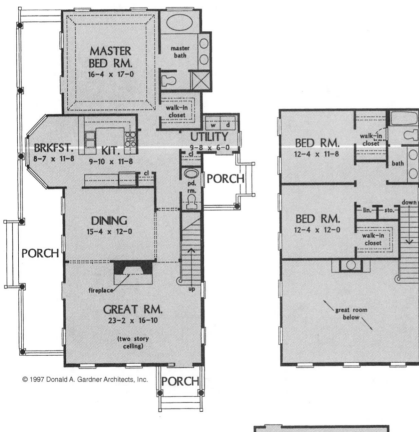

© 1997 Donald A. Gardner Architects, Inc.

MASTER BED RM.
16-4 x 17-0

master bath

walk-in closet

w | d

UTILITY
9-8 x 6-0

BRKFST.
8-7 x 11-8

KIT.
9-10 x 11-8

d

cl

PORCH

pd. rm.

DINING
15-4 x 12-0

PORCH

fireplace

up

GREAT RM.
23-2 x 16-10

(two story ceiling)

PORCH

BED RM.
12-4 x 11-8

walk-in closet

bath

lin. | sto.

down

BED RM.
12-4 x 12-0

walk-in closet

great room below

Width 38'-0"
Depth 64'-4"

GARAGE
22-4 x 25-4

DESIGN 7647

First Floor: 1,545 square feet
Second Floor: 560 square feet
Total: 2,105 square feet

A graceful home with old Southern charm, this two-story offers a sleek design for narrow (or any!) lots. Enter to an impressive two-story great room with a fireplace, followed by a spacious dining room. The U-shaped kitchen is designed for efficiency and easily serves both the dining room and the sunny bayed breakfast room. The first-floor master suite offers privacy as well as an elegant tray ceiling, a walk-in closet and a pampering bath. Two more bedrooms (each with a walk-in closet), a roomy full bath, and storage and linen closets are located on the second floor. The detached two-car garage and the full-length covered porch add much to the livability of this attractive design.

DESIGN 2681

First Floor: 1,350 square feet
Second Floor: 1,224 square feet
Total: 2,574 square feet

This Early American farmhouse features the simple gable rooflines, shuttered multi-pane windows and pilastered front door of the era. While the front door welcomes guests to the foyer, the porch entrance will be enjoyed by family members, giving them immediate access to the casual living space of the house. A massive see-through fireplace is the focal point of this area, providing warmth and fireglow to the family living and dining rooms. Beam ceilings add to the country atmosphere. As in Colonial times, the best room, or parlor, is placed away from family traffic patterns, sharing the left end of the house with the formal dining room. An efficient U-shaped kitchen easily serves both dining rooms and also provides a snack bar for meals on the go. Sleeping quarters are upstairs and include two family bedrooms sharing a bath and a master suite with a private bath.

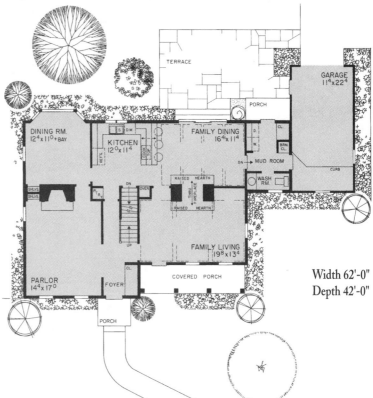

Width 62'-0"
Depth 42'-0"

SOUTHERN GEORGIAN HOMES

GEORGIAN HOUSES IN THE SOUTH WERE DIFFERENT from their counterparts in the North. Brick was the most commonly used exterior material in the Southern Colonies, as compared to clapboard and shingles in the North. Paired end chimneys were more prevalent in the South than in the North, where the central chimney predominated. Generally, Georgian houses of the South were larger than those in the North.

Georgian homes seemed to embody the wealth and also the pride of a prospering nation. Frequently situated at the end of a meticulously landscaped driveway, the proper Georgian house featured a boldly massed design, sometimes marked by a shallow, projecting central section of rough-cut stone. The front entry boasted an imposing arrangement of columns and pediment, often designed as a full-fledged portico. Over the front door could often be found a Palladian window, and a classically detailed cornice edged the roof, which might have a hipped, gabled or gambrel profile. Windows were now numerous, designed with a double-hung sash and easily moved up and down.

Homes became larger as the century progressed, with three stories increasingly common. A greater emphasis was placed on brick permanence and crisp lines, replacing the florid carvings and sweeping curves of Early Georgian detailing. Inside, a long central hallway connected the rooms at the center. The rooms themselves grew in number and now included a separate kitchen, dining room, bedrooms and parlors for receiving guests, signaling a move toward specialized use and a new sense of privacy, which had been virtually unknown in the 17th Century.

DESIGN 2691

First Floor: 1,550 square feet
Second Floor: 1,142 square feet
Total: 2,692 square feet

The original of this brick Georgian adaptation can trace its roots to the 18th Century; the land on which it stands has an older and more interesting history. Located on the James River in Virginia, the land originally belonged to Indian Chief Powhatan, who, in 1614, gave it as a wedding gift to his daughter Pocahontas and John Rolfe. The present-day manor was built in 1720, and is known as Smith's Fort Plantation after a fort that Captain John Smith had built there in 1609. The facade of the house exhibits typical Georgian symmetry. Notice also the segmented arches topping the front door and windows. The floor plan easily divides into formal and informal areas, with a parlor and a gathering room (each with a corner fireplace) across the front and a dining room and breakfast room in back. Upstairs, dormers provide extra light for the master suite and two family bedrooms.

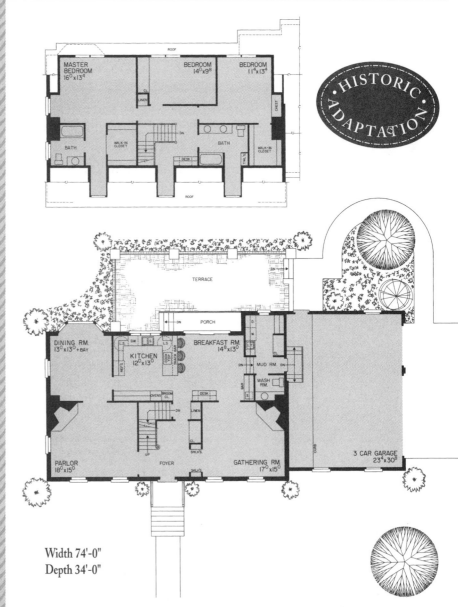

Width 74'-0"
Depth 34'-0"

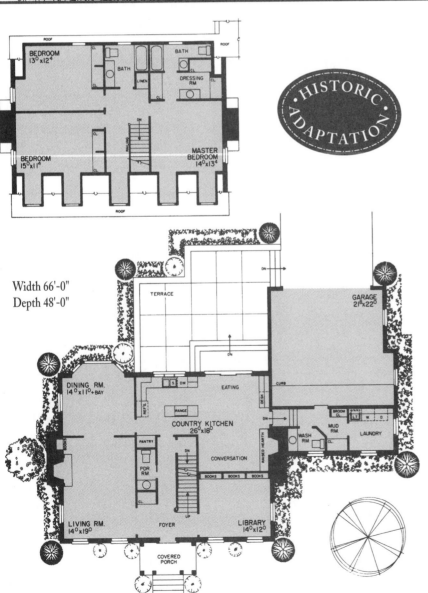

Width 66'-0"
Depth 48'-0"

DESIGN 2688

First Floor: 1,588 square feet
Second Floor: 1,101 square feet
Total: 2,689 square feet

The Shield House in Yorktown, Virginia, dates from 1690 and is typical of many townhouses built by plantation owners to use when they came into town on business. This adaptation includes popular Tudor features such as the pyramidal chimneys and clipped gables, as well as the symmetrically placed windows and pillared porch of Georgian architecture. Inside, the country kitchen will be the center of attraction, with ample space for food preparation, eating and conversation. Family members and guests can easily be tempted outside to enjoy the terrace or into the library for some quiet reading. Notice the fireplaces in the formal living room and kitchen, and the handy washroom near the garage entrance. Upstairs, you will find a comfortable master suite, with a dressing room and twin vanities, and two family bedrooms sharing a full bath.

DESIGN 2638

First Floor: 1,836 square feet
Second Floor: 1,323 square feet
Total: 3,159 square feet

This fine brick Georgian is based on Gunston Hall, the home of George Mason, the author of the Virginia Declaration of Rights and a major contributor to the Bill of Rights of the United States Constitution. Built in 1755 in Lorton, Virginia, the home is highlighted by a pavilioned entrance, angle quoins and bracketed cornices. The first floor is bisected by an elegant central hall, with two large rooms on each side. Each of the rooms—living room, dining room, family room and country kitchen—has a fireplace and built-in cabinetry featuring fine Georgian detailing. Other highlights include sliding doors to the terrace, a work island and beam ceiling in the kitchen and extra storage space in the two-car garage. The blueprints include three- and four-bedroom options.

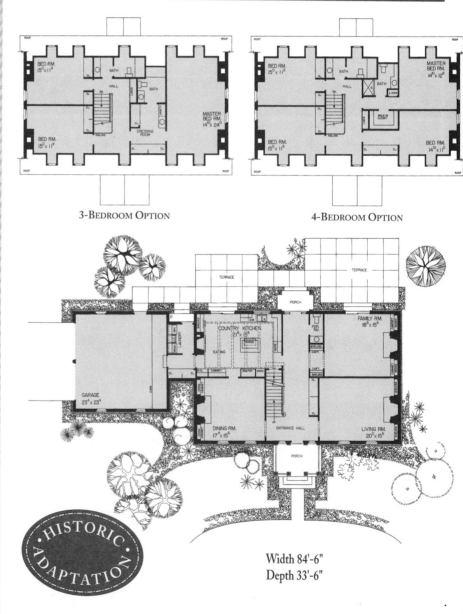

3-BEDROOM OPTION

4-BEDROOM OPTION

Width 84'-6"
Depth 33'-6"

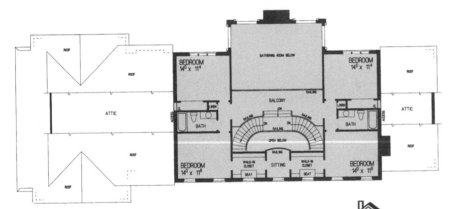

Width 109'-4"
Depth 47'-0"

QUOTE ONE®

Cost to build? See page 198
to order complete cost estimate
to build this house in your area!

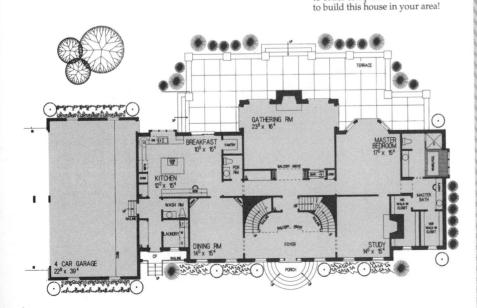

DESIGN 3349

First Floor: 2,807 square feet
Second Floor: 1,363 square feet
Total: 4,170 square feet

L D

Grand Georgian design comes to the forefront in this elegant two-story home. Semi-circular stairs approach an elegant front doorway flanked by arched windows. The foyer features a dramatic double stairway leading to the second floor, where four bedrooms share two full baths. Each of the front bedrooms has a walk-in closet with a window seat and they share a sitting room overlooking the foyer. Downstairs, an impressive master suite features a luxurious bath and a private entrance to a study with a fireplace. Family and guests will appreciate the gathering room with its fireplace and terrace access. To the left of the foyer, the dining room includes corner cabinets, a traditional feature of Colonial homes. The L-shaped kitchen is a delight, with a large center work island, a sunny breakfast area and a walk-in pantry. A four-car garage handles the largest of family fleets.

DESIGN F144

First Floor: 2,843 square feet
Second Floor: 1,308 square feet
Total: 4,151 square feet
Bonus Room: 71 square feet

Authentic details on this gracious Georgian mansion include a dentiled roofline, a ram's-head pediment over the front door, stone quoins and symmetrically arranged windows. The entry foyer opens to the living and dining rooms and the formal stair hall. Note the double access to the stair, making it convenient to the morning room. The sunken family room has plenty of space for entertaining or lounging, plus a focal-point fireplace and access to the terrace. The family chef will appreciate the kitchen, with its work island and walk-in pantry. Note the huge master suite, with a sitting room, twin walk-in closets, terrace access and an optional mini-kitchen and eating area. The second floor contains a guest suite with a walk-in closet and a private bath. Two more bedrooms, a full hall bath and a large walk-on deck complete the plan.

Width 95'-6"
Depth 76'-7"

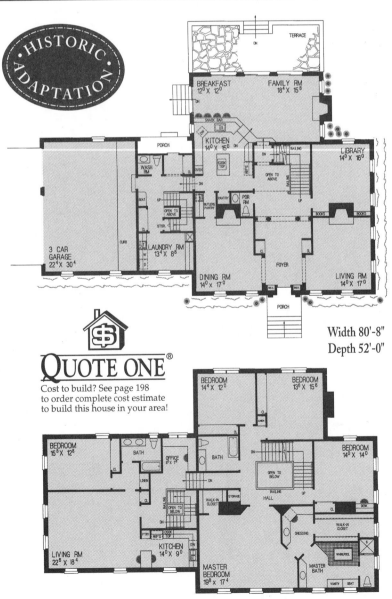

HISTORIC · ADAPTATION

Width 80'-8"
Depth 52'-0"

QUOTE ONE®

Cost to build? See page 198
to order complete cost estimate
to build this house in your area!

DESIGN 2999

First Floor: 2,472 square feet
Second Floor: 2,207 square feet
Guest Apartment: 935 square feet
Total: 5,614 square feet

L D

Many Georgian houses along Maryland's eastern shore were built by prosperous merchants in the 1800s. Widehall, the model for this adaptation, was built in Chesterton around 1770 by Thomas Smyth, the first head of Maryland's revolutionary provisional government. The hip roof supports stylish dormers on all four sides. Note the classic detailing of the facade. The interior begins with a dramatic foyer flanked by formal living and dining rooms. A library with built-in shelves provides a haven for quiet moments. The L-shaped kitchen looks down into a sunken breakfast/family room area. The second floor includes three family bedrooms and a small office as well as a master suite with two walk-in closets, a whirlpool tub and a dressing area. An apartment over the garage is ideal for a live-in relative.

DESIGN 2975

First Floor: 1,656 square feet
Second Floor: 1,440 square feet
Third Floor: 715 square feet
Total: 3,811 square feet

This mansion recalls the home built by George Read II in New Castle, Delaware, around 1791. Its Georgian roots are evident in its symmetry and the Palladian window, keystoned lintels and parapeted chimneys. Notice, however, the roundhead dormer windows, roof balustrades and arched front-door transom, which reflect the Federal styling that was popular at the end of the 18th Century. Three massive chimneys support six fireplaces, including one in each first-floor room and two in the master suite! The country kitchen also boasts an island cooktop, a built-in desk, a pantry and sliding glass doors to the terrace. The second floor contains two family bedrooms, in addition to the luxurious master suite, while the top floor adds a fourth bedroom and a hobby/studio area. The garage includes an L-shaped curb for a worktable and storage.

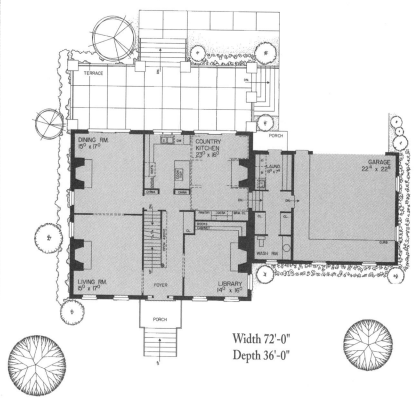

Width 72'-0"
Depth 36'-0"

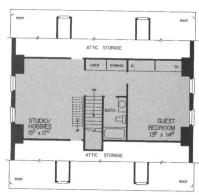

Design by Larry E. Belk Designs

Width 75'-6"
Depth 73'-1"

DESIGN 8139

First Floor: 1,713 square feet
Second Floor: 1,430 square feet
Total: 3,143 square feet

This classic Georgian facade is complemented by an up-to-date floor plan with all the extras. The lovely curved porch opens to a two-story foyer flanked by the formal living and dining rooms. Both rooms feature a fireplace; the large living room also boasts double French doors, which provide access to the covered porch beyond. A charming sun room is situated off the living room, creating a bright area for informal entertaining. The kitchen includes a large pantry, a central work island and a small morning nook that would be perfect for a table for two. A sunny breakfast room is nearby. The master suite includes a large bedroom and a His and Hers master bath complete with separate closets, vanities and toilets. A sitting area with a walk-in cedar closet is shared with two family bedrooms. Please specify crawlspace or slab foundation when ordering.

© Design Traditions

DESIGN T195

First Floor: 2,140 square feet
Second Floor: 1,219 square feet
Total: 3,359 square feet
Bonus Room: 441 square feet

Columned porticos recall the Georgian architecture of post-Revolutionary War America. Formal areas frame the foyer, which opens to a great room with a centered fireplace and dual sets of French doors. The master suite includes a spacious, secluded bath and a private door to the covered rear porch. A bright breakfast area offers its own access to the porch, and opens to the kitchen, which has a pantry and an island cooktop. Three additional bedrooms and a full bath share a balcony hall on the second floor. The attractive two-car garage is attached to the house by a porte cochere and a side porch. Unfinished bonus space over the garage may be developed later. This home is designed with a basement foundation.

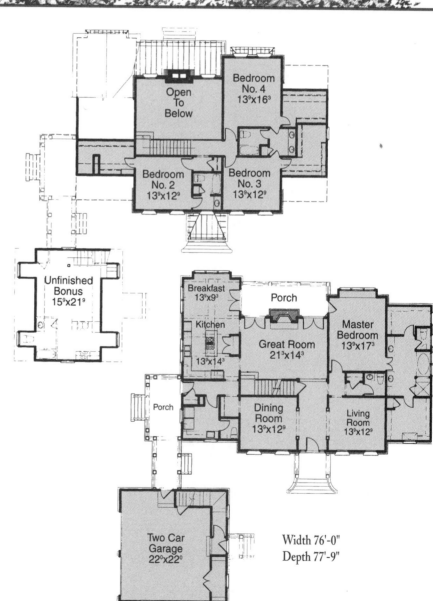

Open To Below

Bedroom No. 4
13⁹x16³

Bedroom No. 2
13⁹x12⁹

Bedroom No. 3
13⁹x12⁹

Unfinished Bonus
15⁹x21⁹

Breakfast
13⁹x9³

Porch

Kitchen
13⁹x14³

Great Room
21³x14³

Master Bedroom
13⁹x17³

Porch

Dining Room
13⁹x12⁹

Living Room
13⁹x12⁹

Two Car Garage
22⁰x22⁰

Width 76'-0"
Depth 77'-9"

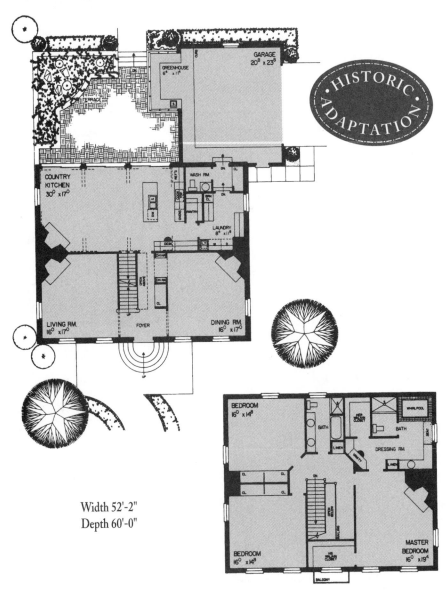

Width 52'-2"
Depth 60'-0"

DESIGN 2982

First Floor: 1,584 square feet
Second Floor: 1,513 square feet
Total: 3,097 square feet

Less ornate than many of its Georgian contemporaries, the facade of the Lightfoot House is broken up only by a wrought-iron balcony over the front door. Curved steps offer a nice contrast to the straight lines of the unshuttered windows. Built in 1730 in Williamsburg, Virginia, the house also features the hip roof and massive chimneys of that era. Inside this adaptation, corner fireplaces provide warmth for the formal living and dining rooms, the country kitchen and the master bedroom. The kitchen is outstanding, with a wall of fanlit sliding glass doors opening to the terrace. A large pantry, a built-in desk and a work island will please the most discerning cook. The fireplace is just one pampering element in a master suite that is sure to please. Two family bedrooms and a bath complete the second floor. The greenhouse extending from the garage adds interest to the rear terrace.

DESIGN F121

First Floor: 1,760 square feet
Second Floor: 2,001 square feet
Total: 3,761 square feet
Optional Lower Lever: 1,760 square feet
Bonus Room: 448 square feet

The brick finish on this stately exterior is further enhanced by the cut stone trim and brick chimneys. The large formal entry is an elegant setting for the four-foot-wide main stair—just one of three stairways that give this home a well-thought-out traffic pattern. Formal rooms on either side of the foyer have fireplaces and are close to a coat closet and powder room. A generous family room (with another fireplace), the morning room and the rear porch are perfect for informal living. Upstairs, a luxurious master suite features His and Hers dressing areas, a fireplace and even a "petit dejeuner" for a quiet breakfast or late-night snack. Two family bedrooms with private baths are just a few steps from a lounge over the porte cochere. Don't overlook the possibilities for future living in the lower level and over the carriage house.

Width 99'-1"
Depth 57'-9"

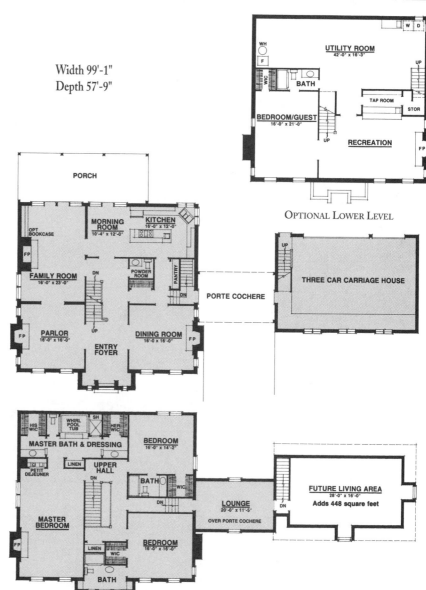

OPTIONAL LOWER LEVEL

© Design Traditions

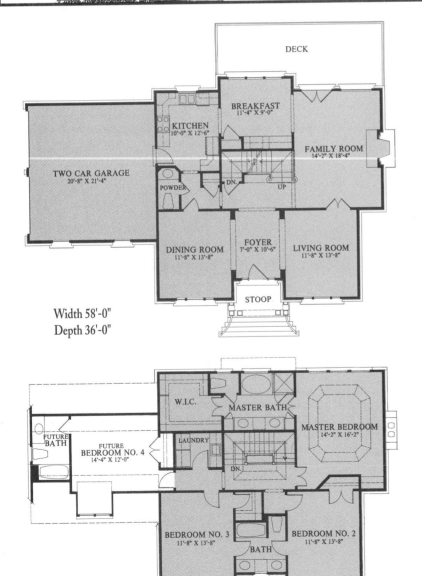

DECK

BREAKFAST
11'-4" X 9'-0"

KITCHEN
10'-0" X 12'-6"

FAMILY ROOM
14'-2" X 18'-4"

TWO CAR GARAGE
20'-8" X 21'-4"

POWDER

DN.   UP

DINING ROOM
11'-8" X 13'-8"

FOYER
7'-0" X 10'-6"

LIVING ROOM
11'-8" X 13'-8"

STOOP

Width 58'-0"
Depth 36'-0"

W.I.C.   MASTER BATH

FUTURE
BATH

LAUNDRY

MASTER BEDROOM
14'-2" X 16'-2"

FUTURE
BEDROOM NO. 4
14'-4" X 12'-0"

DN.

BEDROOM NO. 3
11'-8" X 13'-8"

BATH

BEDROOM NO. 2
11'-8" X 13'-8"

DESIGN T082

First Floor: 1,165 square feet
Second Floor: 1,050 square feet
Total: 2,215 square feet

Classic design knows no boundaries in this gracious two-story home, whose facade includes many Georgian details. From the formal living and dining areas to the more casual family room, the house handles any occasion with ease. A central fireplace provides a focal point in the family room, which also offers French-door access to the rear deck. Of special note on the first floor are the roomy L-shaped kitchen with an attached breakfast area and the guest-pampering powder room. Upstairs are three bedrooms, including a master suite with a fine bath and a walk-in closet. The laundry room is on this level for convenience. A fourth bedroom and another bath can be developed in bonus space as needed. This home is designed with a basement foundation.

© Design Traditions

DESIGN T146

First Floor: 1,609 square feet
Second Floor: 1,583 square feet
Total: 3,192 square feet
Bonus Room: 126 square feet

This home exhibits many Georgian features, including the hip roof, the pediment over the two-story bay, angled brick lintels and porches with columns and balustrades. Inside, the family room stretches from front to back porches and delights with its central hearth. For formal occasions, the living room combines with the dining room to create the perfect atmosphere. The U-shaped kitchen boasts plenty of counter space and easily serves the breakfast room. In the second-floor master suite, double doors lead to the formal bath, which features angled vanities and a whirlpool tub. An unfinished bonus area opens at the rear. Two family bedrooms share a full bath with a dual-bowl vanity. This home is designed with a basement foundation.

Width 49'-3"
Depth 73'-0"

© Design Traditions

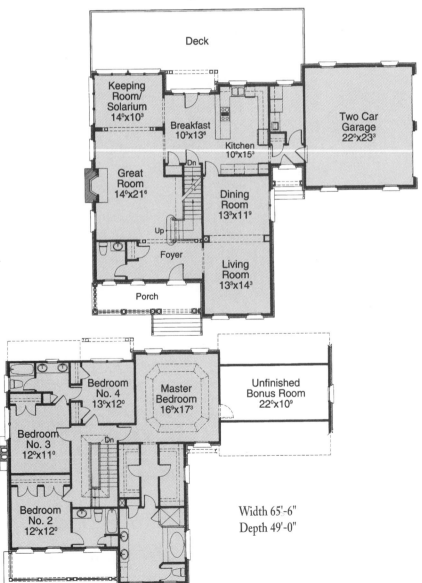

Deck

Keeping Room/ Solarium
14⁰x10³

Breakfast
10⁰x13⁶

Kitchen
10⁰x15³

Two Car Garage
22⁰x23³

Great Room
14⁰x21⁶

Dn

Dining Room
13³x11⁹

Up

Foyer

Living Room
13³x14³

Porch

Bedroom No. 4
13⁰x12⁰

Master Bedroom
16⁰x17³

Unfinished Bonus Room
22⁰x10⁹

Bedroom No. 3
12⁰x11⁰

Dn

Bedroom No. 2
12⁰x12⁰

Width 65'-6"
Depth 49'-0"

DESIGN T166

First Floor: 1,615 square feet
Second Floor: 1,510 square feet
Total: 3,125 square feet
Bonus Room: 255 square feet

Pediments, columns and balustrades are Georgian accents on this stately brick exterior, creating a charming entry to a stylish interior design. The foyer provides a powder room and coat closet for the convenience of guests, who will enjoy being entertained in the formal living and dining rooms. The great room offers a focal-point fireplace and opens to a solarium with views of the rear property. Family and friends will linger over coffee in the bright breakfast nook, which is open to the efficient U-shaped kitchen. The nearby deck poses an invitation to enjoy the outdoors. Upstairs, a generous master suite features twin walk-in closets and a lavish bath. A bonus room off the master bedroom could be made into a nursery or home office. This home is designed with a basement foundation.

DESIGN 7267

First Floor: 1,598 square feet
Second Floor: 1,675 square feet
Total: 3,273 square feet

Covered porches on both levels add interest to this Georgian exterior. Notice the symmetry and intricate detailing that are hallmarks of this genre. The prominent entry opens to the formal living and dining rooms, both of which are brightened by transom windows. The grand family room is highlighted by a fireplace and views of a screened porch with a cozy window seat. The porch is accessed from the breakfast area and leads to the three-car garage along a covered walkway. Open to the breakfast area, an L-shaped kitchen includes a work island with an angled snack bar, a walk-in pantry and plenty of counter space. Upstairs, French doors open to the master suite, which features decorative ceiling details, His and Hers walk-in closets, a large dressing area, dual vanities, a whirlpool bath and a separate shower area. Three family bedrooms, two bathrooms and a bonus room complete the plan.

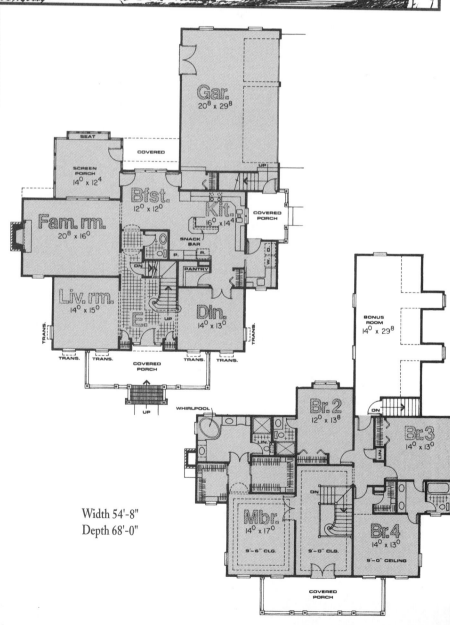

Width 54'-8"
Depth 68'-0"

© Design Traditions

Width 69'-8"
Depth 59'-0"

QUOTE ONE®

Cost to build? See page 198
to order complete cost estimate
to build this house in your area!

DESIGN T049

First Floor: 1,960 square feet
Second Floor: 905 square feet
Total: 2,865 square feet

From its pediment to the columned porch framing the elegant Georgian doorway, this country-style home displays an impressive facade. Inside, Georgian symmetry balances the living room and dining room to the right and left of the foyer. The main level continues into the two-story great room, with its built-in cabinetry, fireplace and large bay window overlooking the rear deck. A dramatic tray ceiling, a wall of glass and access to the rear deck highlight the master bedroom. The master bath features separate vanities and a walk-in closet. To the left of the great room, an island kitchen with a walk-in pantry opens to the breakfast area. Upstairs, three family bedrooms share a railed walkway overlooking the great room. Each bedroom features ample closet space and direct access to a bathroom. This home is designed with a basement foundation.

© Design Traditions

DESIGN T167

First Floor: 1,698 square feet
Second Floor: 1,542 square feet
Total: 3,240 square feet

This Colonial-style home really makes its mark with an elegant brick exterior. Notice the fine detailing of the front door, the dentil trimming on the gable and along the roofline, and the interesting window treatment. Inside, well-defined formal rooms complement casual family areas. A gourmet kitchen includes an island snack bar for meals on the go, and opens into the family room with its focal-point fireplace. A solarium, a screened porch and a deck encourage outdoor activities. The second-floor sleeping quarters include an expansive master suite with a luxurious private bath that features a garden tub and a large walk-in closet. Also on this floor, Bedrooms 3 and 4 share a full bath, while Bedroom 2 has its own bath. This home is designed with a basement foundation.

Width 61'-6"
Depth 51'-0"

© Design Traditions

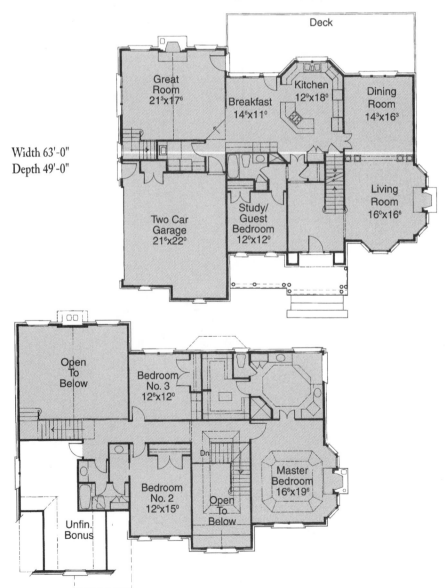

Deck

Great Room 21³x17⁶

Breakfast 14⁶x11⁰

Kitchen 12⁹x18⁰

Dining Room 14³x16³

Living Room 16⁶x16⁶

Two Car Garage 21⁶x22⁰

Study/ Guest Bedroom 12⁰x12⁰

Width 63'-0"
Depth 49'-0"

Open To Below

Bedroom No. 3 12⁶x12⁰

Bedroom No. 2 12⁰x15⁰

Open To Below

Master Bedroom 16⁶x19⁶

Unfin. Bonus

DESIGN T192

First Floor: 1,888 square feet
Second Floor: 1,374 square feet
Total: 3,262 square feet
Bonus Room: 299 square feet

Colonial details on this graceful brick exterior include pediments, a Palladian window and a columned entry with an elegant front door. Columns are found inside, also, where they are used to separate the formal living and dining rooms. A bay window and a fireplace provide light and warmth to this area. Strategically located between formal and casual areas is the gourmet kitchen with a uniquely angled cooktop island and a breakfast area. The two-story great room is appointed with a fireplace, a media corner and a rear staircase. Upstairs, tray ceilings, a lush bath and a romantic fireplace highlight the master suite. Two additional bedrooms and a full bath are found on the second floor, while a fourth bedroom off the foyer could serve as a study instead. This home is designed with a basement foundation.

DESIGN 9364

First Floor: 1,717 square feet
Second Floor: 1,518 square feet
Total: 3,235 square feet

Stately columns highlight the facade of this Southern Colonial home. The open entry allows for views into the formal living and dining rooms and up the tapering staircase. Alcoves flank the staircase, while arched openings enhance the formal areas. The dining room, with built-in hutch space, accesses the kitchen through double doors. The kitchen features an angled snack bar, an island cooktop and an octagonal, glass-enclosed breakfast area. Pocket doors lead from the living room to the huge sunken family room, where you'll find large windows, a fireplace, a built-in entertainment center and built-in bookcases. On the second floor, three family bedrooms make use of two full baths. The master suite features a tiered ceiling, two walk-in closets, a pampering bath and a roomy, bayed sitting area.

Width 78'-0"
Depth 42'-0"

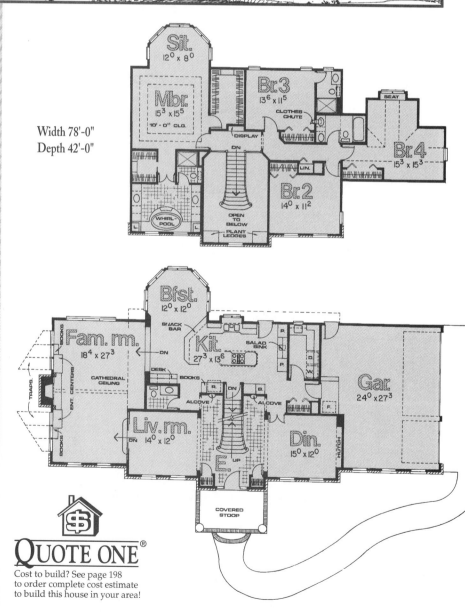

QUOTE ONE®

Cost to build? See page 198
to order complete cost estimate
to build this house in your area!

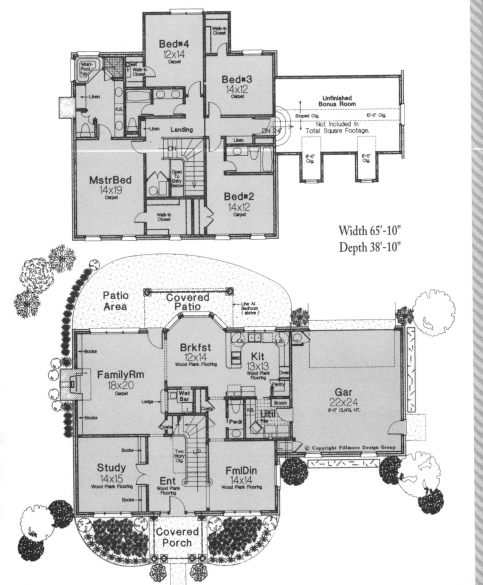

Width 65'-10"
Depth 38'-10"

DESIGN M143

First Floor: 1,573 square feet
Second Floor: 1,449 square feet
Total: 3,022 square feet

A lovely facade graces this striking Georgian, with two pairs of columns supporting the impressive pedimented entry. The hardwood floor in the foyer continues through double doors into a large study with built-in bookshelves and also extends to the right into the formal dining room. The bright, open area across the back holds the family room with a fireplace, the bay-windowed breakfast room and the U-shaped kitchen. Extras include a wet bar in the family room, a pantry, and a powder room and coat closet off the dining room. The master suite, on the second floor, features a walk-in closet and a private bath with a dual-bowl vanity and a corner whirlpool tub. Three family or guest bedrooms access two additional full baths. A large, well-lighted bonus room over the garage is available for future development.

HISTORIC ADAPTATION

DESIGN 2990

First Floor: 2,615 square feet
Second Floor: 1,726 square feet
Guest Suite: 437 square feet
Total: 4,778 square feet

L

St. George Tucker came from Bermuda to Virginia to study law. He served as a judge from 1785 until his death in 1827. His home, located in Williamsburg, Virginia, reflects the "Roman Country House" style of Palladio, identified by its central two-story structure and the lower attached dependencies. A benefit of this sprawling configuration was good cross-ventilation, an important factor in the South then—and in this adaptation. First-floor rooms include a family room with informal dining space at one end of the plan and a formal living room at the other end. In between are the media room, guest powder room, dining room and kitchen. Three second-floor bedrooms include a luxurious master suite with a sitting room and a fireplace, one of five in the house. There is also a guest room with private bath over the garage.

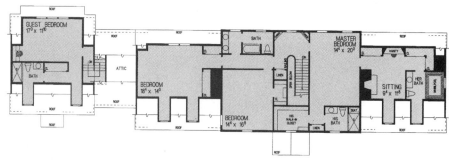

QUOTE ONE®

Cost to build? See page 198 to order complete cost estimate to build this house in your area!

Width 124'-0"
Depth 31'-0"

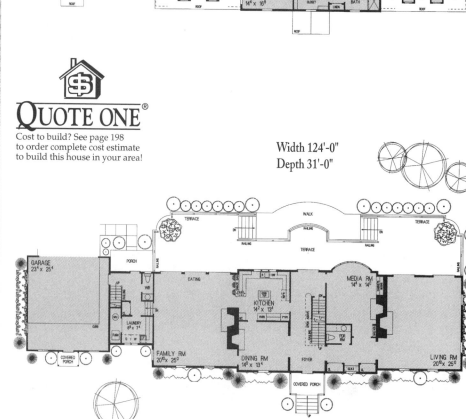

HISTORIC ADAPTATION

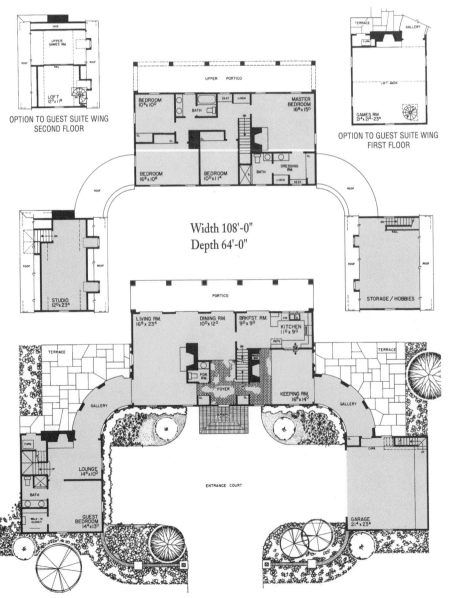

OPTION TO GUEST SUITE WING
SECOND FLOOR

OPTION TO GUEST SUITE WING
FIRST FLOOR

Width 108'-0"
Depth 64'-0"

DESIGN 2665

First Floor: 1,992 square feet
Second Floor: 1,458 square feet
Total: 3,450 square feet
Bonus Room: 893 square feet

George Washington's Mount Vernon began in 1743 as an eight-room cottage. He added to it and improved it over the next 40 years, until it became the stately mansion we know today. The unusual design features curved galleries leading to matching wings. In our adaptation, the living and dining rooms create a large open area, with access to the rear porch for additional entertaining possibilities. A keeping room features a pass-through to the kitchen and a fireplace with a built-in wood box. Four bedrooms, including a master suite with a fireplace, are found upstairs. One wing contains separate guest quarters with a full bath, a lounge area and an upstairs studio. This area can be optionally designed as a game room with a spiral staircase and a loft area. On the other side of the house, the second floor over the garage can be used for storage or as a hobby room.

· HISTORIC · ADAPTATION

DESIGN 3523

First Floor: 1,068 square feet
Second Floor: 982 square feet
Third Floor: 548 square feet
Total: 2,598 square feet

L **D**

Colonial charm enhances this quaint design—notice the pediment and pilasters decorating the front door and dormers, the keystoned lintels and the shuttered small-paned windows. The entry opens to a formal living room, which features a raised-hearth fireplace and opens to a dining room with a bay window. The family room and kitchen form a spacious informal area, enhanced by a built-in desk and a convenient snack bar. The second floor holds a master suite and one family bedroom with a bath. The master bedroom is graced with a huge walk-in closet and a bath with a whirlpool tub and a dual-sink vanity. A studio with dormers is found on the third floor. The full bath here makes this a great guest room or mother-in-law suite.

Width 26'-0"
Depth 40'-0"

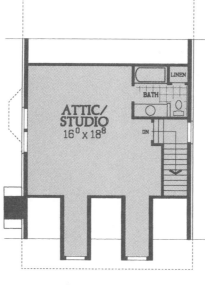

ATTIC/STUDIO 16⁰ x 18⁸

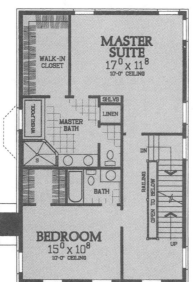

WALK-IN CLOSET
MASTER SUITE 17⁰ x 11⁸ 10'-0" CEILING
SHLVS
LINEN
MASTER BATH
BATH
DN
RAILING
OPEN TO BELOW
UP
BEDROOM 15⁰ x 10⁸ 10'-0" CEILING

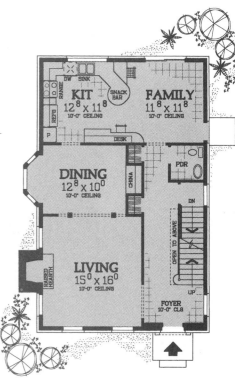

KIT 12⁸ x 11⁸ 10'-0" CEILING
FAMILY 11⁸ x 11⁸ 10'-0" CEILING
SNACK BAR
DW SINK
RANGE
DESK
PDR
DINING 12⁸ x 10⁰ 10'-0" CEILING
CHINA
DN
LIVING 15⁰ x 16⁰ 10'-0" CEILING
RAISED HEARTH
OPEN TO ABOVE
UP
FOYER 10'-0" CLG

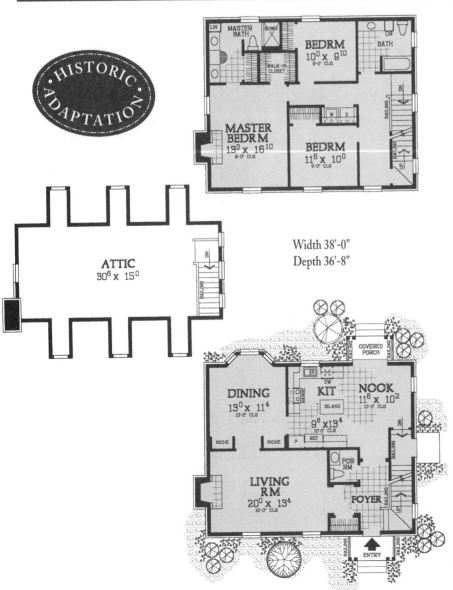

HISTORIC ADAPTATION

MASTER BATH · LIN · SHWR

BEDRM
10⁰ x 9¹⁰
9'-0" CLG

LIN · BATH

WALK-IN CLOSET

RAILING · DN

MASTER BEDRM
13⁰ x 16¹⁰
9'-0" CLG

W · D

RAILING

BEDRM
11⁶ x 10⁰
9'-0" CLG

RAILING · UP

ATTIC
30⁸ x 15⁰

DN · RAILING

Width 38'-0"
Depth 36'-8"

DINING
13⁰ x 11⁴
10'-0" CLG

NICHE

KIT
9⁶ x 13⁴
10'-0" CLG

DW · RANGE · ISLAND

COVERED PORCH

RAILING

NOOK
11⁶ x 10²
10'-0" CLG

DN · RAILING

NICHE · P · REF

PDR RM

LIVING RM
20⁰ x 13⁴
10'-0" CLG

FOYER

RAILING · UP

RAILING

ENTRY

DESIGN 3526

First Floor: 1,056 square feet
Second Floor: 960 square feet
Total: 2,016 square feet
Attic: 659 square feet

L **D**

This classic design offers the perfect blend of modern and traditional—with a gentle nod to Colonial America. Window treatments are interesting, with the pediment over the front entry repeated on the dormers and a Palladian window in the end gable. The columned entry opens to an offset foyer with a stairway. The living area includes a living room with a cozy fireplace and a dining room with a bay window and niches. The kitchen features a work island and an attached nook for casual dining. Upstairs, the master suite boasts a fireplace and a lavish private bath with a walk-in closet and linen storage. Two family bedrooms share a full bath with its own linen closet. The laundry is nearby for convenience. The attic holds over 600 square feet of additional space that can be developed later.

DESIGN 3524

First Floor: 822 square feet
Second Floor: 766 square feet
Total: 1588 square feet
Bonus Room: 405 square feet

L

Perfect for a small lot, this attractive brick home offers Colonial detailing and a practical floor plan. The ground floor is divided into fourths, allowing for three good-sized rooms and an entry area that includes a coat closet, a powder room and stairs to the second floor and the basement. The living room features a raised-hearth corner fireplace and a built-in media shelf, while the dining room offers access to the back yard. The kitchen has counters on three sides as well as a built-in desk, pantry and cutting-block island. The second floor consists of two bedrooms—a master suite offering a walk-in closet, garden tub, dual-bowl vanity and linen closet, and a family bedroom with its own bath and linen closet. Bonus space on the third floor can be used for a third bedroom.

HISTORIC ADAPTATION

Width 28'-8"
Depth 28'-8"

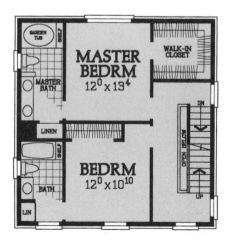

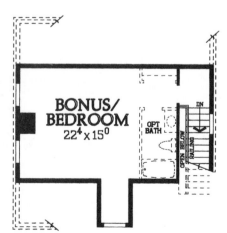

FEDERAL AND GREEK REVIVAL HOUSES

F EDERAL-STYLE HOUSES WERE MORE COMMON IN THE North than the South, and not radically different from Georgians. Federal houses retained the symmetry of the earlier style, but the look was less massive, more elegant. Front entries were still important, often with an elliptical fanlight over the door, and sometimes columns were moved out from the house, creating a portico over the entrance. But, except for the entry, the facade was usually quite plain—corner quoins and pilasters were not used and ornamentation was minimal.

The ellipse became a popular design element, showing up in windows, bays and even in the shapes of rooms. Hip or flat roofs, decorated with a balustrade over the eaves, were popular.

The typical Greek Revival house, popular in all parts of the country, was a two- or three-story symmetrical building that was essentially a copy of a Greek temple, with columns, architraves, friezes and cornices. Exterior walls were made of a variety of materials, but they were invariably white. Columns were always round, not square.

Southern architecture of the period absorbed the Greek Revival and adapted it to post-Georgian styling. Often the pillars were abbreviated to form entry porches or full-width porches supported by square or round columns that were half the height of a two-story house.

Rooflines could be gabled or hipped with a low pitch. A cornice line on the main roof and porch roof often was accentuated with a wide band of trim to represent classic entablature.

Design by R. L. Pfotenhauer

DESIGN F128

First Floor: 1,802 square feet
Second Floor: 1,787 square feet
Total: 3,589 square feet

This design illustrates the transition from Georgian architecture to the more restrained Federal style. The facade is symmetrical, but without much of the Georgian ornamentation. The entry is impressive, however, with pilasters framing a recessed door and an elliptical decoration above. The interior is as satisfying as the exterior, with formal rooms flanking the foyer and plenty of space for informal living. The family room is spacious, and boasts a beam ceiling, a fireplace and access to a wrap-around rear covered porch. The library/media room also has a door to the porch, as well as the option of built-in shelves and window seats. A powder room is nearby for the use of family and guests. A second front door provides a family entrance into the kitchen and its sunny morning room. This area will be a delight to the family cook, with a large pantry, planning desk and island cooktop.

Width 73'-2"
Depth 49'-4"

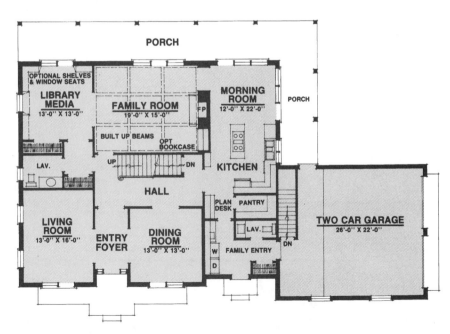

HISTORIC ADAPTATION

Width 64'-0"
Depth 64'-0"

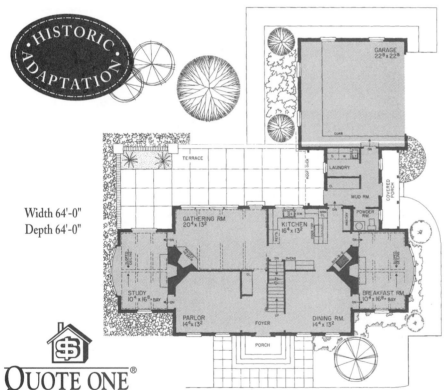

QUOTE ONE®

Cost to build? See page 198
to order complete cost estimate
to build this house in your area!

DESIGN 2662

First Floor: 1,735 square feet
Second Floor: 1,075 square feet
Third Floor: 746 square feet
Total: 3,556 square feet

L

The exterior of this stately brick home exhibits the symmetry and simplicity of Federal styling. The bow windows in the two wings are also hallmarks of that era. Two chimney stacks support fireplaces in the gathering room, the study and the breakfast room, as well as a built-in barbecue in the U-shaped kitchen. The first floor also provides a formal entertaining zone—the parlor and dining room flanking the foyer. A handy mud room with a powder room connects the kitchen to the laundry and to the garage beyond. The second floor is dominated by a sumptuous master suite and two family bedrooms that share a full bath. Five dormers across the third floor provide natural light to two additional bedrooms, either of which might serve as a studio or study space. A full bath with a double vanity finishes this floor.

© Design Traditions

DESIGN T168

First Floor: 1,448 square feet
Second Floor: 1,491 square feet
Total: 2,939 square feet

The semi-circular fanlight in the low-pitched gable echoes the one over the front door, furthering the symmetry that dignifies the exterior of this impressive Colonial home. A curved stairway leads to the entrance, which is decorated by classical pilasters and entablature. Formal living areas are at the front of the house—the living room to the right of the foyer and the dining room to the left. A butler's pantry links the dining room to the island kitchen, which is open to a wonderful great room with a beam ceiling and a fireplace. The nearby breakfast/sunroom provides access to a rear deck. The second floor offers a spacious master suite and three family bedrooms, one of which has a private bath. This home is designed with a basement foundation.

Width 57'-0"
Depth 46'-4"

Deck

Breakfast/Sunroom
11³x9⁹

Kitchen
11³x16⁰

Great Room
21³x15⁹

Two Car Garage
21⁹x21⁰

Dn   Up

Dining Room
12⁶x14⁰

Foyer

Living Room
12⁶x12⁰

Master Bedroom
16⁰x15³

Bedroom No. 2
11³x14⁰

Dn

Bedroom No. 3
12⁰x11⁹

Open To Below

Bedroom No. 4
12⁹x12³

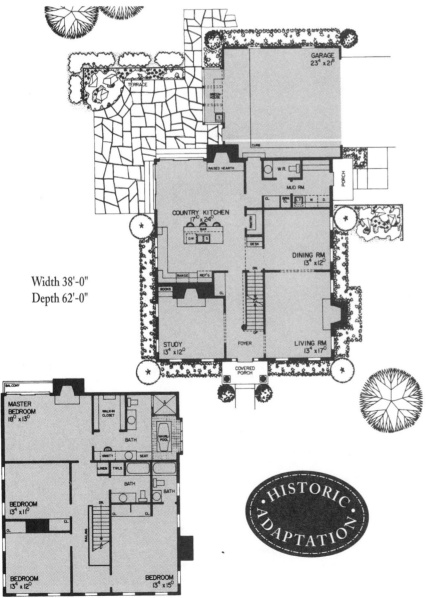

Width 38'-0"
Depth 62'-0"

DESIGN 2979

First Floor: 1,440 square feet
Second Floor: 1,394 square feet
Total: 2,834 square feet

A picture home for a narrow site, this historical adaptation is in so-called "temple form," which marks a transition from Federal to Greek Revival style. Note that the gable end of the house faces the street, as in a Greek temple. Three chimneys support four fireplaces—in the living room, study, kitchen and master bedroom. Family members and guests will love the huge country kitchen, with plenty of room for relaxing, a snack bar for quick meals and sliding glass doors to the terrace. A handy mud room leads to a side porch and the garage. Upstairs, the master suite has a deluxe bath and a private balcony. Three bedrooms and two full baths complete the plan. A basement provides additional space for recreation and storage.

DESIGN 3513

First Floor: 1,855 square feet
Second Floor: 1,287 square feet
Total: 3,142 square feet

L D

This grand entrance is based on that of a home built in 1827 for William Thomas Buckner near Paris, Kentucky. Curved steps lead to a raised front entry that makes a great impression with its rounded roof supported by columns. Light from a Palladian window brightens the two-story foyer, which opens to the formal living and dining rooms—each with a fireplace. Informal living areas are situated to the rear of the plan. Here, a step-saving kitchen harmonizes well with the eating nook and the family room. A covered porch stretches the width of the house, providing opportunities for outdoor activities. Upstairs, two family bedrooms—one with balcony access—share a full bath. The master suite features a built-in desk, a large walk-in closet and a dressing area. Note the unique master bath, which provides space for a clawfoot tub.

HISTORIC · ADAPTATION

QUOTE ONE®

Cost to build? See page 198 to order complete cost estimate to build this house in your area!

Width 56'-10"
Depth 53'-10"

Design by Alan Mascord Design Associates, Inc.

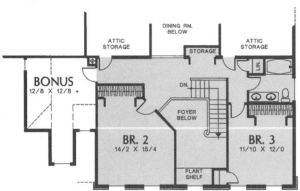

ATTIC STORAGE

DINING RM. BELOW

STORAGE

ATTIC STORAGE

LIN.

BONUS
12/8 X 12/8 +

DN.

FOYER BELOW

BR. 2
14/2 X 15/4

BR. 3
11/10 X 12/0

PLANT SHELF

Width 59'-0"
Depth 54'-0"

SPA

NOOK
10/0 X 8/0

LINEN

MASTER
13/2 X 16/10

VAULTED FAMILY
20/0 X 13/0

BUILT-IN SHELVES

11/8 X 13/0

VAULTED DINING
12/6 X 11/0

LINEN

PAN.

REF.

GARAGE
21/8 X 21/8

D. W.

STOR.

LIVING
13/6 X 12/6

UP

DEN/BR. 4
11/10 X 11/0

DESIGN 9479

First Floor: 1,992 square feet
Second Floor: 703 square feet
Total: 2695 square feet
Bonus Room: 208 square feet

Symmetrically appealing, the exterior of this two-story brick home features a sunburst design in the front-facing gable and a recessed front doorway. The first-floor plan includes formal and informal living areas that radiate around a central kitchen. The den and master suite are in more private areas of the first floor. Special amenities include a light-filled nook off the family room, a hearth flanked by built-in bookshelves, a hall coat closet and a luxurious bath in the master suite. The second level contains two family bedrooms and a full bath, plus a bonus room that can be developed later into a third family bedroom or a playroom for children. Storage abounds on this floor.

© Design Traditions

DESIGN T196

First Floor: 1,959 square feet
Second Floor: 1,408 square feet
Total: 3,367 square feet

An elegant front entry welcomes you to this classically styled home. Inside, a hall leads past the living room—or study—and formal dining room to the spacious family room. You may wish to stop here and enjoy the fireplace, or use the French doors to go out onto the rear covered porch. An island kitchen is convenient to both the dining room and a sunny breakfast room. Guests will be grateful for the privacy of the guest bedroom, located behind the garage and offering access to the porch. The family sleeping zone is upstairs and includes a master suite with a fireplace and a deluxe bath, plus two family bedrooms and an unfinished space for future expansion. This home is designed with a basement foundation.

Width 61'-9"
Depth 62'-9"

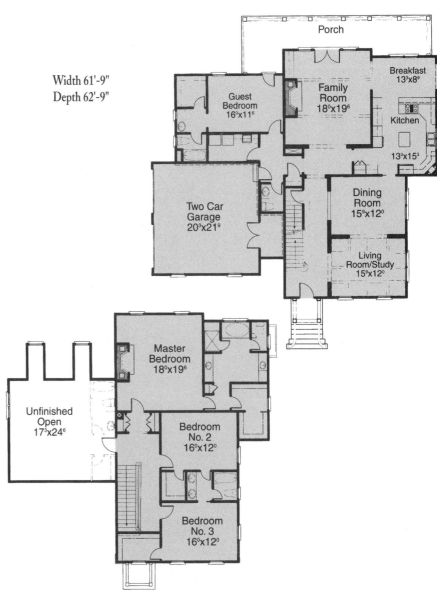

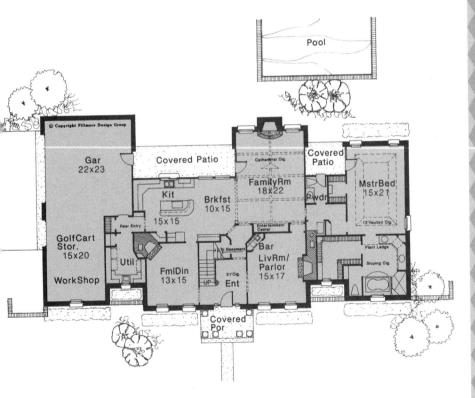

Pool

© Copyright Fillmore Design Group

Gar
22x23

Covered Patio

Covered
Patio

Cathedral Clg.

FamilyRm
18x22

MstrBed
15x21

Kit

Brkfst
10x15

Pwdr

12' Vaulted Clg.

GolfCart
Stor.
15x20

Rear Entry

Plant Ledge

Entertainment
Center

WorkShop

Util

FmlDin
13x15

21' Clg.

UP

Ent

Bar
LivRm/
Parlor
15x17

Sloping Clg.

Covered
Por

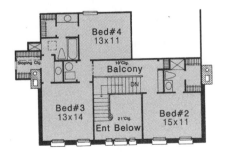

Bed#4
13x11

Sloping Clg.

10' Clg.

Balcony

DN

Bed#3
13x14

21' Clg.

Ent Below

Bed#2
15x11

Width 90'-0"
Depth 53'-10"

DESIGN M137

First Floor: 2,432 square feet
Second Floor: 903 square feet
Total: 3,335 square feet

The elegant symmetry of this Southern design makes it a joy to own. Six columns frame the covered front porch and two chimneys add interest to the roofline. Classic details include decorative lintels over the windows, a central Palladian window and gables with circular inserts. The two-story foyer opens to the formal living room/parlor, which offers a built-in wet bar and a fireplace. A family room with a cathedral ceiling is open to the breakfast area and the U-shaped island kitchen and provides access to a covered patio. A side-entry three-car garage has room for a golf cart and a separate workshop area. The first-floor master suite features vaulted ceilings, a private patio, two walk-in closets and a plant ledge. The three upstairs bedrooms share two baths.

© Design Traditions

DESIGN T157

Square Footage: 2,987

Post-and-beam construction and two gently curving balustrades give a nod to America's past in this Greek Revival-style home. The graceful stairway leads to a columned front porch, which provides French doors to the dining room as well as the formal front entrance. The study, to the left of the foyer, also has access to the front yard. Both the great room and the keeping/family room have fireplaces and access to the rear deck. The U-shaped kitchen is in the center of the house, easily serving all areas. Split sleeping quarters include a master suite with a whirlpool bath and an oversized walk-in closet, plus two family bedrooms sharing a full bath. This home is designed with a basement foundation.

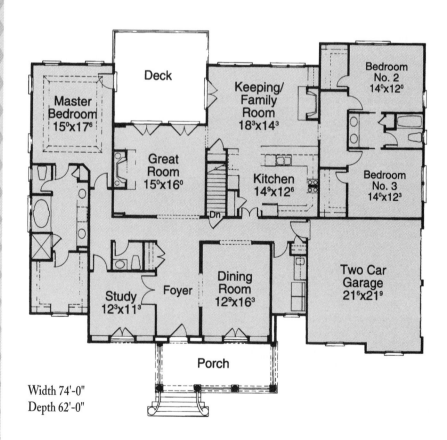

Deck

Master Bedroom
15⁰x17⁶

Great Room
15⁰x16⁰

Keeping/Family Room
18³x14³

Bedroom No. 2
14⁰x12⁰

Kitchen
14⁹x12⁶

Bedroom No. 3
14⁰x12³

Dn

Study
12³x11³

Foyer

Dining Room
12⁹x16³

Two Car Garage
21⁶x21⁹

Porch

Width 74'-0"
Depth 62'-0"

© Design Traditions

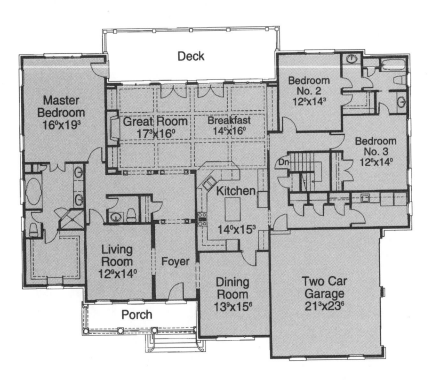

Width 75'-6"
Depth 57'-0"

DESIGN T156

Square Footage: 2,998

This Colonial adaptation includes such classical details as a columned porch and a Palladian window set off by a capstone. The interior is distinctly contemporary. At the heart of the plan lies a light-hearted spirit, with French doors in the great room and the breakfast area to bring in the outdoors. The living and dining rooms are across the front of the house for more formal occasions. The secluded master suite offers a private bath with twin lavatories and a walk-in closet with its own window. Each of the two family bedrooms has a private dressing area with a vanity in their shared full bath. This home is designed with a basement foundation.

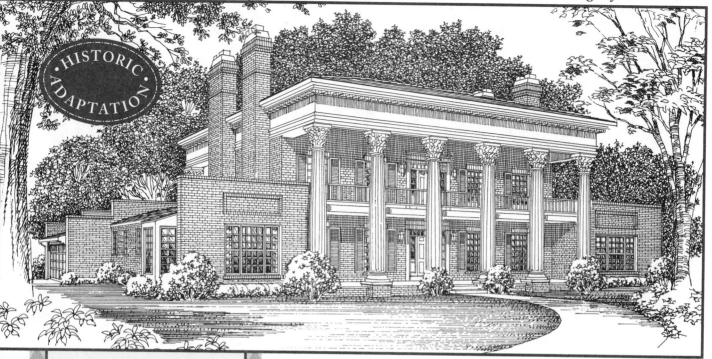

DESIGN 2987

First Floor: 2,822 square feet
Second Floor: 1,335 square feet
Total: 4,157 square feet

Andrew Jackson's dream of white-pillared splendor resulted in the building of The Hermitage from 1819 to 1834 near Nashville, Tennessee. Like its forebear, this adaptation has six soaring Corinthian columns on both the front and the rear, sheltering balconies accessible from the second floor. Two sets of twin chimneys and two projecting wings balance the central portion of the house. The delicate detailing of the facade is exquisite. Living and dining rooms are at the front of the plan, as is the country kitchen, highlighted by a bay window, a through-fireplace to the dining room and a cooktop island/snack bar. The rear covered porch is reached through sliding glass doors in the family room and along the gallery. The amenity-laden master suite fills the right wing, while three other bedrooms are upstairs.

QUOTE ONE®

Cost to build? See page 198 to order complete cost estimate to build this house in your area!

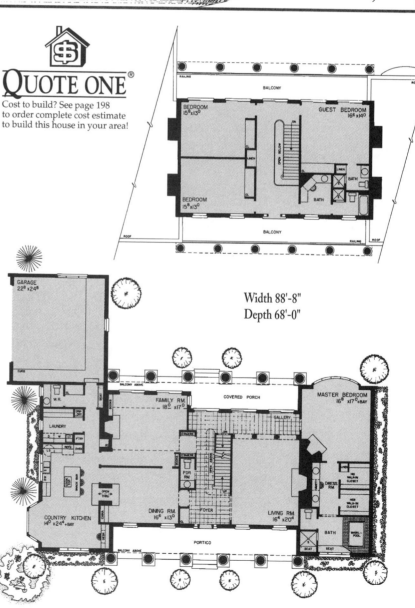

Width 88'-8"
Depth 68'-0"

Width 65'-6"
Depth 64'-0"

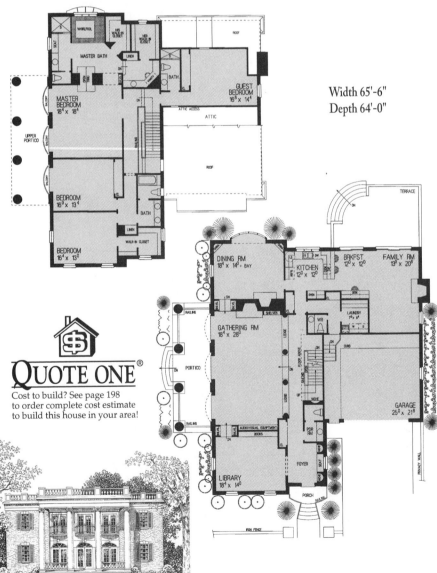

QUOTE ONE®

Cost to build? See page 198
to order complete cost estimate
to build this house in your area!

FRONT VIEW

DESIGN 2993

First Floor: 2,440 square feet
Second Floor: 2,250 square feet
Total: 4,690 square feet

L D

In the 18th Century, Charleston, South Carolina, was known for the "single house," one room deep, with the narrow end facing the street. This adaptation recalls the 1750 home of Robert William Roper, with tall pillars and a handsome brick exterior crowned by a balustrade. The original has a fragment of a Civil War cannon on its roof, sent there in 1865 when the cannon was blown up to keep it from Sherman's troops. (It was deemed safer to leave it there than to try to remove it.) This version adds a family room and a garage to the floor plan. The sunken gathering room opens to the long hall through a colonnade and is flanked by the dining room and a library. Upstairs is a sumptuous master suite with a through-fireplace and three other bedrooms.

DESIGN 3527

First Floor: 2,000 square feet
Second Floor: 2,000 square feet
Total: 4,000 square feet

From the temple-style front to the angled balustrade high up on the roof, this design will be a standout in any neighborhood. Its inspiration is called Melrose, built in the 1840s by a prominent lawyer-turned-planter in Natchez, Mississippi. Determined to build one of the finest houses in Natchez, John T. McMurran enlisted the aid of a Maryland architect, a Philadelphia mason and other renowned craftsmen from New York to New Orleans. Tall columns support porches on two levels on the front and the back of the house. A tiled foyer leads back to the family area, which includes a U-shaped kitchen with a snack bar, a fireplace flanked by window seats and three sets of sliding glass doors to the rear porch. Fireplaces are also found in the formal living and dining rooms and, upstairs, in the master suite with its sumptuous private bath.

Width 50'-0"
Depth 40'-0"

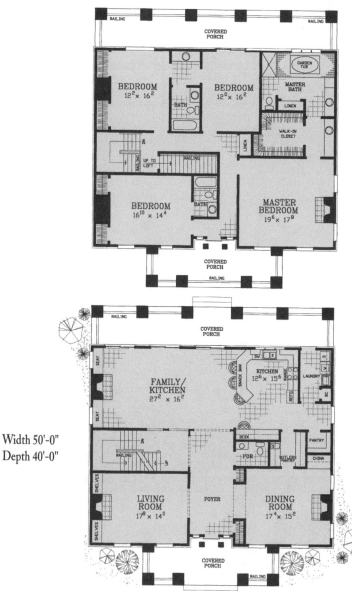

HISTORIC · ADAPTATION

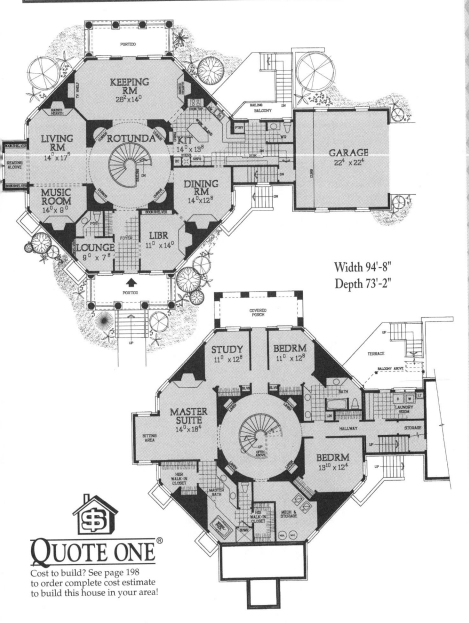

Width 94'-8"
Depth 73'-2"

Quote One®

Cost to build? See page 198
to order complete cost estimate
to build this house in your area!

DESIGN 3509

Main Level: 2,434 square feet
Lower Level: 2,434 square feet
Total: 4,868 square feet

If you're looking to do something a little different for your home-building experience, this adaptation of Jefferson's "Poplar Forest" home may be just the ticket. Named for the tulip poplars that still grow nearby, the red-brick porticoed house was started by Jefferson in 1806, and was laid out as an octagon, a shape he had experimented with in architectural sketches for years. Located near Lynchburg, Virginia, Poplar Forest was Jefferson's retreat from the hustle and bustle of politics. Inside, the rooms radiate out from a central rotunda, which is decorated with round curio niches. Fireplaces adorn all of the major living areas on the upper, entry level—music room, living room, keeping room, dining room and library. The island kitchen is roomy, with a china closet, desk and pantry. Downstairs bedrooms include a master suite with a fireplace, a study and a private luxury bath.

DESIGN E132

First Floor: 3,117 square feet
Second Floor: 1,411 square feet
Total: 4,528 square feet

From the columned front porch to the curved patio in back, this house is filled with elegance and style. The foyer, featuring a graceful curving staircase, opens to the formal living and dining rooms. The focal point of the family room is its fireplace, but windows will beckon you to the covered porch and patio outside. Multiple windows also highlight the kitchen, with its large work island, and the round breakfast room. The master suite is in its own wing to ensure privacy and has a large walk-in closet, an amenity-laden bath and its own entrance to the back porch. A nearby guest room could serve as a study or library. The second floor contains four family bedrooms, two full baths and a sitting room that opens onto a balcony. Please specify crawlspace or slab foundation when ordering.

Width 76'-10"
Depth 68'-10"

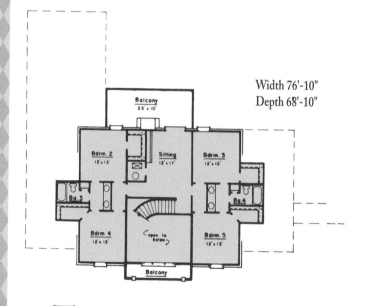

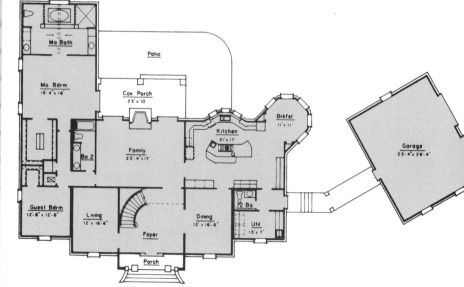

© Design Traditions

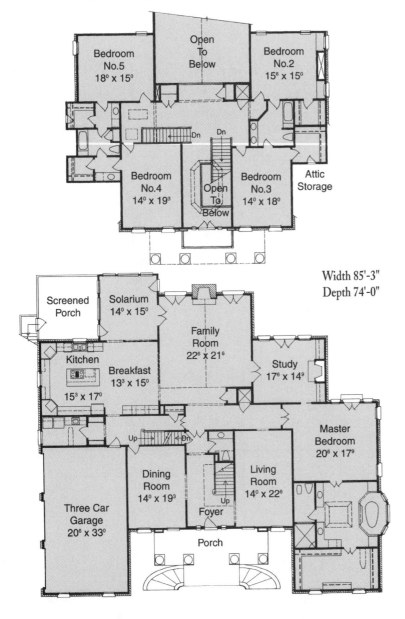

Width 85'-3"
Depth 74'-0"

DESIGN T126

First Floor: 3,902 square feet
Second Floor: 2,159 square feet
Total: 6,061 square feet

The entry to this Greek Revival home is framed by a sweeping double staircase and four large columns topped with a pediment. The two-story foyer is flanked by spacious living and dining rooms. Beyond the foyer, the home is designed with rooms that offer maximum livability. The two-story family room, which has a central fireplace, opens to the study and a solarium. A roomy U-shaped kitchen features a central island cooktop. A staircase off the breakfast room offers convenient access to the second floor. Of the five bedrooms, the master suite is the most impressive, featuring outdoor access and a bath fit for royalty. A walk-in closet with an ironing board will provide room for everything. Four bedrooms upstairs enjoy large proportions. This home is designed with a basement foundation.

DESIGN 2184

First Floor: 1,999 square feet
Second Floor: 1,288 square feet
Total: 3,287 square feet

The tranquility and grace of Greek Revival architecture is evident in this adaptation. Here, fluted columns rise two stories to support a pedimented gable, reminiscent of an ancient Hellenistic temple. The front portico is repeated across the back, with the addition of a private balcony off the second-floor master bedroom. An off-center entrance leaves space for a library in the main part of the house. A graceful stairway follows the curve of the hall, which leads back to the informal rooms—a family room with a fireplace and beam ceiling, an attached breakfast area and the spacious kitchen. Built-ins abound in this design, including china cabinets in the dining room and kitchen. The master suite boasts a pillared lounge with more built-ins and a private dressing room leading to a nearby bath. Two family bedrooms and a second bath complete the plan.

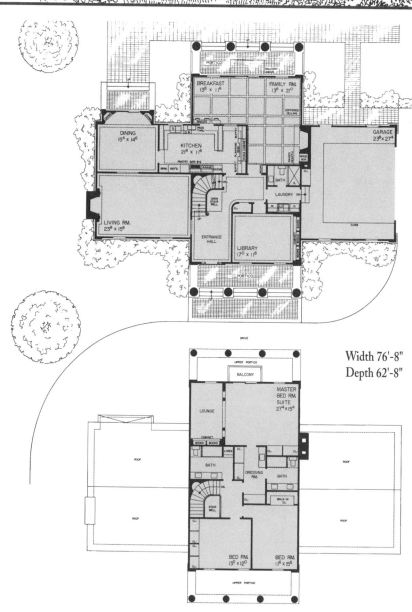

Width 76'-8"
Depth 62'-8"

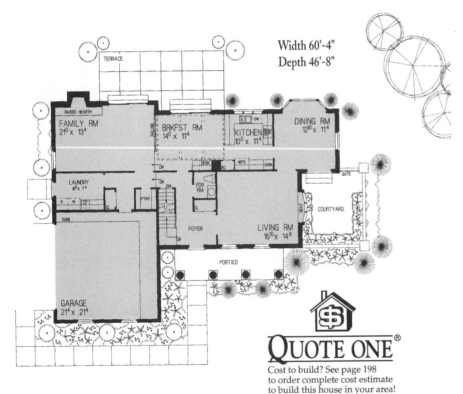

Width 60'-4"
Depth 46'-8"

QUOTE ONE®

Cost to build? See page 198
to order complete cost estimate
to build this house in your area!

DESIGN 3339

First Floor: 1,460 square feet
Second Floor: 1,014 square feet
Total: 2,474 square feet

L

An impressive portico welcomes you to this brick
Greek Revival-style home.
Decorative window treatments and
a classic front door make for an
attractive exterior. A walled court-
yard off the dining room adds outdoor living possibilities, as does the
rear terrace. A formal living room
extends from the front foyer and
leads to the dining room and the
nearby kitchen. A sunken family
room with a raised-hearth fireplace
is separated from the breakfast room
by a railing. Both rooms have access
to the terrace. Upstairs, the master
suite includes a private bath with a
compartmented dressing room and
two vanities. Three family bedrooms share a second bath.

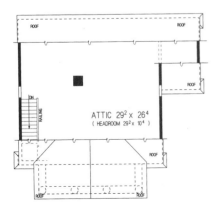

DESIGN 2668

First Floor: 1,206 square feet
Second Floor: 1,254 square feet
Total: 2,460 square feet

L

Here is a frame house whose clapboards, center entrance and symmetrically placed shuttered windows give it a distinctly Georgian ambiance, until a Greek Revival portico with four soaring columns and a denticulated pediment is added. Based on the Roberts-Vaughan House, built in North Carolina in 1790, this design lends itself to a corner or interior lot. Inside, a library offers a quiet retreat to the right of the foyer. To the left is a country kitchen with plenty of room for a table, an island cooktop and a pass-through to the dining room. Between the pantry and the broom closet is a built-in desk. The great room is outstanding, with a high ceiling, a wall of windows and a fireplace. Upstairs, the master suite includes a balcony overlooking the foyer and a bath with twin vanities. Laundry facilities are on this floor, as are a lounge and three family bedrooms sharing a full bath.

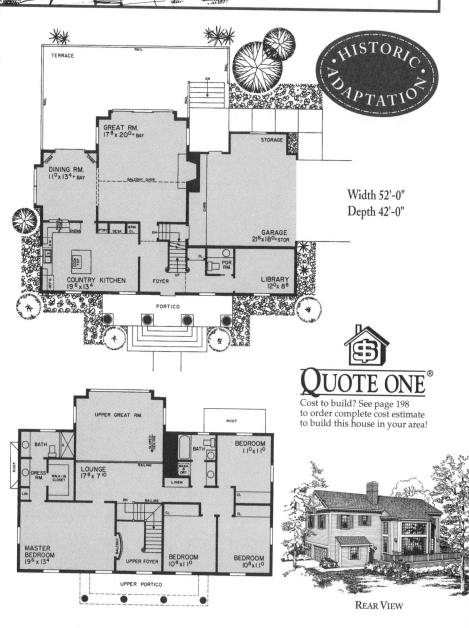

HISTORIC ADAPTATION

Width 52'-0"
Depth 42'-0"

QUOTE ONE®

Cost to build? See page 198 to order complete cost estimate to build this house in your area!

REAR VIEW

Design by Home Planners

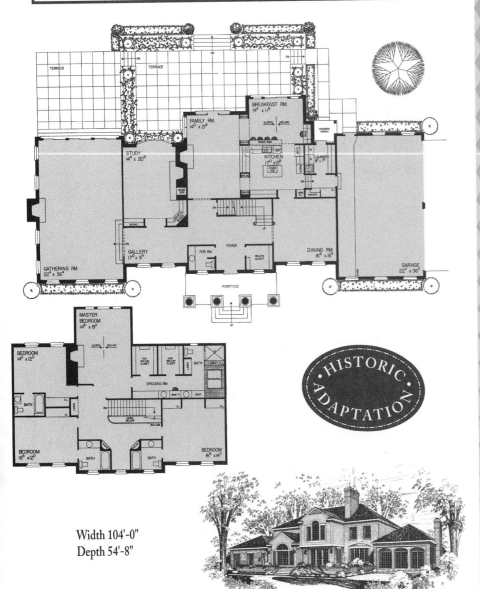

Width 104'-0"
Depth 54'-8"

REAR VIEW

DESIGN 2984

First Floor: 3,116 square feet
Second Floor: 1,997 square feet
Total: 5,113 square feet

L

An echo of Whitehall, built in 1765 in Anne Arundel County, Maryland, resounds in the facade of this home. Its classic symmetry and columned facade herald a grand interior. There's no lack of space, whether entertaining formally or just enjoying a family get-together, and all are kept cozy with fireplaces in the gathering room, study and family room. An island kitchen with an attached breakfast room handily serves the nearby dining room. There is also a snack bar for quick meals. Rear terraces on two levels offer space for outdoor entertaining or just relaxing. There are four bedrooms on the second floor, each with its own bath. The master suite boasts a fourth fireplace, a dressing room, a whirlpool tub and His and Hers walk-in closets.

DESIGN 2991

First Floor: 2,658 square feet
Second Floor: 1,429 square feet
Total: 4,087 square feet

L **D**

Tezcuzo is a plantation house built in 1855 for the Bringiers, French settlers in Louisiana. Located on the Mississippi River, it features a Greek Revival exterior, including the front and rear verandas (or galleries) that were essential to provide relief from the summer heat and humidity. Other typical Southern details, reproduced in this adaptation, are the raised first floor and the pedimented dormers in the hip roof. The updated floor plan begins with a wide foyer flanked by formal living and dining rooms, each with a fireplace. The family room is conveniently open to the island kitchen, where a handy island cooktop with a snack bar serves both areas. A quiet study separates living areas from the master suite, which features His and Hers baths and a bay with a whirlpool tub. The second floor contains three bedrooms, three full baths and a sitting room.

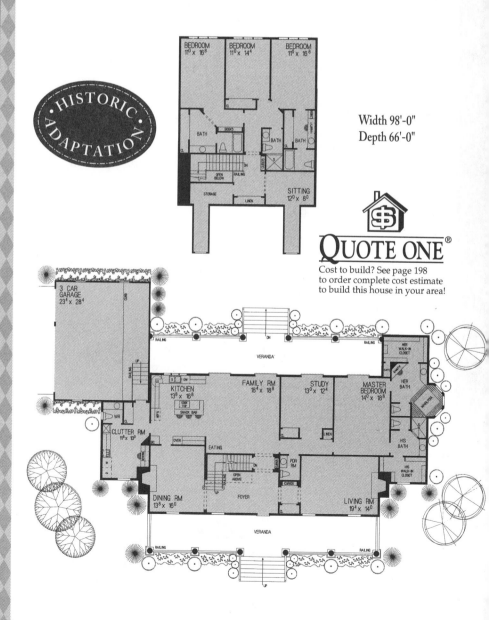

HISTORIC ADAPTATION

Width 98'-0"
Depth 66'-0"

QUOTE ONE®

Cost to build? See page 198 to order complete cost estimate to build this house in your area!

Width 132'-0"
Depth 53'-6"

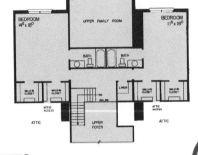

QUOTE ONE®

Cost to build? See page 198
to order complete cost estimate
to build this house in your area!

·HISTORIC· ADAPTATION

DESIGN 2977

First Floor: 4,104 square feet
Second Floor: 979 square feet
Total: 5,083 square feet

L

The exterior of this elegant brick manor depicts classic Georgian symmetry, highlighted by the columned Greek portico. It is based on Homewood, a house built in Baltimore, Maryland, in 1801. The central part of the house contains the four main gathering areas—living room, dining room, family room and library—each with a fireplace. A spacious U-shaped kitchen boasts a work island, a snack bar and a pantry. Sleeping quarters are well spread out, with a guest suite in the left wing and two family bedrooms upstairs. The master suite is in the right wing, and is complete with a fireplace, a lavish bath and sliding glass doors to a back porch. It also offers private access to an adjoining lounge/exercise area and an atrium.

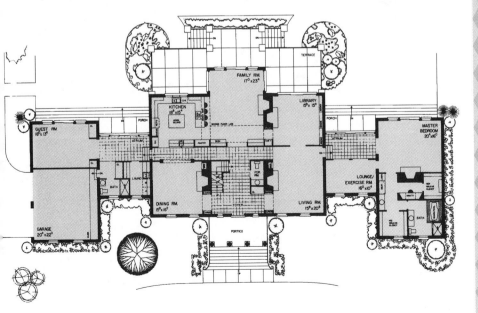

DESIGN 2693

Square Footage: 3,462

The white-pillared one-story house is a significant Kentucky contribution to the architectural heritage of the South. This imposing Greek Revival design recalls Rose Hill, built near Lexington around 1820. The exterior is of brick, with shuttered windows. A classical portico with four Ionic columns leads to a paneled door with an elliptical fanlight and flanking sidelights. The rear of the home features upper and lower terraces enclosed by a low brick wall. Inside, the formal living and dining rooms, the library and the country kitchen each boast a fireplace and built-ins. The sleeping zone includes two family bedrooms with walk-in closets, a shared bath and a bay-windowed master suite. The master bath has His and Hers walk-in closets and vanities, a whirlpool tub and a separate shower. The utility zone offers a multipurpose clutter room and an extra bedroom or a sewing room.

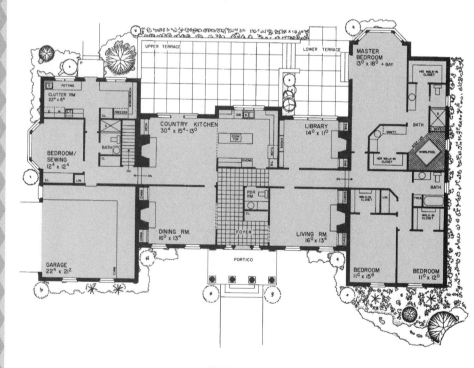

Width 100'-2"
Depth 58'-10"

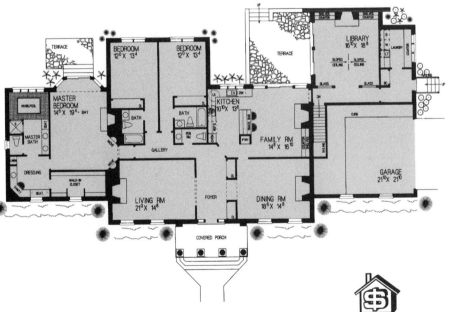

Width 104'-4"
Depth 52'-4"

QUOTE ONE®

Cost to build? See page 198
to order complete cost estimate
to build this house in your area!

DESIGN 2997

Square Footage: 3,442

L **D**

An Ionic portico and a fan-lighted door highlight the exterior of this Greek Revival cottage, an adaptation of Overlook, a home built in Macon, Georgia, in 1835. Four chimneys support five fireplaces, including one in the master bedroom. The homeowners will also appreciate the expansive master bath and dressing area, as well as access to a private rear terrace. Two additional bedrooms each adjoin a full bath. Living areas include formal living and dining rooms and a family room separated from the kitchen by a snack bar. A library with a fireplace, a sloped ceiling and built-in shelves is tucked away in the rear of the home. Sliding glass doors lead from the library and the family room to a second terrace.

DESIGN 3525

Square Footage: 2,195

L

The original of this impressive Greek Revival home was built in Waterville, New York, in the 1830s. It is believed to be the birthplace of George Eastman, the father of modern photography. The facade is dominated by a large front-facing gable and four fluted Doric columns. The single side wing was a common feature of Greek Revival homes built in the Northeast. The tiled foyer opens to the formal living and dining rooms, and leads back to an open informal area. The well-appointed kitchen features an eating nook and a snack bar that it shares with the family room. The sleeping wing contains two bedrooms—a master suite with a walk-in closet and a private bath, and a family bedroom that shares a hall bath with the media room. A rear covered porch adds oudoor dining and relaxing possibilities.

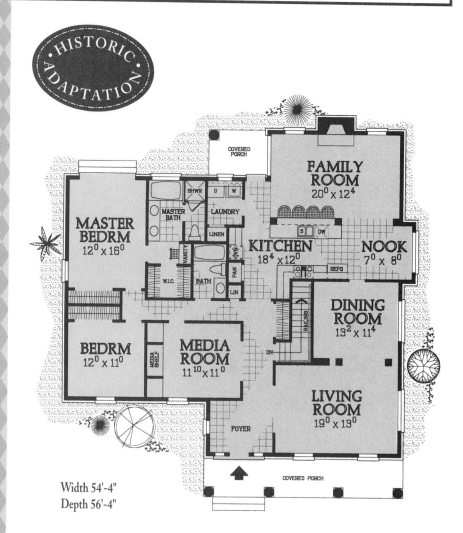

Width 54'-4"
Depth 56'-4"

DECK

DECK

FP

BEDROOM
11'-0'' x 10'-0''

LIVING
ROOM
16'-0'' x 14'-0''

KITCHEN
12'-0'' x 14'-0''

MASTER
BEDROOM
16'-0'' x 14'-0''

WIC

BATH

VAULTED CEILING

VAULTED CEILING

BATH

FAMILY
ENTRY

BEDROOM
11'-0'' x 10'-0''

ENTRY
FOYER

DINING
ROOM
12'-0'' x 14'-0''

DN

LAUNDRY

W   D

TWO-CAR GARAGE
21'-0'' x 21'-0''

PORCH

Width 62'-8"
Depth 36'-0"

DESIGN F117

Square Footage: 1,550

A handsome porch dressed up with Greek Revival details warmly welcomes visitors to this one-story home. From the entry, one is struck by the volume of space provided by the vaulted ceiling in the dining room/living room area. With a fireplace for warmth and access to a rear deck for outdoor entertaining, there is ample space here for family and guests. The nearby kitchen has an interesting angled counter, a door to the deck and room for an informal eating area. The secluded master bedroom also sports a vaulted ceiling and is graced with a private compartmented bath, a walk-in closet and its own deck. Two family bedrooms share a full bath, which is also readily accessible by guests. Adjacent to the two-car garage is a good-sized laundry room.

When You're Ready To Order . . .

Let Us Show You Our Home Blueprint Package.

Building a home? Planning a home? Our Blueprint Package has nearly everything you need to get the job done right, whether you're working on your own or with help from an architect, designer, builder or subcontractors. Each Blueprint Package is the result of many hours of work by licensed architects or professional designers.

QUALITY

Hundreds of hours of painstaking effort have gone into the development of your blueprint set. Each home has been quality-checked by professionals to insure accuracy and buildability.

VALUE

Because we sell in volume, you can buy professional-quality blueprints at a fraction of their development cost. With our plans, your dream home design costs only a few hundred dollars, not the thousands of dollars that custom architects charge.

SERVICE

Once you've chosen your favorite home plan, you'll receive fast, efficient service whether you choose to mail or fax your order to us or call us toll free at 1-800-521-6797. For customer service, call toll free 1-888-690-1116.

SATISFACTION

Over 50 years of service to satisfied home plan buyers provide us unparalleled experience and knowledge in producing quality blueprints. What this means to you is satisfaction with our product and performance.

ORDER TOLL FREE 1-800-521-6797

After you've looked over our Blueprint Package and Important Extras on the following pages, simply mail the order form on page 205 or call toll free on our Blueprint Hotline: 1-800-521-6797. We're ready and eager to serve you. For customer service, call toll free 1-888-690-1116.

Each set of blueprints is an interrelated collection of detail sheets which includes components such as floor plans, interior and exterior elevations, dimensions, cross-sections, diagrams and notations. These sheets show exactly how your house is to be built.

Among the sheets included may be:

Frontal Sheet
This artist's sketch of the exterior of the house gives you an idea of how the house will look when built and landscaped. Large ink-line floor plans show all levels of the house and provide an overview of your new home's livability, as well as a handy reference for deciding on furniture placement.

Foundation Plan
This sheet shows the foundation layout includ-

SAMPLE PACKAGE

ing support walls, excavated and unexcavated areas, if any, and foundation notes. If slab construction rather than basement, the plan shows footings and details for a monolithic slab. This page, or another in the set, may include a sample plot plan for locating your house on a building site.

Detailed Floor Plans

These plans show the layout of each floor of the house. Rooms and interior spaces are carefully dimensioned and keys are given for cross-section details provided later in the plans. The positions of electrical outlets and switches are shown.

House Cross-Sections

Large-scale views show sections or cut-aways of the foundation, interior walls, exterior walls, floors, stairways and roof details. Additional cross-sections may show important changes in floor, ceiling or roof heights or the relationship of one level to another. Extremely valuable for construction, these sections show exactly how the various parts of the house fit together.

Interior Elevations

Many of our drawings show the design and placement of kitchen and bathroom cabinets, laundry areas, fireplaces, bookcases and other built-ins. Little "extras," such as mantelpiece and wainscoting drawings, plus moulding sections, provide details that give your home that custom touch.

Exterior Elevations

These drawings show the front, rear and sides of your house and give necessary notes on exterior materials and finishes. Particular attention is given to cornice detail, brick and stone accents or other finish items that make your home unique.

Frontal Sheet

Foundation Plans

Detailed Floor Plans

Exterior Elevations

Interior Elevations

House Cross-Sections

Important Extras To Do The Job Right!

Introducing eight important planning and construction aids developed by our professionals to help you succeed in your home-building project.

MATERIALS LIST

(Note: Because of the diversity of local building codes, our Materials List does not include mechanical materials.)

For many of the designs in our portfolio, we offer a customized materials take-off that is invaluable in planning and estimating the cost of your new home. This Materials List outlines the quantity, type and size of materials needed to build your house (with the exception of mechanical system items). Included are framing lumber, windows and doors, kitchen and bath cabinetry, rough and finish hardware, and much more. This handy list helps you or your builder cost out materials and serves as a reference sheet when you're compiling bids. A Materials List cannot be ordered before blueprints are ordered.

SPECIFICATION OUTLINE

This valuable 16-page document is critical to building your house correctly. Designed to be filled in by you or your builder, this book lists 166 stages or items crucial to the building process. It provides a comprehensive review of the construction process and helps in making choices of materials. When combined with the blueprints, a signed contract, and a schedule, it becomes a legal document and record for the building of your home.

QUOTE ONE®

Summary Cost Report / Materials Cost Report

A new service for estimating the cost of building select designs, the Quote One® system is available in two separate stages: The Summary Cost Report and the Materials Cost Report.

Make even more informed decisions about your home-building project with the second phase of our package, our Materials Cost Report. This tool is invaluable in planning and estimating the cost of your new home. The material and installation (labor and equipment) cost is shown for each of over 1,000 line items provided in the Materials List (Standard grade) which is included when you purchase this estimating tool. It allows you to determine building costs for your specific zip-code area and for your chosen home design. Space is allowed for additional estimates from contractors and subcontractors, such as for mechanical materials, which are not included in our packages. This invaluable tool is available for a price of $110 ($120 for a Schedule E plan) which includes a Materials List. A Materials Cost Report cannot be ordered before blueprints are ordered.

The Quote One® program is continually updated with new plans. If you are interested in a plan that is not indicated as Quote One®, please call and ask our sales reps, they will be happy to verify the status for you. To order these invaluable reports, use the order form on page 205 or call 1-800-521-6797.

The Summary Cost Report is the first stage in the package and shows the total cost per square foot for your chosen home in your zip-code area and then breaks that cost down into ten categories showing the costs for building materials, labor and installation. The total cost for the report (which includes three grades: Budget, Standard and Custom) is just $19.95 for one home, and additionals are only $14.95. These reports allow you to evaluate your building budget and compare the costs of building a variety of homes in your area.

CONSTRUCTION INFORMATION

If you want to know more about techniques—and deal more confidently with subcontractors we offer these useful sheets. Each set is an excellent tool that will add to your understanding of these technical subjects.

Plan-A-Home®

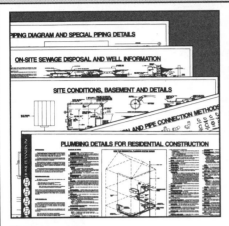

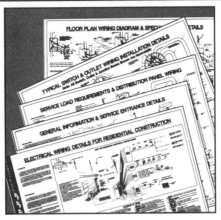

PLUMBING

The Blueprint Package includes locations for all the plumbing fixtures in your new house, including sinks, lavatories, tubs, showers, toilets, laundry trays and water heaters. However, if you want to know more about the complete plumbing system, these 24x36-inch detail sheets will prove very useful. Prepared to meet requirements of the National Plumbing Code, these six fact-filled sheets give general information on pipe schedules, fittings, sump-pump details, water-softener hookups, septic system details and much more. Color-coded sheets include a glossary of terms.

ELECTRICAL

The locations for every electrical switch, plug and outlet are shown in your Blueprint Package. However, these Electrical Details go further to take the mystery out of household electrical systems. Prepared to meet requirements of the National Electrical Code, these comprehensive 24x36-inch drawings come packed with helpful information, including wire sizing, switch-installation schematics, cable-routing details, appliance wattage, door-bell hookups, typical service panel circuitry and much more. Six sheets are bound together and color-coded for easy reference. A glossary of terms is also included.

Plan-A-Home® is an easy-to-use tool that helps you design a new home, arrange furniture in a new or existing home, or plan a remodeling project. Each package contains:

- **More than 700 reusable peel-off planning symbols** on a self-stick vinyl sheet, including walls, windows, doors, all types of furniture, kitchen components, bath fixtures and many more.

- **A reusable, transparent, 1/4-inch scale planning grid** that matches the scale of actual working drawings (1/4-inch equals 1 foot). This grid provides the basis for house layouts of up to 140x92 feet.

- **Tracing paper** and a protective sheet for copying or transferring your completed plan.

- **A felt-tip pen,** with water-soluble ink that wipes away quickly.

Plan-A-Home® lets you lay out areas as large as a 7,500 square foot, six-bedroom, seven-bath house.

CONSTRUCTION

The Blueprint Package contains everything an experienced builder needs to construct a particular house. However, it doesn't show all the ways that houses can be built, nor does it explain alternate construction methods. To help you understand how your house will be built—and offer additional techniques—this set of drawings depicts the materials and methods used to build foundations, fireplaces, walls, floors and roofs. Where appropriate, the drawings show acceptable alternatives. These six sheets will answer questions for the advanced do-it-yourselfer or home planner.

MECHANICAL

This package contains fundamental principles and useful data that will help you make informed decisions and communicate with subcontractors about heating and cooling systems. The 24x36-inch drawings contain instructions and samples that allow you to make simple load calculations and preliminary sizing and costing analysis. Covered are today's most commonly used systems from heat pumps to solar fuel systems. The package is packed full of illustrations and diagrams to help you visualize components and how they relate to one another.

To Order, Call Toll Free 1-800-521-6797

To add these important extras to your Blueprint Package, simply indicate your choices on the order form on page 205 or call us Toll Free 1-800-521-6797 and we'll tell you more about these exciting products. For customer service, call toll free 1-888-690-1116.

D The Deck Blueprint Package

Many of the homes in this book can be enhanced with a professionally designed Home Planners' Deck Plan. Those home plans highlighted with a **D** have a matching or corresponding deck plan available which includes a Deck Plan Frontal Sheet, Deck Framing and Floor Plans, Deck Elevations and a Deck Materials List. A Standard Deck Details Package, also available, provides all the how-to information necessary for building *any* deck. Our Complete Deck Building Package contains 1 set of Custom Deck Plans of your choice, plus 1 set of Standard Deck Building Details all for one low price. Our plans and details are carefully prepared in an easy-to-understand format that will guide you through every stage of your deck-building project. This page contains a sampling of 12 of the 25 different Deck layouts to match your favorite house. See page 202 for prices and ordering information.

SPLIT-LEVEL SUN DECK
Deck Plan D100

BI-LEVEL DECK WITH COVERED DINING
Deck Plan D101

WRAP-AROUND FAMILY DECK
Deck Plan D104

DECK FOR DINING AND VIEWS
Deck Plan D107

TREND SETTER DECK
Deck Plan D110

TURN-OF-THE-CENTURY DECK
Deck Plan D111

WEEKEND ENTERTAINER DECK
Deck Plan D112

CENTER-VIEW DECK
Deck Plan D114

KITCHEN-EXTENDER DECK
Deck Plan D115

SPLIT-LEVEL ACTIVITY DECK
Deck Plan D117

TRI-LEVEL DECK WITH GRILL
Deck Plan D119

CONTEMPORARY LEISURE DECK
Deck Plan D120

■ *The Landscape Blueprint Package*

For the homes marked with an ■ in this book, Home Planners has created a front-yard landscape plan that matches or is complementary in design to the house plan. These comprehensive blueprint packages include a Frontal Sheet, Plan View, Regionalized Plant & Materials List, a sheet on Planting and Maintaining Your Landscape, Zone Maps and Plant Size and Description Guide. These plans will help you achieve professional results, adding value and enjoyment to your property for years to come. Each set of blueprints is a full 18" x 24" in size with clear, complete instructions and easy-to-read type. Six of the forty front yard Landscape Plans to match your favorite house are shown below.

Regional Order Map

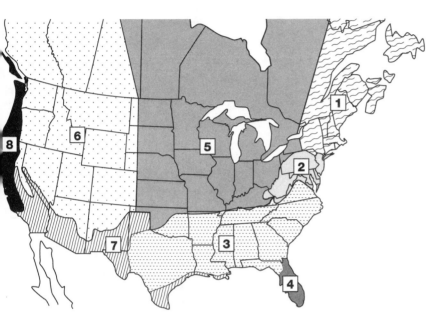

Most of the Landscape Plans shown on these pages are available with a Plant & Materials List adapted by horticultural experts to 8 different regions of the country. Please specify Geographic Region when ordering your plan. See page 202 for prices, ordering information and regional availability.

Region	1	Northeast
Region	2	Mid-Atlantic
Region	3	Deep South
Region	4	Florida & Gulf Coast
Region	5	Midwest
Region	6	Rocky Mountains
Region	7	Southern California & Desert Southwest
Region	8	Northern California & Pacific Northwest

CAPE COD COTTAGE
Landscape Plan L202

GAMBREL-ROOF COLONIAL
Landscape Plan L203

CENTER-HALL COLONIAL
Landscape Plan L204

CLASSIC NEW ENGLAND COLONIAL
Landscape Plan L205

COUNTRY-STYLE FARMHOUSE
Landscape Plan L207

TRADITIONAL SPLIT-LEVEL
Landscape Plan L228

Price Schedule & Plans Index

House Blueprint Price Schedule
(Prices guaranteed through December 31, 1999)

Tier	1-set Study Package	4-set Building Package	8-set Building Package	1-set Reproducible Sepias	Home Customizer® Package
A	$390	$435	$495	$595	$645
B	$430	$475	$535	$655	$705
C	$470	$515	$575	$715	$765
D	$510	$555	$615	$775	$825
E	$630	$675	$735	$835	$885

Prices for 4- or 8-set Building Packages honored only at time of original order.

Additional Identical Blueprints in same order ....$50 per set
Reverse Blueprints (mirror image) ....$50 per set
Specification Outlines ....$10 each
Materials Lists (available only from those designers listed below):
▲ Home Planners Designs...$50
† Design Basics Designs..$75
◆ Donald Gardner Designs...$50
■ Design Traditions Designs...$50
✱ Alan Mascord Designs...$50
≠ Greg Marquis Designs $50
● Homes for Living Designs..$50

Materials Lists for "E" price plans are an additional $10.

Deck Plans Price Schedule

CUSTOM DECK PLANS

Price Group	Q	R	S
1 Set Custom Plans	$25	$30	$35

Additional identical sets $10 each
Reverse sets (mirror image) $10 each

STANDARD DECK DETAILS
1 Set Generic Construction Details ....$14.95 each

COMPLETE DECK BUILDING PACKAGE

Price Group	Q	R	S
1 Set Custom Plans, plus 1 Set Standard Deck Details	$35	$40	$45

Landscape Plans Price Schedule

Price Group	X	Y	Z
1 set	$35	$45	$55
3 sets	$50	$60	$70
6 sets	$65	$75	$85

Additional Identical Sets.....................................$10 each
Reverse Sets (mirror image)...............................$10 each

Index

To use the Index below, refer to the design number listed in numerical order (a helpful page reference is also given). Note the price index letter and refer to the House Blueprint Price Schedule above for the cost of one, four or eight sets of blueprints or the cost of a reproducible sepia. Additional prices are shown for identical and reverse blueprint sets, as well as a very useful Materials List for some of the plans. Also note in the Index below those plans that have matching or complementary Deck Plans or Landscape Plans. Refer to the schedules above for prices of these plans. All Home Planners' plans can be customized with Home Planners' Home Customizer® Package. These plans are indicated below with this symbol: 🏠. See page 205 for information. Some plans are also part of our Quote One® estimating service and are indicated by this symbol: 🏠 . See page 198 for more information.

To Order: Fill in and send the order form on page 205—or call toll free 1-800-521-6797 or 520-297-8200.

DESIGN	PRICE	PAGE	CUSTOMIZABLE	QUOTE ONE®	DECK	DECK PRICE	LANDSCAPE	LANDSCAPE PRICE	REGIONS
▲2101	B	34	🏠						
▲2131	B	72	🏠		D117	S	L203	Y	1-3,5,6,8
▲2145	A	52	🏠	🏠			L209	Y	1-6,8
▲2146	A	53	🏠		D114	R	L203	Y	1-3,5,6,8
▲2184	C	186	🏠						
▲2191	C	46	🏠				L222	Y	1-3,5,6,8
▲2395	B	53	🏠				L201	Y	1-3,5,6,8
▲2397	C	73	🏠						
▲2520	B	26	🏠		D105	R	L201	Y	1-3,5,6,8
▲2522	C	106	🏠						
▲2542	D	108	🏠				L208	Z	1,2,5,6,8
▲2556	C	99	🏠		D103	R			
▲2571	A	24	🏠		D114	R	L202	X	1-3,5,6,8
▲2610	C	87	🏠	🏠	D114	R	L204	Y	1-3,5,6,8
▲2615	D	30	🏠	🏠	D106	S	L211	Y	1-8
▲2622	A	44	🏠		D103	R	L200	X	1-3,5,6,8
▲2631	B	62	🏠		D112	R	L201	Y	1-3,5,6,8
▲2632	B	78	🏠						
▲2635	A	59	🏠						
▲2636	A	58	🏠						
▲2638	C	146	🏠						
▲2639	C	105	🏠		D114	R	L215	Z	1-6,8
▲2642	B	37	🏠						
▲2643	C	70	🏠						
▲2644	B	77	🏠						
▲2649	C	39	🏠						
▲2653	C	80	🏠				L209	Y	1-6,8
▲2656	B	74	🏠		D105	R	L203	Y	1-3,5,6,8
▲2657	B	50	🏠	🏠			L200	X	1-3,5,6,8
▲2659	B	85	🏠	🏠	D113	R	L205	Y	1-3,5,6,8
▲2662	C	171	🏠	🏠			L216	Y	1-3,5,6,8
▲2664	B	136	🏠		D113	R			
▲2665	D	165	🏠						
▲2668	B	188	🏠	🏠			L214	Z	1-3,5,6,8
▲2681	B	142	🏠						
▲2683	D	22	🏠	🏠	D101	R	L214	Z	1-3,5,6,8
▲2687	C	82	🏠		D117	S	L204	Y	1-3,5,6,8
▲2688	B	145	🏠						
▲2689	B	76	🏠						
▲2691	B	144	🏠						
▲2692	C	36	🏠						
▲2693	D	192	🏠						

Before You Order . . .

Before filling out the coupon at right or calling us on our Toll-Free Blueprint Hotline, you may want to learn more about our services and products. Here's some information you will find helpful.

Quick Turnaround

We process and ship every blueprint order from our office within two business days. Because of this quick turnaround, we won't send a formal notice acknowledging receipt of your order.

Our Exchange Policy

Since blueprints are printed in response to your order, we cannot honor requests for refunds. However, we will exchange your entire first order for an equal number of blueprints at a price of $50 for the first set and $10 for each additional set; $70 total exchange fee for 4 sets; $100 total exchange fee for 8 sets . . . *plus* the difference in cost if exchanging for a design in a higher price bracket or *less* the difference in cost if exchanging for a design in lower price bracket. One exchange is allowed within a year of purchase date. **(Sepias are not exchangeable.)** All sets from the first order must be returned before the exchange can take place. Please add $18 for postage and handling via ground service; $30 via Second Day Air; $40 via Next Day Air.

About Reverse Blueprints

If you want to build in reverse of the plan as shown, we will include an extra set of reverse blueprints (mirror image) for an additional fee of $50. Although lettering and dimensions will appear backward, reverses will be a useful aid if you decide to flop the plan.

Revising, Modifying and Customizing Plans

The wide variety of designs available in this publication allows you to select ideas and concepts for a home to fit your building site and match your family's needs, wants and budget. Like many homeowners who buy these plans, you and your builder, architect or engineer may want to make changes to them. Some minor changes may be made by your builder, but we recommend that most changes be made by a licensed architect or engineer. If you need to make alterations to a design that is customizable, you need only order our Home Customizer® Package to get you started. As set forth below, we cannot assume any responsibility for blueprints which have been changed, whether by you, your builder or by professionals selected by you or referred to you by us, because such individuals are outside our supervision and control.

Architectural and Engineering Seals

Some cities and states are now requiring that a licensed architect or engineer review and "seal" a blueprint, or officially approve it, prior to construction due to concerns over energy costs, safety and other factors. Prior to application for a building permit or the start of actual construction, we strongly advise that you consult your local building official who can tell you if such a review is required.

About the Designers

The architects and designers whose work appears in this publication are among America's leading residential designers. Each plan was designed to meet the requirements of a nationally recognized model building code in effect at the time and place the plan was drawn. Because national building codes change from time to time, plans may not comply with any such code at the time they are sold to a customer. In addition, building officials may not accept these plans as final construction documents of record as the plans may need to be modified and additional drawings and details added to suit local conditions and requirements. We strongly advise that purchasers consult a licensed architect or engineer, and their local building official, before starting any construction related to these plans.

Local Building Codes and Zoning Requirements

At the time of creation, our plans are drawn to specifications published by the Building Officials and Code Administrators (BOCA) International, Inc.; the Southern Building Code Congress (SBCCI) International, Inc.; the International Conference of Building Officials; or the Council of American Building Officials (CABO). Our plans are designed to meet or exceed national building standards. Because of the great differences in geography and climate throughout the United States and Canada, each state, county and municipality has its own building codes, zone requirements, ordinances and building regulations. Your plan may need to be modified to comply with local requirements regarding snow loads, energy codes, soil and seismic conditions and a wide range of other matters. In addition, you may need to obtain permits or inspections from local governments before and in the course of construction. Prior to using blueprints obtained from us, we strongly advise that you consult a licensed architect or engineer—and speak with your local building official—before applying for any permit or beginning construction. We authorize the use of our blueprints on the express condition that you strictly comply with all local building codes, zoning requirements and other applicable laws, regulations, ordinances and requirements. **Notice:** Plans for homes to be built in Nevada must be re-drawn by a Nevada-registered professional. Consult your building official for more information on this subject.

Foundation and Exterior Wall Changes

Most of our plans are drawn with either a full or partial basement foundation. Depending on your specific climate or regional building practices, you may wish to change this basement to a slab or crawlspace. Most professional contractors and builders can easily adapt your plans to alternate foundation types. Likewise, most can easily change 2x4 wall construction to 2x6, or vice versa.

Disclaimer

We and the designers we work with have put substantial care and effort into the creation of our blueprints. However, because we cannot provide on-site consultation, supervision and control over actual construction, and because of the great variance in local building requirements, building practices and soil, seismic, weather and other conditions, WE CANNOT MAKE ANY WARRANTY, EXPRESS OR IMPLIED, WITH RESPECT TO THE CONTENT OR USE OF OUR BLUEPRINTS, INCLUDING BUT NOT LIMITED TO ANY WARRANTY OF MERCHANTABILITY OR OF FITNESS FOR A PARTICULAR PURPOSE.

Terms and Conditions

These designs are protected under the terms of United States Copyright Law and may not be copied or reproduced in any way, by any means, unless you have purchased Sepias or Reproducibles which clearly indicate your right to copy or reproduce. We authorize the use of your chosen design as an aid in the construction of one single family home only. You may not use this design to build a second or multiple dwellings without purchasing another blueprint or blueprints or paying additional design fees.

How Many Blueprints Do You Need?

A single set of blueprints is sufficient to study a home in greater detail. However, if you are planning to obtain cost estimates from a contractor or subcontractors—or if you are planning to build immediately—you will need more sets. Because additional sets are cheaper when ordered in quantity with the original order, make sure you order enough blueprints to satisfy all requirements. The following checklist will help you determine how many you need:

____ Owner

____ Builder (generally requires at least three sets; one as a legal document, one to use during inspections, and at least one to give to subcontractors)

____ Local Building Department (often requires two sets)

____ Mortgage Lender (usually one set for a conventional loan; three sets for FHA or VA loans)

____ TOTAL NUMBER OF SETS

Toll Free 1-800-521-6797

Regular Office Hours:
8:00 a.m. to 8:00 p.m. Eastern Time, Monday through Friday
Our staff will gladly answer any questions during regular office hours. Our answering service can place orders after hours or on weekends.

If we receive your order by 4:00 p.m. Eastern Time, Monday through Friday, we'll process it and ship within two business days. When ordering by phone, please have your charge card ready. We'll also ask you for the Order Form Key Number at the bottom of the coupon.

By FAX: Copy the Order Form on the next page and send it on our FAX line: 1-800-224-6699 or 1-520-544-3086.

Canadian Customers
Order Toll-Free 1-800-561-4169

For faster service and plans that are modified for building in Canada, customers may now call in orders directly to our Canadian supplier of plans and charge the purchase to a charge card. Or, you may complete the order form at right, adding 40% to all prices and mail in Canadian funds to:

The Plan Centre 60 Baffin Place
Unit 5
Waterloo, Ontario N2V 1Z7

OR: Copy the Order Form and send it via our Canadian FAX line: 1-800-719-3291.

The Home Customizer®

"This house is perfect...if only the family room were two feet wider." Sound familiar? In response to the numerous requests for this type of modification, Home Planners has developed **The Home Customizer® Package**. This exclusive package offers our top-of-the-line materials to make it easy for anyone, anywhere to customize any Home Planners design to fit their needs. Check the index on page 202-203 for those plans which are customizable.

Some of the changes you can make to any of our plans include:

- exterior elevation changes
- kitchen and bath modifications
- roof, wall and foundation changes
- room additions and more!

The Home Customizer® Package includes everything you'll need to make the necessary changes to your favorite Home Planners design. The package includes:

- instruction book with examples
- architectural scale and clear work film
- erasable red marker and removable correction tape
- ¼"-scale furniture cutouts
- 1 set reproducible, erasable Sepias
- 1 set study blueprints for communicating changes to your design professional
- a copyright release letter so you can make copies as you need them
- referral letter with the name, address and telephone number of the professional in your region who is trained in modifying Home Planners designs efficiently and inexpensively.

The price of the **Home Customizer® Package** ranges from $605 to $845, depending on the price schedule of the design you have chosen. **The Home Customizer® Package** will not only save you 25% to 75% of the cost of drawing the plans from scratch with a custom architect or engineer, it will also give you the flexibility to have your changes and modifications made by our referral network or by the professional of your choice. Now it's even easier and more affordable to have the custom home you've always wanted.

 For information about any of our services or to order call 1-800-521-6797.

BLUEPRINTS ARE NOT RETURNABLE

For Customer Service, call toll free 1-888-690-1116.

ORDER FORM

 HOME PLANNERS, LLC
Wholly owned by Hanley-Wood, Inc.
3275 WEST INA ROAD, SUITE 110
TUCSON, ARIZONA 85741

THE BASIC BLUEPRINT PACKAGE
Rush me the following (please refer to the Plans Index and Price Schedule in this section):

_____ Set(s) of blueprints for plan number(s) _____. $_____
_____ Set(s) of sepias for plan number(s) _____. $_____
_____ Home Customizer® Package for plan(s) _____ $_____
_____ Additional identical blueprints in same order @ $50 per set. $_____
_____ Reverse blueprints @ $50 per set. $_____

IMPORTANT EXTRAS
Rush me the following:

_____ Materials List: $50 (Must be purchased with Blueprint set.)
$75 Design Basics. Add $10 for a Schedule E plan Materials List. $_____
_____ **Quote One**® Summary Cost Report @ $19.95 for 1, $14.95 for each additional, for plans _____ $_____
Building location: City _____ Zip Code _____
_____ **Quote One**® Materials Cost Report @ $110 Schedule A-D; $120 Schedule E for plan_____ $_____
(Must be purchased with Blueprints set.)
Building location: City _____ Zip Code _____
_____ Specification Outlines @ $10 each. $_____
_____ Detail Sets @ $14.95 each; any two for $22.95; any three for $29.95; all four for $39.95 (save $19.85). $_____
❏ Plumbing ❏ Electrical ❏ Construction ❏ Mechanical
(These helpful details provide general construction advice and are not specific to any single plan.)
_____ Plan-A-Home® @ $29.95 each. $_____
DECK BLUEPRINTS
_____ Set(s) of Deck Plan _____. $_____
_____ Additional identical blueprints in same order @ $10 per set. $_____
_____ Reverse blueprints @ $10 per set. $_____
_____ Set of Standard Deck Details @ $14.95 per set. $_____
_____ Set of Complete Building Package (Best Buy!)
Includes Custom Deck Plan _____.
(See Index and Price Schedule)
Plus Standard Deck Details $_____
LANDSCAPE BLUEPRINTS
_____ Set(s) of Landscape Plan _____. $_____
_____ Additional identical blueprints in same order @ $10 per set. $_____
_____ Reverse blueprints @ $10 per set. $_____
Please indicate the appropriate region of the country for Plant & Material List. (See Map on page 201): Region _____

POSTAGE AND HANDLING	1-3 sets	4+ sets
Signature is required for all deliveries.		
DELIVERY (Requires street address - No P.O. Boxes)		
•Regular Service (Allow 7-10 business days delivery)	❏ $15.00	❏ $18.00
•Priority (Allow 4-5 business days delivery)	❏ $20.00	❏ $30.00
•Express (Allow 3 business days delivery)	❏ $30.00	❏ $40.00
CERTIFIED MAIL	❏ $20.00	❏ $30.00
If no street address available. (Allow 7-10 days delivery)		
OVERSEAS DELIVERY		
Note: All delivery times are from date Blueprint Package is shipped.	fax, phone or mail for quote	

POSTAGE (From box above) $_____
SUB-TOTAL $_____
SALES TAX (AZ, CA, DC, IL, MI, MN, NY & WA residents, please add appropriate state and local sales tax.) $_____
TOTAL (Sub-total and tax) $_____

YOUR ADDRESS (please print)

Name _____

Street _____

City _____State_____Zip _____

Daytime telephone number (_____) _____

FOR CREDIT CARD ORDERS ONLY
Please fill in the information below:
Credit card number _____
Exp. Date: Month/Year _____

Check one ❏ Visa ❏ MasterCard ❏ Discover Card ❏ American Express

Signature _____

Please check appropriate box: ❏ Licensed Builder-Contractor
❏ Homeowner

 ORDER TOLL FREE!
1-800-521-6797 or 520-297-8200

Order Form Key
TB57

Helpful Books & Software

Home Planners wants your building experience to be as pleasant and trouble-free as possible. That's why we've expanded our library of Do-It-Yourself titles to help you along. In addition to our beautiful plans books, we've added books to guide you through specific projects as well as the construction process. In fact, these are titles that will be as useful after your dream home is built as they are right now.

ONE-STORY

1 448 designs for all lifestyles. 860 to 5,400 square feet. 384 pages $9.95

TWO-STORY

2 460 designs for one-and-a-half and two stories. 1,245 to 7,275 square feet. 384 pages $9.95

VACATION

3 345 designs for recreation, retirement and leisure. 312 pages $8.95

MULTI-LEVEL

4 214 designs for split-levels, bi-levels, multi-levels and walkouts. 224 pages $8.95

COUNTRY

5 200 country designs from classic to contemporary by 7 winning designers. 224 pages $8.95

MOVE-UP

6 200 stylish designs for today's growing families from 9 hot designers. 224 pages $8.95

NARROW-LOT

7 200 unique homes less than 60' wide from 7 designers. Up to 3,000 square feet. 224 pages $8.95

SMALL HOUSE

8 200 beautiful designs chosen for versatility and affordability. 224 pages $8.95

BUDGET-SMART

9 200 efficient plans from 7 top designers, that you can really afford to build! 224 pages $8.95

EXPANDABLES

10 200 flexible plans that expand with your needs from 7 top designers. 240 pages $8.95

ENCYCLOPEDIA

11 500 exceptional plans for all styles and budgets—the best book of its kind! 352 pages $9.95

AFFORDABLE

12 Completely revised and updated, featuring 300 designs for modest budgets. 256 pages $9.95

ENCYCLOPEDIA 2

13 500 Completely new plans. Spacious and stylish designs for every budget and taste. 352 pages $9.95

VICTORIAN

14 160 striking Victorian and Farmhouse designs from three leading designers. 192 pages $12.95

ESTATE

15 Dream big! Twenty-one designers showcase their biggest and best plans. 208 pages. $15.95

LUXURY

16 154 fine luxury plans-loaded with luscious amenities! 192 pages $14.95

COTTAGES

17 25 fresh new designs that are as warm as a tropical breeze. A blend of the best aspects of many coastal styles. 64 pages. $19.95

BEST SELLERS

18 Our 50th Anniversary book with 200 of our very best designs in full color! 224 pages $12.95

SPECIAL COLLECTION
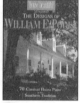
19 70 Romantic house plans that capture the classic tradition of home design. 160 pages $17.95

COUNTRY HOUSES

20 208 Unique home plans that combine traditional style and modern livability. 224 pages $9.95

CLASSIC

21 Timeless, elegant designs that always feel like home. Gorgeous plans that are as flexible and up-to-date as their occupants. 240 pages. $9.95

CONTEMPORARY

22 The most complete and imaginative collection of contemporary designs available anywhere. 240 pages. $9.95

EASY-LIVING

23 200 Efficient and sophisticated plans that are small in size, but big on livability. 224 pages $8.95

SOUTHERN

24 207 homes rich in Southern styling and comfort. 240 pages $8.95

SUNBELT

25 215 Designs that capture the spirit of the Southwest. 208 pages $10.95

WESTERN

26 215 designs that capture the spirit and diversity of the Western lifestyle. 208 pages $9.95

ENERGY GUIDE

27 The most comprehensive energy efficiency and conservation guide available. 280 pages $35.00

Design Software

BOOK & CD ROM

28 Both the Home Planners Gold book and matching Windows™ CD ROM with 3D floorplans. $24.95

3D DESIGN SUITE

29 Home design made easy! View designs in 3D, take a virtual reality tour, add decorating details and more. $59.95

Outdoor Projects

OUTDOOR

30 42 unique outdoor projects. Gazebos, strombellas, bridges, sheds, playsets and more! 96 pages $7.95

GARAGES & MORE

31 101 Multi-use garages and outdoor structures to enhance any home. 96 pages $7.95

DECKS

32 25 outstanding single-, double- and multi-level decks you can build. 112 pages $7.95

Landscape Designs

EASY CARE	FRONT & BACK	BACKYARDS	BEDS & BORDERS	BATHROOMS	KITCHENS	HOUSE CONTRACTING	WINDOWS & DOORS

33 41 special landscapes designed for beauty and low maintenance. 160 pages $14.95

34 The first book of do-it-yourself landscapes. 40 front, 15 backyards. 208 pages $14.95

35 40 designs focused solely on creating your own specially themed backyard oasis. 160 pages $14.95

36 Practical advice and maintenance techniques for a wide variety of yard projects. 160 pages. $14.95

37 An innovative guide to organizing, remodeling and decorating your bathroom. 96 pages $9.95

38 An imaginative guide to designing the perfect kitchen. Chock full of bright ideas to make your job easier. 176 pages $14.95

39 Everything you need to know to act as your own general contractor...and save up to 25% off building costs. 134 pages $14.95

40 Installation techniques and tips that make your project easier and more professional looking. 80 pages $7.95

ROOFING	FRAMING	VISUAL HANDBOOK	BASIC WIRING	PATIOS & WALKS	TILE	PLUMBING	TRIM & MOLDING

   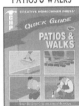    

41 Information on the latest tools, materials and techniques for roof installation or repair. 80 pages $7.95

42 For those who want to take a more-hands on approach to their dream. 319 pages $19.95

43 A plain-talk guide to the construction process; financing to final walk-through, this book covers it all. 498 pages $19.95

44 A straight forward guide to one of the most misunderstood systems in the home. 160 pages $12.95

45 Clear step-by-step instructions take you from the basic design stages to the finished project. 80 pages $7.95

46 Every kind of tile for every kind of application. Includes tips on use installation and repair. 176 pages $12.95

47 Tackle any plumbing installation or repair as quickly and efficiently as a professional. 160 pages $12.95

48 Step-by-step instructions for installing baseboards, window and door casings and more. 80 pages $7.95

Additional Books Order Form

To order your books, just check the box of the book numbered below and complete the coupon. We will process your order and ship it from our office within 48 hours. Send coupon and check (in U.S. funds).

YES! Please send me the books I've indicated:

☐ 1:VO	$9.95	☐ 25:SW	$10.95
☐ 2:VT	$9.95	☐ 26:WH	$9.95
☐ 3:VH	$8.95	☐ 27:RES	$35.00
☐ 4:VS	$8.95	☐ 28:HPGC	$24.95
☐ 5:FH	$8.95	☐ 29:PLANSUITE	$59.95
☐ 6:MU	$8.95	☐ 30:YG	$7.95
☐ 7:NL	$8.95	☐ 31:GG	$7.95
☐ 8:SM	$8.95	☐ 32:DP	$7.95
☐ 9:BS	$8.95	☐ 33:ECL	$14.95
☐ 10:EX	$8.95	☐ 34:HL	$14.95
☐ 11:EN	$9.95	☐ 35:BYL	$14.95
☐ 12:AF	$9.95	☐ 36:BB	$14.95
☐ 13:E2	$9.95	☐ 37:CDB	$9.95
☐ 14:VDH	$12.95	☐ 38:CKI	$14.95
☐ 15:EDH	$15.95	☐ 39:SBC	$14.95
☐ 16:LD2	$14.95	☐ 40:CGD	$7.95
☐ 17:CTG	$19.95	☐ 41:CGR	$7.95
☐ 18:HPG	$12.95	☐ 42:SRF	$19.95
☐ 19:WEP	$17.95	☐ 43:RVH	$19.95
☐ 20:CN	$9.95	☐ 44:CBW	$12.95
☐ 21:CS	$9.95	☐ 45:CGW	$7.95
☐ 22:CM	$9.95	☐ 46:CWT	$12.95
☐ 23:EL	$8.95	☐ 47:CMP	$12.95
☐ 24:SH	$8.95	☐ 48:CGT	$7.95

Canadian Customers
Order Toll-Free 1-800-561-4169

Additional Books Sub-Total $_____
ADD Postage and Handling $ __3.00__
Sales Tax: (AZ, CA, DC, IL, MI, MN, NY & WA residents, please add appropriate state and local sales tax.) $_____
YOUR TOTAL (Sub-Total, Postage/Handling, Tax) $_____

YOUR ADDRESS (Please print)

Name _____

Street _____

City _____ State _____ Zip _____

Phone (_____) _____—_____

YOUR PAYMENT
Check one: ☐ Check ☐ Visa ☐ MasterCard ☐ Discover Card
Required credit card information:

Credit Card Number _____

Expiration Date (Month/Year) _____/_____

Signature Required _____

 Home Planners, LLC
Wholly owned by Hanley-Wood, Inc.
3275 W. Ina Road, Suite 110, Dept. BK, Tucson, AZ 85741

TB57

Glossary

ARCADE Row of arches supported by columns.

ARCH Curving structure comprised of wedge-shaped blocks, supported at the sides.

BALUSTER Small column or pillar that supports a rail.

BALUSTRADE Series of balusters joined by a rail, used for porches and balconies.

BAY WINDOW Projecting window, usually at least three-sided.

BEAM CEILING Ceiling with exposed beams, either real or ornamental.

BELT COURSE Horizontal band on the outside walls of a building, usually defining interior floor levels.

BOARD-AND-BATTEN Frame construction of vertical boards, with the cracks covered by narrow wood strips (battens).

BRACKET Triangular or inverted L-shaped piece supporting the overhang of a roof.

CASEMENT WINDOW Window type with sashes that swing out from the structure.

CLAPBOARDS Wooden exterior covering in which each row of boards partially overlaps the row below it.

CLERESTORY WINDOW Upper-story, usually multi-pane, window.

COFFER Recessed panel in a ceiling.

CORBEL Projecting piece that supports a beam.

CORNICE Molded projection that tops off the part to which it is attached.

CROSS GABLE Gable at a right angle to the house's main gable, usually facing the front.

CUPOLA Small domed roof or turret, usually built upon the main roof.

DENTIL One of a series of small blocks arranged in a row like a set of teeth.

DORMER Projecting window set in the sloping plane of a roof.

DOUBLE-HUNG WINDOW Window with two sashes that can be opened from the top, the bottom or both.

DOUBLE PORTICO Two-story porch, usually with columns and a pediment.

EAVE Lower edge of the part of the roof that overhangs a wall.

ENTABLATURE Horizontal structure on top of a column, consisting of architrave, frieze and cornice.

FACADE Face of a building.

FANLIGHT Semicircular window usually found above a door or large set of multi-pane windows.

FENESTRATION The way in which windows are arranged in a wall.

FINIAL Ornament fixed to the top of a spire, gable, pediment, roof or other structure.

FLUSH SIDING Smooth wood siding with no overlapping of boards.

FRENCH DOOR Door with a large area of glass, usually multi-pane.

GABLE Triangle-shaped part at the end of a ridged roof.

GABLE ROOF A roof that slopes on only two sides.

GAMBREL Ridged roof having two slopes on each side, with the lower slope having the steeper pitch.

HALF HOUSE Small Cape Cod-style house, characterized by two windows to one side of the front door.

HALF-TIMBERING Ornamentation on walls in which spaces between timber framing have been filled with masonry or other material.

HEARTH Floor directly in front of a fireplace and the floor of a fireplace where the fire is built.

HIP ROOF Roof with four sides, each uniformly pitched.

LINTEL Horizontal piece spanning the top of an opening such as a door or window.

MANSARD ROOF Roof with two slopes on all four sides.

MOLDING Band used as ornamentation for a wall or other surface.

PALLADIAN WINDOW Window with a large arched center and rectangular flanking pieces.

PEDIMENT Triangular surface of a gable or a similar form over a door, a window or a row of columns.

PENDANT Decorative form hanging from an eave or elsewhere.

PENT ROOF Small roof ledge placed between the first and second floors of a house.

PILASTER Rectangular column projecting outward from a wall.

PORTICO Entrance porch, usually with columns and a pediment.

QUOINS Decorative pieces of stone or brick at the corners of buildings.

SALTBOX Style of house which has a gabled roof with the rear slope much longer than the front.

SHED ROOF Roof with a single slope.

SIDELIGHTS Narrow windows flanking a door.

SLIDING GLASS DOOR Door with one stationary and one moving panel, both of glass.

TRANSOM Small window over a door.

VERANDA Open porch with a roof.

VISIT THE PAST, BUILD FOR THE FUTURE

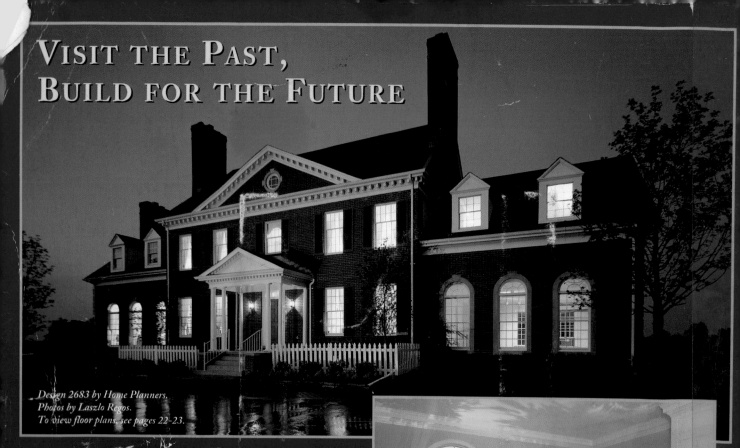

Design 2683 by Home Planners.
Photos by Laszlo Regos.
To view floor plans, see pages 22-23.

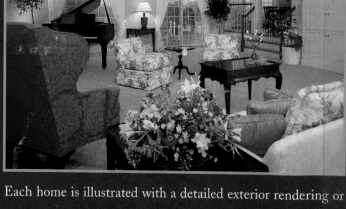

THERE MAY BE NO STYLE OF ARCHITECTURE with a stronger hold on the American imagination than Colonial. This collection offers almost 200 designs combining up-to-date floor plans with Early American exteriors, including Cape Cod cottages, gracious Georgian and Federal styles, comfortable farmhouses and Greek Revival mansions. More than 90 designs are based on actual historic homes, with information about the original house and its inhabitants. Look for the "Historic Adaptation" seal to learn more about:

- **PARSON CAPEN HOUSE (1682)**
- **JOHN PAUL JONES HOUSE (1758)**
- **PAUL REVERE HOUSE (1676)**
- **MOUNT VERNON (1743)**
- **THE HERMITAGE (1834)**
- **WOODROW WILSON'S BIRTHPLACE (1846)**

Each home is illustrated with a detailed exterior rendering or photograph and easy-to-read floor plans. Complete sets of construction-ready plans are available for each design.

- **INTRODUCTION TO COLONIAL STYLES**
- **32 FULL-COLOR PAGES**
- **GLOSSARY**

ISBN 1-881955-47-8

9 781881 955474

EAN

$9.95
($13.95 Canada)

ISBN 1-881955-47-8

0 29129 95547 3

UPC

HOME PLANNERS, LLC
Wholly owned by Hanley-Wood, Inc.
3275 W. INA RD., SUITE 110, TUCSON, ARIZONA 85741
www.homeplanners.com